I DREAM OF JONI

ALSO BY HENRY ALFORD

And Then We Danced: A Voyage Into the Groove

Would It Kill You to Stop Doing That?: A Modern Guide to Manners

How to Live: A Search for Wisdom from Old People (While They Are Still on This Earth)

Out There: One Man's Search for the Funniest Person on the Internet

Big Kiss: One Actor's Desperate Attempt to Claw His Way to the Top

Municipal Bondage

I DREAM OF JONI

A Portrait of JONI MITCHELL in 53 Snapshots

Henry Alford

G

GALLERY BOOKS

New York Amsterdam/Antwerp London
Toronto Sydney New Delhi

G

Gallery Books
An Imprint of Simon & Schuster, LLC
1230 Avenue of the Americas
New York, NY 10020

First Gallery Books hardcover edition January 2025

GALLERY BOOKS and colophon are registered trademarks of Simon & Schuster, LLC

Interior design by Jaime Putorti

Manufactured in the United States of America

10 9 8 7 6 5 4 3 2 1

Library of Congress Cataloging-in-Publication Data

Names: Alford, Henry, 1962– author. | Mitchell, Joni. Lyrics. Selections.
Title: I dream of Joni: a portrait of Joni Mitchell in 53 snapshots/Henry Alford.
Description: First Gallery Books hardcover edition. | New York: Gallery Books, 2025. | Includes bibliographical references and index. | Summary: "The eternal singer-songwriter Joni Mitchell is seen anew, portrayed through a witty and comprehensive exploration of anecdotes, quotes, and lyrics by "the most graceful of humorists" (Vanity Fair) and author of And Then We Danced"—Provided by publisher.
Identifiers: LCCN 2024020267 (print) | LCCN 2024020268 (ebook) | ISBN 9781668019504 (hardcover) | ISBN 9781668019511 (paperback) | ISBN 9781668019528 (ebook)
Subjects: LCSH: Mitchell, Joni—Anecdotes. | Mitchell, Joni—Quotations.
Classification: LCC ML410.M6823 A75 2025 (print) | LCC ML410.M6823 (ebook) |
DDC 782.42164092—dc23/eng/20240430
LC record available at https://lccn.loc.gov/2024020267
LC ebook record available at https://lccn.loc.gov/2024020268

ISBN 978-1-6680-1950-4
ISBN 978-1-6680-1952-8 (ebook)

I DREAM OF JONI

PROLOGUE

1

In the presence of the great, we are sometimes very small.

It's January 19, a Saturday night, and Joni Mitchell and her band are in Champaign, Illinois, where they are playing the 16,218-capacity Assembly Hall. The weather, as if in homage to the singer-songwriter whose most famous song, "Both Sides Now," is sometimes incorrectly referred to as "Clouds," is, appropriately, cloudy.

The crowd is a roiling swirl of bell-bottoms and political disaffection and hairstyles these people will later regret: it's 1974. The Watergate scandal has cast a seamy yellow light on the presidency; Pringles have taught the world that potato chips are now stackable. We're at peak Joni. Sure, her personal life at the moment is, per usual, zigzaggy like an EKG, but her professional life is groovy beyond measure. Even though Mitchell is someone who judges her work on artistic rather than commercial terms, it can't be lost on her how spectacularly well her last three albums have gone. Let me mansplain for you.

Court and Spark, the album that she released just two days earlier, is being met with rhapsodic reviews and, spurred on by the hits "Help Me" and "Free Man in Paris," will eventually go double platinum—a remarkable feat given that the album is (a) a densely layered suite of sophisticated, interconnecting songs and (b) backed by a jazz band. In a musical landscape rife with woozy nostalgia—Barbra Streisand cooing about "The Way We Were," Jim Croce longing to capture "Time in a Bottle"—Mitchell's blasts of thorny ambivalence are like a breathless wake-up call from your complicated and mystique-drenched older sister.

On the album before *Court and Spark,* 1972's *For the Roses,* Mitchell pulled off a weird and highly uncharacteristic little victory. After David Geffen, her friend and agent, had repeatedly pointed out to her that her songs were hits for other singers but not for her—most famously, Judy Collins's cover of "Both Sides Now," but also Crosby, Stills, Nash & Young with "Woodstock," and even the heavy metal band Nazareth with "This Flight Tonight"—Mitchell wrote a song for herself that she hoped would chart. Determining that deejays were an important part of the hit-making process, she cannily decided to celebrate their medium by writing a love song from the point of view of a radio, teasing out the similarities between these electronic appliances and lovestruck humans (e.g., both get turned on, both send out signals, both create static); then she gave the tune a long intro and a long outro so that deejays could talk over them. Her scheme worked: "You Turn Me On, I'm a Radio" hit #25 on *Billboard.*

Meanwhile, the album *Blue,* Mitchell's 1971 masterpiece that would forever mark her as a purveyor of searing self-disclosure, was performing its own quiet miracle: year after year it veritably toppled dormitories across the country via collective sobbing.

Bob Dylan spent a weekend listening to *Blue* and then wrote the song "Tangled Up in Blue." Four of the songs on *Blue*, each of them played on a droney Appalachian stringed instrument called a dulcimer, are so beguiling that, almost fifty years later, Joni superfan Harry Styles tracked down the woman who made and sold Mitchell her dulcimer and bought four of them himself; he gave his 2022 Album of the Year–winning *Harry's House* the same title as a Joni song. Taylor Swift called *Blue* her favorite record ever and named her 2012 album *Red* in homage to it.

But performing at big arenas like tonight's Assembly Hall: oof, Joni hates it. It's hard to tune her guitars with this much amplification. Also, it's a weird sensation to have thousands of people at your feet—when you look out into the darkened crowd, it feels like you are the intended meal for an ocean of teeth.

But the biggest hassle with arenas is the randomness that you get with an audience this big: Mitchell's bracing authenticity as a performer ("I'm a Method actor," she has said) wants silence—or, at least, relative calm. On various occasions over the past four or five years, restless audiences have caused her to stop mid-song to reprimand the audience, cut her set short, or even walk off stage—like the time she decided the crowd at the 1969 Atlantic City Pop Festival didn't like her music, or when the guy at the Isle of Wight show in 1970 jumped up on stage and announced, "This is a hippie concentration camp!"

Is that what's happening tonight? During a break between songs, one audience member takes it upon himself to yell out a song request, but it's not a Joni song this guy wants, it's a song by someone who's not even on the bill, Jefferson Airplane's singer Grace Slick. The guy screams, "'White Raaaaaabbit'!"

Dude. Are you *trying* to harsh Joni's mellow?

Awkward.

Fortunately, Joni's sense of composure kicks in.

"Sweetheart," she says into the mic, "I'm slick but I'm not *that* Slick."

2

November 14, 1993. Joni's hometown, Saskatoon, in Saskatchewan, Canada, at a country club called the Willows Club. Mitchell is being presented a lifetime achievement award from the Saskatchewan Recording Industry.

The host and interviewer of the evening, trying to keep his introduction short, pares Mitchell's many accolades down to a single one—not the group of immortal songs that she has written; not her having brought a new emotional candor to pop music or her having helped blur the divide between pop songs and art songs; not the illustrious people like Swift and Elton John and Prince who claim her as an influence; not the sky-high integrity that is the result of having self-produced her own albums and having almost always followed her muse rather than public taste; not the two lyrics of hers that have been included in *Bartlett's Familiar Quotations* ("They paved paradise and put up a parking lot" from "Big Yellow Taxi" and "We are stardust, we are golden/ And we've got to get ourselves back to the garden" from "Woodstock"); not the fact that her illnesses over the course of her life—from the forceps, as Joni might put it, to the stone—have required her to learn how to walk three times; not the three-octave range or the five Grammys to that date or the fact that the covers of most of her studio albums have featured her own artwork; not the fact that she is so beloved that, in 1977, she was allowed to fill an entire album side with a largely improvised, sixteen-minute-long, Aaron Copland–esque orchestral suite, some of whose lyrics address the tenuous interface between Indigenous people in rural Canada and Joni's childhood beach ball; not the fact that her nursery rhyme–ish song "The Circle Game" is so culturally ubiquitous—sung or referenced on seemingly any TV show peddling white, middle-class nostalgia, including *The Brady Bunch, thirtysomething, The Wonder Years*—that Mitchell has come to refer to it, in a heavy Brooklyn accent, as "Soycle Game"; but, rather, this: radio announcers don't even need to say Joni's name when they play her songs because her voice and musicianship and lyrics are so unique.

Mitchell is no fan of awards—they always seem to come at the wrong time, as if the presenters know that they should honor her, but not why they should. She can seem cool if not downright arctic when people celebrate her: in the middle of a tribute concert at the Hammerstein Ballroom in 2000, Mitchell, seated in the audience, ate a banana.

But coolness was not her tone at the Saskatchewan event. Here, surrounded by her parents and old friends and well-wishers, she was loose and gracious and utterly lovable. The more she talked, the more her Canadian accent and rounded vowels started to come oot, eh? Like, you were almost expecting to hear aboot something super-local like a salmon festival over in Medicine Hat, eh?

Radiant with sun-streaked hair and lots of silver jewelry, Mitchell apologized for her hoarse voice ("I was up last night being rowdy") and alluded to her chronic insomnia ("I keep vampire hours"). She reminisced about the seventh-grade poetry teacher, Arthur Kratzmann, who inspired her to write poetry; she apologized to her high school art teacher for having dozed off during his class once after she'd stayed up all night listening to the radio. She referred to her "first husband"—she's had two—and added, "I'm like the Elizabeth Taylor of rock here."

Q and A time. A man in the audience raised his hand and said he had a stupid question; Joni joked that she loves stupid questions. The stupid question was "How did you become such a fabulous songwriter?" Joni launched into a spate of self-deprecation about the power of Irish blarney, but then she autocorrected, saying that she'd like to try to say something useful instead. The rest of her answer was indeed useful—she advocated finding a work that you admire and studying it intensely; then creating something of your own wherein you emulate the spirit of the work that inspired you; and then assessing how your work falls short of its inspiration. Finally: "Narrow the gap. Just keep narrowing the gap."

As the audience contemplated the ways in which gap-narrowing might revolutionize their own lives—you could almost hear a roomful of people each forming the conclusion, "Maybe it's *not* a random collection of chicken casserole recipes but a *novel*!"—a second man in the audience asked a variant of the songwriting question, but went broader focus, addressing creativity itself.

"My question is, Why do you do it?" he said. "Obviously, you're good at it. You *can* do it. But are you driven by something you don't know where it comes from? The energy to create all this art—are you producing it, or . . . Where is it coming from?"

All eyes on Joni. As any committed Joni fan in the audience realized, there's a really interesting possible answer to this question—a really interesting and juicy possible answer—but it's not one that Mitchell talks about much, and even if she were to, it probably wouldn't come out in a public setting, particularly a public setting that includes her parents.

Nervously glancing over at her mother and father seated in front of her, Mitchell made the split-second decision to punt. She told the question asker, "I really like doing it. I mean, uh . . ." She nodded her head twice. ". . . I really like doing it. All you have to do is give up a little television."

As the audience laughed, Mitchell lit a consoling cigarette—she was a four-pack-a-day smoker until her aneurysm in 2015—and then turned to the host to say, "I guess that's a wrap, eh?"

Though no one in the room acknowledged it, this moment may have been the most newsworthy part of the awards ceremony: one of the world's most celebrated oversharers had opted to undershare.

The INCIDENT

3

Alberta and Saskatchewan. The 1940s and '50s. We see a woman with sparkling, intense eyes: Joni's mother.

Like a character in a Dickens novel, Joni's mother was possessed of a first name that seemed to distill her essential traits—bourgeois aspiration and mild disappointment—into one adorable, easily digestible bundle.

Myrtle.

When Joni was young, Myrtle Anderson sniffed at her neighbors' housekeeping habits and vacuumed the Andersons' garage daily. Granted, the prairie is a dusty place. But the gentle and archetypical roar of your average Hoover? Let us collectively replace that soothing sound with a muffled *tsk-tsk*—because what exactly are you vacuuming when you vacuum daily? You're not laying siege to an accumulation of particulates or dead skin lying beneath you. You're not sucking up a deeper level of dust now that your infant vacuum cleaner is a day older and a day stronger. No, you're making a powerful statement about the *future* of dust.

"I was a little afraid of Myrtle as a kid," retired teacher Sharolyn Dickson, who has been friends with Mitchell since the sixth grade, told me. "She was *that* kind of straitlaced. She was quite disapproving of some of the things that Joni was interested in doing."

Repressed but hot-blooded, as Joni would describe her years later, Myrtle was a former schoolteacher married to a grocer and bandleader/trumpet instructor with a strong competitive streak. Bill Anderson, the son of a violin maker, was from a Norwegian family with possible, though disputed, ancestry in the nomadic tribe known as the Sami (which would explain the high cheekbones). The Andersons, lower-middle-class Protestants, lived under infinite sky and endless wheat fields on the Canadian prairie—first in Fort Macleod, Alberta, where their only child, Roberta Joan, was born on November 7, 1943. Then the family moved on to two small towns, sometimes living without electricity or running water, before settling in the Saskatchewan city of Saskatoon when Joan was eleven.

Even today, Saskatoon, a city of about 285,000, bears vestiges of the prairie: while walking around the heart of its downtown one day in 2023, I stumbled on—just across the street from a glassy, eighteen-floor office building, and hard by a Cineplex with fifteen screens—two white hares munching grass in a parking lot. During my stay I spent a lot of time staring into dark, cavernous storefronts, trying to figure out if they were open. I formed the opinion, You'd definitely have to make your own fun here.

Joni's friend Sharolyn Dickson drove me around Saskatoon one afternoon, showing me her and Joni's childhood haunts, including the swimming pool on Avenue H, whose jukebox young Joan liked to dance to. ("One of the things you notice when you spend time with her," Sharolyn told me, "is someone will put some music on"—here Sharolyn looked down at her shoulders, which she had started swaying to imagined music—"and this is where it starts.")

When we stopped in front of an imposing brick building that Sharolyn identified as Nutana, her and Joni's high school, Sharolyn told me, "We weren't allowed to go in the front door, that was for the teachers. We had to use the side door."

"That's crazy," I said.

"There were a lot of things like that. Even for the teachers: there was a men's staff room and a women's staff room."

O, the decorous 1950s. For a future renegade and visionary like Joni, maybe growing up in a city that had been founded by a temperance society—not to mention being reared by a mother who shared the same birthday as Queen Victoria—was the ideal cradle. When a childhood friend once asked Joni "Why do we have such square parents?" Joni, as if aping Marlon Brando in *The Wild One,* explained, "To have something to rebel against."

Living amid an expanse of sky and grassland may have aided the process of rebellion: "If you go to Vancouver or Toronto and mention Saskatchewan or Manitoba, people say, 'Oh, that's kind of a wasteland.' Which we're trying to overcome," Saskatoon's young mayor, Charlie Clark, a longtime Joni fan, told me when I interviewed him at City Hall. "I moved from Vancouver to Winnipeg to Toronto to Saskatoon, and the idea of what kind of car I drive and what kind of house I live in was way less important here than it was in bigger cities. Maybe it does foster an ability for people to focus on who they are as opposed to trying to fit into some of those externally driven things."

But figuring yourself out sometimes pits you against the people who raised you. As Mitchell's biographer David Yaffe told me, "Sometimes she felt contempt for her parents, and sometimes she wanted to protect them." After all, Myrtle's squareness wasn't wholly restrictive. She nurtured her young daughter's artistic talents—she let Joan paint a tree on her bedroom wall, she taught Joan to press wildflowers in scrapbooks. Prone to quoting Shakespeare, Myrtle had Joan recite Shakespeare sonnets. She taught her daughter, as the song "Let the Wind Carry Me" on *For the Roses* would put it, the deeper meaning. It was not lost on either Myrtle or Joan that Myrtle's own mother, Sadie, who played the organ in a Presbyterian church and wrote poetry, had come from a long line of classical musicians but, upon marrying, had been forced to bide her time as a resentful farmer's wife. When Sadie was upset, she'd play her organ at home in a minor key, "so my mother grew up," as Joni explained to an audience at Le Hibou Coffee House in Ottawa in March of 1968, "not being able to stand anything that had a minor key in it anywhere." When Sadie and her husband had a fight one night, he threw all of Sadie's gramophone records on the floor. Sadie, enraged, kicked a door off its hinge.

Though Irish blood flowed through Myrtle's veins, too, her ministrations were gentler. Hers was the language of wary caution and faint disapproval, especially in the face of her impulsive, athletic daughter. A health nut, Myrtle preached nutrition and exercise, but disapproved of dancing and displays of emotion. She thought guitars were hillbillyish and that swearing was common. She hated makeup. She thought cats belonged outdoors. "You're too sensitive," she told her daughter. "You've got to learn to control your emotions."

On this last score, Myrtle was probably onto something: when Joni saw the movie *Bambi* at age four or five, she was traumatized by the forest fire scene, as many children are. But Joni's reaction lingered. "I couldn't exorcise the vision," she said years later. "For days, maybe a week afterwards, I was down on the floor drawing fire and deer running, day after day after day."

Typically, though, Joan's hypersensitive antennae took her to sunnier places. When, at a birthday party at age seven, Joan heard Edith Piaf for the first time, she got goose bumps and dropped her cake fork. When Joan saw the Kirk Douglas movie *The Story of Three Loves* a few years later, she was so struck by the film's music, Rachmaninoff's *Rhapsody on a Theme of Paganini*, that she went to a department store's listening booth and started obsessively listening. ("Up until I was thirteen, comedy was all that mattered to me," Joni has said. "Why didn't I become a writer of funny songs? Because of that beautiful melody.")

But the signal event of young Joan's life was her contracting polio at age nine. Joni has said that, were it not for polio, she probably would have taken after her father, a provincial tennis champion, and become an athlete; she was often picked first for sports teams, and she'd already shown signs of being a talented bowler.

Her bout with polio started strangely: while looking into a mirror one morning, she thought she looked different, and concluded, "You're a woman now." (Her gamine outfit may have played a part here: she was wearing pegged pants, a blue sweater, and a red-and-white gingham blouse with a sailor's collar.) The next day she had trouble getting out of bed and collapsed. Her back was twisted forward and to the right, and her balance was off.

She was flown to St. Paul's Hospital in Saskatoon (she later wrote in her Grade 5 notebook that, from the air, the towns looked like "topaz brooches on the black velvet land"). A colony of annexed trailers for polio victims had been set up outside the hospital. Therein, doctors told Mitchell that she might never walk again. Her back arched so high that an adult male could put two fists under it; once in her hospital bed, she was told that if she moved, the polio might spread. For the next six weeks, she was treated daily with scalding hot compresses: nurses would bring a cauldron of hot flannel rags to Joni's bedside and then, using tongs, apply the rags to Joni's limbs almost to the point of blistering. Gradually, Joni has said, "I unfurled."

During those six weeks, her father did not visit, and Myrtle visited only once: wearing a mask, Myrtle, with a haunted look in her eyes, handed Joan a Christmas tree and then beat a hasty retreat. Though this kind of limited interaction with one's family was common for polio patients, it couldn't have helped the feelings of abandonment that Joan was already feeling while lying in her bed, haunted by the menacing wheeze of the worst-case scenarios located near her in another trailer, the patients in iron lungs: if the disease spread to her lungs, she'd end up in one. Worse, she shared a room with a boy who had the same symptoms as Joan, and the boy died.

Joan self-soothed with a coloring book, filling in the outlines of the Christmas carolers depicted therein by dipping cotton swabs in gentian violet, an antiseptic being used to treat her mouth ulcers.

At night she sometimes found herself singing at the top of her lungs; Joni has said that this was the first time she ever sang for people.

She told the Christmas tree "I am not a cripple" and vowed to the tree that if she got better, she'd do something special with her life.

The feelings of abandonment that we experience as children have a sneaky habit of reoccurring throughout our lives; how will Joan's time in the polio ward reverberate? While it's tempting, but probably too easy, to hold this emotionally scarring incident responsible for the Joni Mitchell songbook's preoccupation with travel and flight, another aspect of Mitchell's subsequent output is more traceable: polio will alter the way Joni later plays guitar, inadvertently leading to the creation of the signature Joni Mitchell sound. The neural damage from polio will make it difficult for Joni to play certain chords on her guitar, particularly an F chord, so she'll opt to use open tuning on her guitar strings, which will be easier on her left hand (with open tuning, you typically make a chord by pressing down on the strings with a single finger rather than with three or four). Open tuning makes guitars sound swollen with overtones, thus creating a richer sound than you get from standard tuning; it's like laying a chord on top of another chord. Open tuning is a longtime favorite of blues musicians, many of the earliest of whom played banjos, which are open-tuned; it's also a favorite of Keith Richards, who usually composes in open G.

But Joni will take open tuning one step further. As Roger McGuinn, the front man of the Byrds whose jangly intro to the Byrds' cover of "Mr. Tambourine Man" is one of the most famous guitar riffs in rock history, told me, "Joni has all these innovative tunings." Over the course of Mitchell's career, she'll invent more than fifty of her own open tunings; she'll sometimes use the ambient sounds of her environment—the sound of surf, the hum of a dishwasher—as their base.

Twenty years later, when she is performing at the Los Angeles club the Troubadour, Joni says, "Sometimes it takes a personal crisis to turn you on the spiritual path. During your childhood and your teens you go through many crises. Everybody should go through it: it's a good experience. After a crisis you go through a reevaluation of yourself."

The hospital sent Joan home in a wheelchair, but she refused to use it once she'd returned. Myrtle homeschooled Joan for a year. Joan practiced dancing daily, using the doorknob of her bedroom door as her dance partner. According to Sheila Weller's book *Girls Like Us*, ten-year-old Joan started having secretions—a reaction, she would later learn, to an antibiotic she was taking—so Myrtle took her to a doctor. After performing an external gynecological exam on Joan, the doctor subtly accused her of having had sex: "You've been a naughty girl, haven't you?" But when Joan shot her mother a look of pleading bewilderment, Myrtle took the doctor's side. (When Joni mentioned the incident to her mother years later, Myrtle said, "Poppycock! I never did that." But maybe Myrtle was only preaching caution—after all, Myrtle's favorite way of chiding Joan when Joan got on her nerves was to say "Don't have kids when you get grown.")

Fortunately, Joni learned early on how to step away from the fray in order to gain perspective. She'd started smoking cigarettes at age nine when a friend brought some Black Cat cork cigarettes to church choir practice one day. After practice, a small group of intrepid young choristers had sneakily lit up on a frozen pond; some of them rent the crisp Canadian air with gales of coughing, and one girl vomited. But not Joan. "I took one hit and went, 'This is great.'" She felt "really smart and clear."

She started hiding her cigarettes under her family's house. Whenever she needed a break, she'd grab her smokes, get on her bike, and ride out to the prairie in order to smoke and stare at birds.

She'd later describe these moments as "the best part of my childhood."

4

"The first time I heard 'Both Sides Now' was on the phone in 1967 during the middle of the night. I got a call from [singer-songwriter] Tom Rush, who was very excited. Tom, a great fan of Joni's, had earlier introduced me to her and to her fine song 'The Circle Game.'

"'Joni has a new song, and I want you to hear it. I think you'll love it.' He put Joni on the phone, and she sang 'Both Sides Now.'

"I immediately fell in love with the song and knew it was a classic. I had to sing it. On September 28, 1967, I recorded 'Both Sides Now' at Columbia Studios in New York."

—*Trust Your Heart: An Autobiography*,
by Judy Collins, 1987

"I had begun to hear of Joni Mitchell by then. She had a good following in the Village and in Canada and many cities in the States. She didn't have a recording contract at the time, and one night one of her ardent fans (I remember it being Tom Rush, but he always denies it) called me at 3 a.m. and had Joni play me 'Both Sides Now.'

I immediately began to weep. I said I had to record it, she said she wanted me to, as she didn't have a contract at that time, and was eager for her songs to get out to the public."

—*Singing Lessons: A Memoir of Love, Loss, Hope, and Healing,* by Judy Collins, 1998

"One night, in the spring of 1967, I was fast asleep when the phone rang at three in the morning. Al [Kooper, the founder of the group Blood, Sweat & Tears, known for their hits "Spinning Wheel" and "You've Made Me So Very Happy"] said a few words about being sorry to be calling so late and then told me he had met a great songwriter and wanted me to hear her sing an amazing song. He put Joni Mitchell on the phone.

"He and Joni had met up at the show he was doing (I think she had a crush on one of the band members). Al said he went home with her when she told him she was a songwriter and had some songs he might like.

"'I thought, well, if she can't write songs, she's pretty good-looking! I figured I could only lose a night's sleep out of the deal,' he told me later.

"My good luck is that when they got to Joni's place, instead of jumping into bed with him, she sang him 'Both Sides Now.' Al had already been in the music business a long time, and he knew a lot of singers. It was my luck that instead of calling Janis [Ian] or Buffy [Sainte-Marie] or Carolyn [Hester] or the other Judy [Henske], he called me.

"After Joni sang me 'Both Sides Now,' I put the phone down and wept. I had never heard a song that I felt was so beautiful, and it would change both our lives.

"The next day, this time with [Elektra Records honcho] Jac [Holzman], I heard Joni play the song again. . . . I wept once more, as I would when I heard many of her songs."

—*Sweet Judy Blue Eyes: My Life in Music*,
by Judy Collins, 2011

"And then, of course, Joni Mitchell, whose music found its way to me through the good turn of a friend named Al Kooper, who called me at four in the morning—I thought it was three, but he reminded me recently that it was four—you know how your memory is about the sixties—and he called me and put her on the line, and she played 'Both Sides Now' for me on the phone."

—Judy Collins on *Talk of the Nation*,
July 22, 2009

"Somebody called me and put me on the phone with her, and she sang me 'Both Sides Now.'"

—Judy Collins interviewed on NoDepression.com, 2014

"[Al Kooper] called me up and said, 'I know you're looking for songs for your next album, and you have to hear this.' He put Joni on the phone, and she played 'Both Sides Now.' It was—and still is—one of the most singable, the most memorable songs I've ever heard. I got dressed and went right over. She had a little apartment on the Lower East Side [ed: Mitchell lived, rather, in Chelsea, as referenced in her song "Chelsea Morning"], full of cut glass and candles, very Joni. The three of us stayed up all night playing songs."

—Judy Collins interview in *American Songwriter*, October 26, 2020

"The first time that I heard the song I was in bed, it was three o'clock in the morning. I was absolutely slam-dunk drunk, I can tell you that. Why I woke up, I don't know. The guy who started Blood, Sweat & Tears called me. He and I were very good friends, Al Kooper. It was three in the morning and the phone rang and it was Al. I said, 'What's the matter? Are you in trouble? Can I help you?' And he said, 'No, *you're* in trouble.' He said, 'I met this girl at the club, and her name is Joni Mitchell. She came there because she was in love with the drummer and then she told me that she writes songs and I said, 'Woah, you're a very good-looking girl—woman—what else do you do?' And she said, 'I write songs, that's about it.' He said—it was now about two in the morning probably—he said, 'What shall we do, how can I hear them?' She said, 'Why don't you come to my place?' So he went to her place and she started playing songs and he went out of his mind. He said, 'I've got somebody I have to call, and you have to sing her some of the songs.' So he put Joni Mitchell on the phone and woke me up at three in the morning. And she sang me 'Both Sides Now.' And I said, 'Oh my God, I'll be right over.'"

—Judy Collins on Andy Cohen's Sirius Radio podcast, August 8, 2022

"It was the middle of the night when she called. I was probably drunk. I was definitely passed out."

—Judy Collins in *New York* magazine, February 23, 2022

"One night I was sitting in my favorite bar in the Village, the Dugout. . . . It was the best place to kill a summer night, and I always ran into a few friends I would miss while I was on the road. I was living platonically at folk singer Judy Collins's apartment on the Upper West Side . . . Judy, the number two female folk singer behind Joan Baez, was a wonderful, generous woman. Her apartment was the folk music salon of the mid-sixties. People like Dylan, Leonard Cohen, Phil Ochs, and others would make the pilgrimage to her digs and enjoy her hospitality and earth mothering. This particular night in the Village I was sitting with a new girl in town. She had a crush on Roy Blumenfeld, the drummer from The Blues Project. Unfortunately for her, Roy had a girlfriend who was on to her and extremely jealous. So, this gal is crying in my beer for about three hours, and I don't mind 'cause she's kinda easy on the eyes and nothing else is going on anyway. So they're closing the bar and throwing us out and I offer to walk her home. . . . Since I was covered in the ashes of my failed marriage, this was a pleasant diversion.

"When we got to her door, she invited me in to hear some of her new songs. She was a folk singer. Canadian. Half of a duet with her recently divorced husband, they had achieved a mild popularity and a cult following in various American border cities. She, being real pretty, had me bounding up the stairs like a hound dog, figuring if the songs were lousy, maybe I could salvage the evening some other way. In a few minutes that became the furthest thing from my mind.

"Her songs were incredible and totally original. . . . And she had enough to keep going for hours, most of them brilliant. One song especially killed me, and I thought it would be great for Judy Collins—that a nice way to pay for her hospitality would be to turn her on to it . . . I called Judy up. It was 5:30 a.m. by now, and Judy was pretty pissed off.

"'I have to get up soon and drive all the way to the Newport Folk Festival . . . I can hear this song when I get back . . . ,' she said diplomatically.

"Bang! A great idea hits me. 'Judy, why don't you, room permitting, take this girl with you to the festival. . . . Then, being that you're on the board of directors, you could see if maybe they could fit her in the schedule somewhere . . . ?' Silence at the other end. 'Judy?'

"'Kooper, you bastard. Yeah. I'll do it. Gimme her number. Bye.'

"Just to make sure, I gave the woman Judy's number and told her to call Collins in a couple of hours. I split immediately 'cause I was exhausted and never made it to Judy's place, preferring to crash on a bench in Washington Square Park in the steamy, summer morning rather than get hell for waking her at 5:30 a.m.

"Well, as the saying goes, the rest is history. The girl (Joni Mitchell, of course) played at the 1967 festival, thanks to the last-minute urgings of Judy, and stole the whole show. Judy eventually recorded the song I thought she would like, 'Michael from Mountains.'"

—From Al Kooper's memoir, *Backstage Passes and Backstabbing Bastards*, 1998

"The next day, an excited Joni—packed and ready—waited, in vain, for Judy Collins to show. 'Judy stood me up,' Joni has said, 'and she was my hero, [so] it was kind of heartbreaking. I waited and waited and waited, and she never came. . . . A day went by, and I got a phone call from her, and she sounded kind of sheepish. She said somebody had sung one of my songs in a workshop. It was a terrible rendition she said, but people went crazy. Judy thought I really should be at Newport.' She had a car pick Joni up and take her to the festival [where] an obstruction materialized in the form of Joan Baez and Mimi Fariña's mother, 'Big' Joan Baez. Using her considerable influence, the matriarch had Joni barred from the schedule, presumably fearing that the comely arriviste would steal the thunder from her daughters.

"At this point Judy—who was known as one tough lady—stepped in and pulled weight of her own. Judy told Mrs. Baez, 'If Joni doesn't perform, then *I* won't perform and Leonard [Cohen] won't perform.' By dint of Judy's threat, Joni got onstage at Newport."

—From *Girls Like Us: Carole King, Joni Mitchell, Carly Simon—and the Journey of a Generation,* by Sheila Weller, 2008

"'Both Sides Now' was inspired by a passage from Saul Bellow's *Henderson the Rain King*: 'I dreamed down at the clouds, and thought that when I was a kid I had dreamed up at them, and having dreamed at the clouds from both sides as no other generation of men has done, one should be able to accept his death very easily.' . . .

"[T]he song's lovely melody made it instantly attractive to a diverse range of predatory, hit-hungry artists."

—*Financial Times*, January 20, 2019 [Note: The song has been recorded some 1,573 times, by musicians ranging from Doris Day to Bing Crosby to Pete Seeger to Willie Nelson to Frank Sinatra to Courtney Love to Kiri Te Kanawa to Hugh Masekela to Neil Diamond to Leonard Nimoy to Laurie Anderson to Carly Rae Jepsen, and has been widely heard in films and TV shows, serving as a plot point in 2003's *Love Actually* and 2021's Best Picture, *CODA*. Joni herself can be heard singing it on sixteen of her records.]

"When [Joni Mitchell] recorded an orchestral version of 'Both Sides Now' two years ago, several people asked her how she got Judy Collins to let her have the song."

—*Globe and Mail* (Toronto), October 27, 2001

5

November 2007. Joni is being interviewed by Charlie Rose for his show on public television. Dressed in a charcoal-hued Issey Miyake micro-pleated V-neck blouse accessorized with understated gold jewelry, Joni dutifully answers a question from the hangdog TV host about her artistic influences. Mitchell has answered this question scores of times for various interviewers, usually referencing Rachmaninoff, mid-career Miles Davis (*Nefertiti, In a Silent Way),* Billie Holiday, and Bob Dylan's accusatory screed "Positively 4th Street," whose opening line ("You got a lotta nerve to say you are my friend") made Joni realize that songs could address any topic whatsoever. Less frequently, she has also referenced Debussy; Stravinsky; Duke Ellington; Edith Piaf; the McGuire Sisters; Annie Ross of the jazz vocalese trio Lambert, Hendricks & Ross ("my Beatles"); the Police (for helping her transition from jazz back to pop rock in the 1980s); late-career Marvin Gaye; and Laura Nyro.

This time, Mitchell adds that some of her influences, like Duke Ellington, didn't reveal themselves for decades because "it takes a long time for an artist to ripen." She adds, with a note of disappointment, that the pop music industry, obsessed as it is with youth, doesn't grant performers the amount of time necessary for this ripening.

Somewhat abruptly, Rose changes conversational course.

ROSE: Have you missed anything?

MITCHELL: Missed—in life?

ROSE: Yes, that you thought might happen, you might do?

MITCHELL: Anything I missed I wasn't supposed to have.

ROSE: Is that right? You have a kind of sense of . . .

MITCHELL: Destiny.

6

Saskatoon, the 1950s and '60s.

When you're an only child and spend a lot of time alone, it's easy to attach an excessive amount of meaning to the events that happen to you, because you are under the impression you are the only, only, only person in the world who has ever noticed that, say, there's a town in Ontario called Punkeydoodles Corners.

It's also easy, in turn, to over-examine the passing parade of life for meaning. Joan had a column in the student newspaper at Aden Bowman Collegiate called "Fads and Fashions."

Being a columnist is maybe not what you'd expect from a mediocre student who was using *Reader's Digest* Condensed Books and comic-book versions of literary classics to complete her assignments, and whose ninth-grade yearbook photo was captioned "Her greatest aspiration is not to become a Latin teacher." But Joan had long loved to draw pictures of clothing and had even harbored dreams of becoming a fashion designer. "She really did have an interest in clothing back then," said longtime friend Sharolyn Dickson. "More so than many of us." Joan encouraged her schoolmates to attach silver stars to their blue suede shoes; she suggested that girls wear a necktie of their father's to school. She was so entranced by color and its permutations that she would collect the crepe paper left over from parades, dissolve it in water, and store the results in decorative shampoo bottles.

In her high school yearbook, she satirized insecure, bourgeois shoppers: "Last week I bought a brown shantung dress at Blanche Buchanan's for $28 (a fraction of its former price!). At home, I surveyed myself before my vanity mirror. 'Trés chic,' I muttered, although, somehow, without the cooing of the vendeuses, the creation seemed to give me the distinction and interesting contours of a large bran muffin."

As a fellow student wrote in Mitchell's copy of the yearbook, "Winged words flow from her pen." Mitchell also designed a pair of culottes in high school. Girls weren't allowed to wear Bermuda shorts or pants to classes, so Joan designed a box-pleated skirt that was essentially a pair of Bermuda shorts with flaps over them. When she gave a pair of them to her friend Ruthie, it created jealousy in their friend group. "She also made her own poodle skirts," Dickson told me. "She would get the fabric and turn it into something wonderful." (Joan's interest in clothing and its distribution would flare up again in the early 1970s when she got in the habit of going into Beverly Hills boutiques ten minutes before closing, staying for an hour, and then going out to dinner with the boutique's salesperson.)

If writing columns and creating culottes was a way for a young person to forge an identity, so was name-changing. Gifted art students at Aden Bowman Collegiate took classes at Saskatoon Technical Collegiate with an Abstract Expressionist painter named Henry

Bonli. Joan and Bonli argued a fair amount—he was an Abstract Expressionist, and Joan, as anyone who has seen the covers of Joni's albums knows, was, and is, as a painter, largely figurative. But one thing Joan loved about Bonli was his name. Enamored of the sight of "Bonli" on a canvas—and perhaps additionally inspired by the name of the pop singer Joni James, who was on the radio a lot at the time—Joan shed her *a* and took on an *i*.

When writing her new name, did young Joni dispense with the traditional dot over the *i* and go the full monty with a circle? Uh, we're talking about someone who designed her own culottes. Yes.

7

November 19, 1975. A hotel lobby in Worcester, Massachusetts. Joni has been performing as part of Bob Dylan's Rolling Thunder Revue, a traveling concert that, with little advance notice, will play in small theaters and town halls—Dylan wanted to "play for the people"—all the while raising money for Rubin "Hurricane" Carter, an imprisoned boxer convicted of murder who is trying to get an appeal.

Rolling Thunder featured, among others, Dylan, Joan Baez, Mitchell, Roger McGuinn from the Byrds, Roberta Flack, poet Allen Ginsberg, and *Nashville* actress Ronee Blakley; the finale concert at Madison Square Garden also included Muhammad Ali and Coretta Scott King, Martin Luther King's widow.

Rolling Thunder was famous for having been especially drug-soaked—even Joni, who had never been much of a druggie, joked at one point that she should be paid in cocaine. The tour had a shaggy, anything-goes vibe to it—at least one of the tour's shows saw a Cherokee medicine man standing onstage and stroking a feather in time to the music; in one town along the way, Ginsberg's recitation of a poem, to a ballroom full of mahjong players, found him screaming about bearded vaginas. Baez will later call the tour "a floating ship of crazies"; Mitchell will call it "mad," "a circus"; Ronee Blakley will call it "a heavenly catastrophe."

Martin Scorsese was filming Rolling Thunder; actor and playwright Sam Shepard was along for the ride, too, writing dialogue for an art film Dylan was making en route, as well as keeping a journal that's full of sentences like "A hundred bucks' worth of Valiums are delivered to the Niagara Hilton like so much Chicken Delight."

Dylan also invited on the tour a journalist named Larry "Ratso" Sloman, who will ultimately turn his reporting into the book *On the Road with Bob Dylan*. It's Ratso and his book that we'll be following.

While the tour was stationed in Worcester for the night, Ratso Sloman walked up to Joni in the lobby of her hotel, introduced himself, and told Joni that he'd been trying to interview her for years but that her manager had told him that Joni hates the press.

No, no, Joni protested to Ratso—it's not journalists that she doesn't like, it's the interview format.

Joni and Ratso continued chatting as they walked past a beautiful indoor garden. Ratso said, "We got a friend in common. Leonard Cohen. Him, Dylan, and Kinky Friedman are my three favorite male songwriters."

At the time, Ratso was, or recently had been, on assignment for a publication that Joni wasn't talking to, *Rolling Stone*. In February 1972, the magazine had published "Hollywood's Hot 100," a chart of all the influences and romantic liaisons between various people in the Los Angeles music scene; Joni had been hurt to see herself named "the Queen of El Lay," represented on the chart as a lipsticked kiss surrounded by broken hearts emanating from former flames James Taylor, Graham Nash, and David Crosby. (Mitchell in 1996 about the chart: "I mean, I can't date? Am I a sinner for dating? That was kind of shocking.") She was convinced that the publication was out to blackball her; for about eight years, she did her best to avoid talking to its reporters. (It can't have helped that *Rolling Stone*'s review of her debut record in 1968 had included the whopper "she's like a sand dune: you like the idea of her.") Her antipathy toward the magazine—shared by music critic Ellen Willis, who in 1970 called *Rolling Stone* "viciously anti-woman"—will reach its zenith in the mid-1990s when, trying to maneuver her way unaided into a very crowded industry event, Mitchell sees *Rolling Stone* honcho Jann Wenner smirk at her, so she throws a drink in Wenner's face and tells him "Kiss my ass!"

Whether or not Mitchell transferred this distrust onto Ratso Sloman is unclear. He had started the tour on assignment from the magazine; but he reneged when he determined that his editors only wanted to know how much money Dylan was making, and stayed on the tour so he could turn his reporting into his book. When I talked to Ratso in 2023, he told me that he didn't think Joni had associated him with the magazine all that much at the time. Likening himself to a mascot for Dylan's Rolling Thunder—during the tour Sloman had earned the nickname Ratso from Joan Baez, who thought he looked like Ratso Rizzo, Dustin Hoffman's character in *Midnight Cowboy*—he said, "Joni saw that I was backstage a lot and that I was friendly with the band. I don't think I had that kind of smear—the *Rolling Stone* smear."

Nevertheless, six nights later on the tour, in Augusta, Maine,

Ratso's efforts to interview Joni failed again. Joni had just come off stage. ("Every single time the place goes up in smoke like a brush fire," Shepard would write of her Rolling Thunder appearances. The *Ann Arbor Sun* said of one appearance, "The audience blew its top. . . . After two numbers, she vacated the spotlight, ignoring the carnivorous roar calling for her return.") She was wearing a military uniform and a badge. Ratso has written that he sidled up and asked her if she wanted to do an interview.

"With who?"

"With me."

"Why do I want to do an interview with you?" Joni said. "I'm not even third on your list."

"I told you you're first on my list."

"No, you didn't. You mentioned three people—Bob, Leonard, and Kinky—and you didn't even mention me."

"But . . ."

Joni told him she didn't want to do an interview with anybody.

Ratso reminded her that he'd been bugging her manager for two years.

Ratso Sloman's persistence on the tour will not go unnoticed: at one point, two security guards, in an effort to keep Ratso away from the tour's performers, will dump him on a hotel's couch. Ratso will later confess that he was "clinically manic, out of my mind, and totally rock-and-roll" on the tour. Rolling Thunder's tour manager, Chris O'Dell, told me, "He was a nuisance. But everyone knew that Bob really liked him."

Backstage in Augusta, Mitchell reiterated to Sloman that she dislikes the interview format. Shaking her head no, she added, "I'm much jiver than my work and I'd rather have people think that my work is me."

Ratso went out into the house to watch Dylan's set. Shortly thereafter, Joni, who would forever compare and contrast herself with His Bobness—when giving interviews, she'll do impersonations of him; she'll say he fell asleep when she played him *Court and Spark* shortly after she'd finished recording it; she'll tell an audience in 2023, "There's nothing better he likes than to see me fuck up"—walked up to Ratso and said, "Want to do an interview?"

Ratso joked that he only interviewed stars.

Mitchell grabbed Sloman by the arm and took him behind the stage, to a corridor where they sat in chairs.

Joni said, "I'm interviewing you, OK?"

"You don't have any notes. Don't you prepare?" asked Ratso, who was copiously tape-recording all his interviews on the tour.

Joni told Ratso that not only did she not have notes—she didn't even know who Ratso was. (Ratso has a master's degree in sociology from University of Wisconsin, where he specialized in deviance and criminology. Years later, he would go on to cowrite two of radio host Howard Stern's memoirs, two of boxer Mike Tyson's, and one by Red Hot Chili Pepper Anthony Kiedis.)

Joni asked Ratso if he was a Dylan fan. He said he was, and reminded her that he thought Dylan, Leonard Cohen, and Kinky Friedman were the three most important male songwriters: "I make that distinction because I can't really compare male and female songwriters, it's a different experience."

Joni asked why he made a distinction between male and female songwriters.

Ratso said it was a "different perspective."

Joni asked him if he was interested in what women think.

Ratso assured her he was.

Joni continued, "I would think that men would be curious about what women think in the confines of their rooms late at night."

In 1973, *Roe v. Wade* had legalized first-trimester abortion, and (female) tennis player Billie Jean King had defeated (male) Wimbledon champion and noisome troglodyte Bobby Riggs in the Battle of the Sexes; in 1974, the president of the National Organization for Women and other women's group leaders had met with President Ford in the White House.

Ratso tried to assure her that he was interested in women's thoughts, but said he made a distinction between being able to appreciate a point of view and actually experiencing that point of view.

Joni asked, "Don't you think that you have any femininity in your spirit at all?"

Ratso said he did.

Joni wondered if he was comfortable expressing this femininity—was he afraid to cry?

Sloman told her that he cried a lot. Joni asked for clarification.

Ratso assured her that he cried when necessary, adding that he is a Cancer who had Saturn in his constellation for a long time. Joni, who is a Scorpio, said that this was logical, given the moon's power over tides, and given how much of the human body is water.

Then Joni asked if Ratso saw more similarities between her songs and Joan Baez's and Ronee Blakley's than between her songs and Dylan's and Cohen's. "You know, I really think that you have limited your experience by a preconception. We do this all the time. I have to be aware of my preconceptions."

Ratso said that the three women were simply examples of . . .

". . . I asked you a question first," Joni pointed out. "I said, 'Do you think there is more in common in the work of us three women . . .'"

". . . As females, as prototypical female songwriters."

"I asked you a question and you answered it and I'm confronting you with that question again. I'll ask it again, do you think I have more in common in my work with Ronee and Joan than I do with any of the other men on your list, you said no before." (Joni: *so* Scorpio.)

Finally, Ratso admitted that, of all the songwriters in question, Joni probably had the most in common with fellow Canadian Leonard Cohen.

Joni accused Ratso of not having listened to the music she played during the show; he said he had listened, but it was difficult to hear lyrics during performances. She said, "I'm challenging you to an error of perception in yourself that you're missing the meat of what I do by putting me into a category."

This is, after all, the songwriter whose most signature song suggests that, after a careful consideration of clouds, love, and life from various vantage points—respectively, up and down, give and take, and win and lose—the only certainty you come away with is that you don't know anything about clouds, love, or life.

Ratso said it was not a question of categorization—it was simply that he found it impossible to fully empathize with a female perspective; Joni countered that in a lot of her songs she's an omniscient narrator or neutral observer. (She has often described herself as a playwright. She sees herself as a storyteller who spins yarns that are only sometimes based on her own experiences.)

"But you're always looking from your eyes," Sloman said.

"Well, what other place are you going to look from?"

They parried back and forth a few more times until Mitchell, upset, stood and started to leave. Sloman tried to stop her. Mitchell told him she didn't want to talk to him anymore because his point of view was "too narrow," and walked off. (When I interviewed Sloman, I asked him how pissed off Mitchell had been. He replied, "She didn't give me a cold shoulder at breakfast the next day.")

Two weeks later on the tour, after Rolling Thunder's final show at Madison Square Garden, Ratso and musician Steven Soles found themselves hanging out in Joni's room at the Westbury Hotel. Joni was playing them some new songs—"In France They Kiss on Main Street," and "Coyote," a song inspired by having trysted with the married Sam Shepard on the tour right on the heels of Shepard having an affair with tour manager O'Dell.

The Shepard affairs. When, during her fling with Shepard, O'Dell had noticed that the playwright's affections seemed to be waning, she had gone to his hotel room. She sat on his bed to talk to him, whereupon she heard the room's door behind her click shut: Joni, who'd been hiding in the bathroom, was making a hasty exit. O'Dell decided to gracefully bow out of the competition. "Everybody knew about it all," O'Dell told me. "That wasn't OK. I was working. I had a job to do. I couldn't afford that. It was really easy to make that decision." A few days after the hotel room scene, when O'Dell had to visit Mitchell in her dressing room to discuss some upcoming stops on the tour, Mitchell asked O'Dell to sit. Mitchell told her, "You know, I really admire the way you're handling this thing. You seem so confident and able to deal with this. I really respect that. I wish I could do the same."

O'Dell, who would go on to write a memoir about working in the music industry called *Miss O'Dell*, told me, "She was very gracious about it. I have a great deal of respect for her for that. To even say it out loud. Joni and I became friends after that. We'd laugh about it, how awkward it was. How silly it was because he was married. 'Well, *that* was crazy!'"

Years later, Mitchell will downgrade her affair with Shepard to a passing fancy; given that the classically handsome Shepard was arguably, in 1975, the eighth or ninth hottest man on the planet, it will seem an amusingly self-protective bit of understatement when Mitchell says of him retrospectively, "For me, on coke, I found him very attractive."

Back at the Westbury Hotel during Rolling Thunder, Ratso asked Joni to play "Coyote," and Joni said she was still working on the lyrics. Ratso joked that there would be more coyotes out on the road; Joni, taking the comedic bait, said that she would collect their pelts, "shameless hussy that I am!" They both started laughing, and soon Joni had launched into an improvised version of "Coyote," spurred on by Ratso's whooping and hollering, with Joni singing about how she's a chronicler of highly nuanced—and universal—feelings.

At the song's end, Ratso said, "You knew what I was saying that day. You just blew it all out of proportion. I was just saying that I got different eyes."

"And I was saying don't come around me until you widen your scope a little . . ."

Joni added that she was feeling exhausted. It had been a long night for her—she'd been fighting the flu the whole tour. She put her hand onto her head and said, "I feel like I've absorbed so much, being in the middle of a human experiment, and I've absorbed so much information, I haven't had time to sort it out yet."

She fell over onto the bed.

When Sloman finished writing *On the Road with Bob Dylan,* he sent copies of the manuscript to Dylan and to Mitchell. Dylan's collaborator Howard Alk called Sloman and left a message saying "I gave it to Bob. He read it one night and then I read it. We couldn't believe it, but you did it! You actually wrote this thing and we love it." Sloman was thrilled. Dylan would go on to call the book "the *War and Peace* of rock and roll."

But then, as Sloman explained to me in 2023, "I'm in bed a couple days later and I get a phone call. I'm half-asleep. It's, like, five in the morning, or two o'clock LA time. It's Joni and she says, 'Ratso, I can't believe it—why do you have me saying these things?'" Sloman reminded her that he had tape-recorded all their conversations. "I told her, 'Joni, you said all that stuff. I didn't make anything up.'" Considering the possibility that Mitchell had read only her own quotes and not the whole book, Sloman told her, "Look, do me a favor, go back and reread it, especially the preface and the end where I quote Ouspenskii talking about Gurdjieff. I think if you put it in that context, it'll make more sense to you." In these two brief sections of the book, Sloman quotes the Russian philosopher and esotericist Pyotr Ouspenskii talking about a dance that the Russian mystic George Gurdjieff had choreographed, and how Gurdjieff had intended the dance to be an allegory through which its dancers would come to know themselves better. Sloman told me, "So Joni did it. And she called me back and said, 'You're absolutely right.' Because if you read the whole book carefully, you get the idea of this traveling circus that reveals people's identities."

Ratso remained friends with Joni after the tour. He helped her find an apartment in New York; he took her to restaurants in Little Italy. "In some ways, she's very forthcoming, much more than you'd expect from a celebrity of that stature," he told me. "Very down to earth."

In the early nineties, Joni and Ratso started working together on Joni's memoirs. They'd meet at Joni's house in Bel Air; Ratso collected about seven hours of tape.

But when Joni's and Ratso's lawyers got on the phone with each other in order to negotiate terms for their clients, the negotiations became protracted.

So protracted that Joni got cold feet.

8

2008. A regal, sixty-five-year-old Mitchell, dressed in white linens and a tan cap, is at a dinner party near her second home, a rustic hideaway on the Sunshine Coast of British Columbia. An archipelago, the Sunshine Coast is accessible only by boat or plane. This remote part of the world throbs with a gnarled enchantment—during my trip there two summers ago, the area's many moss-encased tree trunks kept coaxing my imagination hobbit-ward.

At the 2008 dinner party, Mitchell was holding court, occasionally dispensing wisdom or opinion in the manner of a much-loved, all-knowing empress. This social stance is not unusual for her: in 2023, I interviewed Rosanna Arquette, a close friend of Mitchell's for more than thirty years, about what it's like to spend time with Mitchell, whom I've never met. I asked Arquette, "If you had to describe Joni to someone who's never met her, how would you describe her?"

"I would say, She's the goddess of music."

"No, I mean more What's she like in a room?"

"She tells stories. You sit and you listen," Arquette said. "Everybody sits at her feet. Bows down and listens."

As with many autodidacts, Mitchell does not wear her erudition lightly. In 1988, an interviewer from *New Musical Express* reported, "I haven't been in the room five minutes and Joni Mitchell is quoting great chunks of Nietzsche at me"; when the *New York Times* talked to her in 1998, Mitchell, whom David Crosby once called "about as modest as Mussolini," compared herself to Mozart, Picasso, and William Blake, and her lyrics to the Bible.

Joni's mellow at the dinner party in British Columbia was ruffled when she overheard one of the other guests, Mitchell biographer Michelle Mercer, who was working on her book *Will You Take Me as I Am*, asking the person sitting next to her, a Reiki healer, whether she ever tries to be funny when conducting healings. Mercer explained to her dinner companion, "Humor can be seen as a sign of enlightenment—it might make your clients trust you."

Joni was not having it. She raised her voice and laid into Mercer: "Humor is no sign of enlightenment," she said. "Humor is necessary, but it's not a sign of anything. Don't put it that way, because it's ignorant."

The room filled with five hundred pounds of gravity, as if the dinner party had just landed on Jupiter.

It's not that Mitchell's companions hadn't heard this kind of tone-shifting pronouncement from her before. But wasn't this the same person who, famously, had sung "Laughing and crying / You know it's the same release"? Moreover, if we consider the various life stages of Joni Mitchell—roughly speaking, Kid Joni, Coffeehouse Joni, Laurel Canyon Joni, Jazzy Joni, Bitter 1980s and 1990s Joni, and Beloved Queen of the Universe Joni—it felt a little late in the day, here in 2008, for our Beloved Queen to be issuing a blast of eighties- and nineties-style Bitter. Hadn't everyone . . . moved on?

The comment was equally strange because, despite Mitchell's reputation as an enabler of the world's sorrows, humor has always been an important part of her work—the world will still be listening to "Big Yellow Taxi" in a hundred years partly because the song's levity makes its heavy message delightful, unlike Mitchell's later attempts at the same theme in other songs, in the eighties and nineties, or on 2007's *Shine*. Similarly, having "The Circle Game" protagonist's *cart*wheels morph into *car* wheels as he ages is a burst of wit that keeps that song from collapsing into "On Top of Old Smokey" territory. Or look at the sly satire of many of the songs on *The Hissing of Summer Lawns* and *Turbulent Indigo*; or the more overt comedy of "You Turn Me On, I'm a Radio" or "Talk to Me," which spoofs Joni's chattiness and has her impersonating a chicken.

The following evening, Mitchell apologized to Mercer for "going after" her. Mitchell confessed to her, "I get kind of agitated. I'm finally going in for a 'treatment' so that I won't be so rrrr-rrrr-rrrr, so terrier-like."

Mercer responded diplomatically, "At least I know where you stand."

"Oh, you *never* have to worry about that with me."

9

If you ever find yourself with a little pocket of time to kill, say on a quiet Thursday evening when all of your loved ones are in thrall to prestige television, you can do worse than to contemplate Myrtle teaching Shakespeare sonnets to young Joan. When I did it recently, I imagined the two of them sitting in the kitchen in Saskatoon, tackling Sonnet 13, the one that starts "O! That you were yourself! But, love, you are," the sonnet that basically says, You're awesome, but awesomeness fades, so pass your awesomeness on to your children. Who would do otherwise? "None but unthrifts."

The image of two headstrong women wrestling with reproachful iambs captured my imagination. But even more beguiling to me was imagining young Joan subsequently viewing one of her schoolmates committing an act of negligence—say, leaving his bike out in the rain, or leaving a movie after the first five minutes—and then pronouncing, through her sacred fog of cigarettes and mild disdain, "What an unthrift!"

Given the pedagogical nature of Joni's early experiences with literature, not to mention that her songs are simultaneously deep but relatable to a wide range of ages, it makes a lot of sense that her music would seep into the educational system. Those of us who grew up in the seventies know all too well the feeling of sitting in a hard wooden chair, or around a spitty campfire, warbling "The Circle Game" almost to the point of lightheadedness.

As it turns out, during that same decade, many third-grade students in New Jersey were required to study the lyrics of "Big Yellow Taxi" when the song was made part of their curriculum.

A short, punchy folk song that is built on the repeated image of paradise being paved over and turned into a parking lot, shifting in its last verse to the personal—the singer's "old man," or lover, is taken away by a taxi, as if to say, The environment isn't the only thing that perishes when neglected—Joni wrote "Big Yellow Taxi" in 1968 on her first trip to Hawaii, less than a year before 3 million gallons of oil would spill into the waters off Santa Barbara, and that pollution would cause Ohio's Cuyahoga River literally to burst into flames. On awakening in her high-rise Oahu hotel room one morning, she opened the curtains, saw an endless parking lot, and cried. The song has gone on to be recorded by at least 569 other artists, including Cher, Amy Grant, Keb' Mo', Green Day, Counting Crows, and Harry Styles; Janet Jackson sampled it, and Bob Dylan rewrote and then mumble-sang it.

"Big Yellow Taxi" has a spirit of fun and a comic concision that belies the song's fairly rigorous lyrical agenda. After all, this is a song that asks its listener (a) to appreciate what you have before it disappears, (b) to lament the decimation of the natural world, (c) to scorn the profit motive, (d) to embrace the rigors of organic farming by accepting spots on apples, and (e) to rue the late-night departure of your lover by yellow taxi.

It's *a lot* to ask of an eight-year-old.

10

1979. Mitchell is in her house in Bel Air when the phone rings. It's her friend Warren Beatty. Mitchell liked to refer to Beatty as "Pussycat," a jocular reference to his pickup line, "What's new, Pussycat?" (Among Mitchell's other charming turns of phrase are "Hot *dog*!" to express excitement and calling someone "a real smooth cookie.")

Beatty, whom Mitchell had met through her agent and the head of her record label, David Geffen, was doing preproduction work on his movie *Reds*. Anxious to talk to people who were alive in the 1910s, the period during which most of *Reds* takes place, Beatty was calling Mitchell because he wondered if she might put him in touch with her friend Georgia O'Keeffe, who was born in 1887.

Mitchell felt slightly inhibited about connecting Beatty with the great modernist artist. Mitchell's friendship with O'Keeffe was neither long-lived nor easy; accounts of the brief amount of time the two women spent together invariably sound like Mitchell is trying to reconcile herself to a fifty-six-years-her-senior version of herself: Granny Joni. After all, both women were severely beautiful, prairie-raised, cloud-obsessed painters and feminist role models who were born in November, had had rocky experiences at art school, and had posed nude—not to mention prickly, self-made, highly influential artistic pioneers and semi-hermits often irritated by people's reaction to their work, particularly with respect to gender. (Of critics' constant likening of her paintings of flowers to female genitalia, O'Keeffe once wrote in an exhibition catalog, "When you took time to really notice my flower you hung all your own associations with flowers on my flower, and you wrote about my flower as if I think and see what you think and see of the flower—and I don't." Which sounds like a liner note from an early Joni album.)

The two women's friendship had started two years earlier, when, without notice, Mitchell had dropped off on O'Keeffe's doorstep in Abiquiú, New Mexico, copies of her most recent album, *Hejira,* and her book of drawings, *Morning Glory on the Vine.* (Getting in touch with people whose work you admire was a skill that Mitchell had picked up from Beatty.) Mitchell had included a note with her gift: "I want you to have this book—it is a collection of growing pains. The work it contains is not quite ripe. Nevertheless—I want you to have it out of my respect, admiration, and identification with some elements of your creative spirit."

O'Keeffe, spurred on by her fifty-eight-year-younger companion and assistant Juan Hamilton's interest in Mitchell, wrote back.

Dear Joni Mitchell,

I wanted to write you and thank you for the record and the book you left, but I did not have an address. My friend, Juan Hamilton, thought I might like to meet you also and got your address from someone in Los Angeles. If you would like to come and visit for a day or two, please write or call Juan . . .

Hoping you have not gotten washed away by the Aclifornia [sic] rains.

Sincerely,

Georgia O'Keeffe

O'Keeffe's letter languished in a sack of fan mail at Mitchell's house for many months before Mitchell read it. However, the two women finally connected, and Mitchell, who was working on her album *Mingus*, her collaboration with the jazz great, at the time, ended up staying with the ninety-year-old O'Keeffe for five days in the summer of 1978.

During the stay, Mitchell was slightly put off at their initial dinner because O'Keeffe launched into a critique of a previous guest—"Well, Warhol was here, he wasn't much." To the current guest, this felt judgey.

Let's hear from the houseguest here: "Everything was home cooked and delicious, and I had the distinct feeling she was checking me out. The funny thing was I'd bought all these Indian things—ankle bells and rattles—in Santa Fe on my way there. I was just dying to go up to my room and try them on. But I didn't want to appear rude and just leave her there, and she kept chatting away. But in the end I thought, What the hell, so I put them all on and then let out a few chants and leapt around the room. She just stood there leaning on her cane, staring at me, saying, 'You're a pretty curious visitor.'"

The next day, O'Keeffe woke Mitchell up early—as you'll remember, Joni keeps vampire hours—and they went for a long walk in the country with Hamilton. "She was amazingly energetic for a woman in her nineties. She's racing along this road, and of course I'm chain-smoking all the way, trying to keep up with her. She suddenly stops and says, 'You shouldn't smoke.' Her housekeeper, Juan, said in surprise, 'Georgia, you don't usually tell people what they should do.' And Georgia turned to me and said sternly, 'Well, you should live.'" Which must have sounded very stern to someone who has called nicotine a "grounding herb."

The two women seemed to find more common ground when it came to their mutual interests in painting and music. "I would have liked to have been a musician, too, but you can't do both," O'Keeffe told Mitchell at one point, probably alluding to the fact that in the first half of the twentieth century, it was an uphill battle to prosper as a woman in *one* male-dominated field, let alone two. "Oh, yes, you can," Mitchell told her—whereupon O'Keeffe leaned in like a delighted little kid and said, "Really?" (Mitchell: "I thought, The old bird is gonna be taking up the fiddle any minute now!")

Did they have fun together? Did Mitchell attain new insights into O'Keeffe's spare, hypnotic work? Did Mitchell try to attach one of her ankle bells to one of O'Keeffe's animal skulls? Mitchell's accounts of the stay make it sound less like summer camp or a dance party than an extended visit to the DMV. Joni would go on to paint a series of paintings inspired by the time she spent with O'Keeffe, but would destroy all of them, save for one, a picture of O'Keeffe's rain barrel, which Mitchell exhibited at her retrospective of paintings at the Mendel Art Gallery in Saskatoon in 2000, even though "My cat peed on it."

But if Mitchell's visit with O'Keeffe was a trip to the DMV, it was one that ended with Mitchell getting her proverbial license: months later, back in LA, she picked up a copy of *ARTnews* magazine in which an interviewer asked O'Keeffe what she would like to come back as if she were ever reincarnated. "In another life," O'Keeffe answered, "I would come back as a blond soprano who could sing high, clear notes without fear."

Hot *dog.*

But, to go back to the phone call from Beatty, it wasn't Mitchell's and O'Keeffe's shared orneriness that made Mitchell hesitant to hand over her older friend's phone number so that Beatty could grill O'Keeffe on influenza and the advent of rayon. Rather, it was something more akin to the two women's shared mode of perception: "I don't know," Mitchell responded to Beatty's request. "Georgia might say, 'Ah, yes, it was a very . . . *yellow* time period.'"

What's intriguing about this reference to yellow is that it sounds exactly like the kind of thing that Mitchell herself might say, particularly if she were in the recording studio. Joni's approach in the studio, whereat she has typically worked as her own producer, ably assisted by her longtime engineer Henry Lewy, is largely intuitive. She doesn't read music: as she told *Downbeat*, the magazine about jazz and the blues, in 1979, "I didn't know—and don't to this day—what key I'm playing in, or the names of my chords, I don't know the numbers, letters, or the staff. I approach it very paintingly, metaphorically." (Mitchell's process takes time: while mixing *Court and Spark*, she would spend about eight hours on a track, whereas industry standard at the time was more like three hours.)

The chief recipients of these metaphors are her musicians. "OK, Herbie—you're the ice cubes rattling in a glass," she told pianist and jazz legend Herbie Hancock when they were recording "Be Cool" on 2002's *Travelogue*; when trying to create the perfect aural equivalent for the lyrics in 1974's *Court and Spark* cut "Trouble Child," wherein Mitchell invokes waves breaking on the shore of Malibu, she asked the piano player Joe Sample to play "a Japanese wave."

"A Japanese wave?" he asked, baffled.

"Yeah, like *Doodle oodle loo breeow*," Mitchell said, making an ascending arc with her hand that folded back on itself when she hit the *breeow*.

You know, *that* kind of Japanese wave.

This process of adding layers to her musical compositions is similar to how Joni paints. With songs, she typically starts with a melody, then adds words, and then takes it into the studio; with paintings, she starts with a sketch and then starts applying successive coats of color.

The musician with whom Mitchell most often talked in metaphors was renowned saxophonist Wayne Shorter, who passed away in 2023. Prone to playing short bursts of birdlike notes—a possible accommodation that the former U.S. Army sharpshooter had made due to having asthma—Shorter, like Herbie Hancock, had played for Joni's musical idol, jazz legend Miles Davis, the icon of cool, take-no-shit sophistication who is widely considered the most influential jazz musician ever. Mitchell has said that Shorter was one of only two geniuses she's ever played with (the other being jazz drummer Brian Blade, of whom she's said, "He watches my shoulders, so he knows where I'm going to go next"). "Hearing Joni and Wayne talk," Herbie Hancock wrote in his memoir, "is like an out-of-body experience."

A typical cue that Mitchell might have given Shorter is "OK, you know, you come in here and you get out here, and when you come in, you come in as sad as you can possibly be, and you have to go out really young."

Shorter was similarly metaphorical: when he played on Hancock and Tina Turner's extraordinary cover of "Edith and the Kingpin," Mitchell's song about a pimp and one of his workers, Shorter told producer Hancock what his sax would sound like: "I'm going to be the guys that are at the bar that are kind of looking at the chicks and kind of whispering to each other." He sometimes told Mitchell during recording sessions, "I'm a string section now!" Prior to bringing the members of the quartet he started in 2000 on stage, Shorter would tell audiences, "See you at the movies." Brian Blade, who drummed in that quartet, told me he remembered Shorter once saying, "I want to be a duck. A duck that's sort of dead in the water, up top."

For Shorter's skittering, keening solos, Mitchell typically had Shorter do about ten takes, each of which was vastly different from the others—which is exactly why she adored Shorter's work—and then she collaged her favorite bits together: "Basically I have Wayne come in with his crayons and scribble all over my canvas, and then I paint over the ones I don't want, to get my space back." At the end of a session, Shorter might tell Mitchell, "Now, sculpt."

Mitchell has said that when she was recording *Travelogue* in 2000, Shorter was originally unavailable. "So I said to him, 'Wayne, you've got to play on this, otherwise I'll get your competitor.' And he went, 'No, no, no, don't do that. I'm the only one that can crawl across your shit.' And it's true. He just crawls across it like a fly, you know."

Mitchell knew that Shorter was a kindred spirit the first time they played together, in 1976. They were in London, recording *Don Juan's Reckless Daughter*. Prior to one take, Shorter explained to Mitchell how he was going to approach the song: "I'm going to play it like you're at Hyde Park and there's a nanny and a baby and a boat, and the baby puts the boat on the pond, and the wind is just nudging it. It's just nudging it."

Mitchell thought, "Oh my God, this guy."

11

October 11, 2022. The actress Jamie Lee Curtis was sitting in a radio studio in London, giving an interview to a British show called *Greatest Hits Radio*. Because Curtis has starred in two classic films in which characters assume alternate identities, the interviewer asked her, "If you could sort of do the *Trading Places* or *Freaky Friday* with another female artist . . . who would that have been?"

Curtis responded without hesitation. "Joni Mitchell," she said. "Joni Mitchell, Joni Mitchell, Joni Mitchell, Joni Mitchell, Joni Mitchell, Joni Mitchell, Joni Mitchell, Joni Mitchell, Joni Mitchell, Joni Mitchell."

To be sure, a singer-songwriter would be a potential source of envy to an actress because the former has more control over her material—as Faye Dunaway once said to Joni, "You're lucky because you can create your own roles." But the pull that Joni exerts over the famous people who are her fans goes deeper than that, as evidenced by k.d. lang saying that Joni is "the single most important artistic influence" in her life, or by Elvis Costello saying in 1997 that he had bought every one of Mitchell's records since her debut, or by Kate Bush saying that Joni "stands alone" or Chaka Khan saying "Her music saved my life."

That Mitchell has inspired countless numbers of musicians is less noteworthy than the fact that these acolytes are so diverse: What do disco queen Donna Summer, opera phenom Renée Fleming, Disney stalwart Alan Menken, pop stars Madonna and Lorde, children's entertainer Raffi, New Wave luminaries Joe Jackson and Chris Stein and Kate Pierson, "Sailing" and "Arthur's Theme" schmaltz purveyor Christopher Cross, Broadway tunesmith Sara Bareilles, sultry jazzer Diana Krall, indie darling Phoebe Bridgers, funk master Prince, bluesy rocker Lucinda Williams, and Maynard James Keenan, who founded the heavy metal band Puscifer, have in common? All have cited Mitchell as an influence.

Some of these famous fans are not shy about their fandom. When Joni and drummer Brian Blade gave a last-minute show at the tiny venue Fez in New York City in 1995, one audience member—Chrissie Hynde of the Pretenders—kept yelling "Let it out, Joni!" and "Go for it, bitch!" between songs. According to some reports, when fellow audience member Carly Simon asked Hynde to stop, Hynde grabbed Simon around the throat and stage-whispered, "That's a *real* singer up there!," whereupon someone in the audience suggested, "Why don't you have another drink, Chrissie?" and Simon left the venue. But according to a post signed "Love, Carly" on Carly Simon's website, Simon didn't recognize Hynde and asked her to pipe down, whereupon Hynde playfully choked Simon, saying "You're great, too, Carly—get up there, you need to do this, too," so Simon switched seats because this all was happening in the middle of a song.

Mitchell has famous fans who are not musicians, too, of course. Nobel Prize winner Kazuo Ishiguro, author of *The Remains of the Day*, said in 2015 that, forty-six years after its release, he still listens to *Hejira* "over and over again"; when asked that same year by the *New York Times Book Review* what books were on his nightstand, he mentioned books by Homer, Carson McCullers, Flannery O'Connor, as well as *Joni Mitchell: In Her Own Words*.

It makes perfect sense that Mitchell has influenced or inspired rafts of other sensitive singer-songwriters—people like Stevie Nicks or Tori Amos or Sarah McLachlan or Norah Jones or Shawn Colvin or Seal or Haim or SZA. It also makes sense that any sensitive singer-songwriter who is prone to mimicry, like Dar Williams, might even have to force herself to *stop* listening to Mitchell, to thwart mitosis. But even folks who you wouldn't imagine being swayed by Joni's music have fallen prey to its charms. In 2005, we learned that one of President George W. Bush's advisers had put Joni's cover of Leiber and Stoller's "(You're So Square) Baby I Don't Care" on the president's iPod (Joni's reaction: "Oh, God," followed by laughter, followed by "I wish they'd put in 'Dog Eat Dog,' you know?")

Similarly, you wouldn't necessarily peg Jimmy Page, the founder of Led Zeppelin, as a Joni fan. But when asked once about writing immortal songs like his "Stairway to Heaven," Page confessed, "I have to do a lot of hard work before I can get anywhere near those stages of consistent, total brilliance. I don't think there are too many people who are capable of it. Maybe one. Joni Mitchell . . . She brings tears to my eyes. What more can I say?" (Led Zeppelin's song "Going to California" is said to be a tribute to Joni; after singing the lines "To find a queen without a king / They say she plays guitar and cries and sings" at concerts, Robert Plant would sometimes add "Joni.")

In a 2022 interview on Yahoo.com, hard rocker Courtney Love, whose cover of "Both Sides Now" is a virtually unrecognizable three minutes and fifty-eight seconds of sonic distortion and moody caterwauling, suggested that Joni's music was important to her friend Lana Del Rey's 2019 album, *Norman Fucking Rockwell!*. Love said of Del Rey, "She described a record she wanted to make to me, and I'm like, 'Oh you mean *Hissing of Summer Lawns*. She's like, 'What's that?' I'm like, 'It's a Joni Mitchell record.' She's like, 'Who's that?'" So Love proceeded to give Del Rey "all the Joni" and it "changed her fucking whole thing."

What's lovely about all these famous fans is the way that their appreciation of Joni ends up normalizing them—how it makes them seem like you or me. Legendary soprano Renée Fleming, one of the few stars of opera to achieve name recognition beyond the classical music world, has said that when she met her idol for the first time—the idol whose records helped Fleming to develop her voice because, in high school, Fleming liked to harmonize high up above Joni—she knew she had two choices. "I could fall at her feet and grovel, sobbing hysterically, or I could say, 'How nice to meet you.'"

She went with the latter.

12

Maidstone, Saskatchewan. Probably 1947 or 1948. The tiny (two blocks, one church, one hotel) hamlet of three hundred or so people that the Andersons will live in until they move to Saskatoon in 1954 when Joan is eleven.

Myrtle had just gotten a phone call from the grocery store: a brick of Neapolitan ice cream had come in. So Myrtle sent little Joan over to pick it up. As Joan approached the store, though, she saw something that dazzled her: having tied up their horses nearby, ten Indigenous people, probably Cree, all wearing beautiful beaded leather, were silently sitting on the store's steps and porch.

Joan couldn't go in the store. Not because she was frightened. Rather, she was transfixed by the group's solemnity and self-possession and quiet majesty, all borne out by their gorgeous clothing.

(Joni's love of Indigenous cultures will continue through her life, and in 2018, she was given the honorary Indigenous name Sparkling White Bear Woman. "Some Indigenous people consider her a prophet because of her love of the earth," Mitchell's friend since childhood Sharolyn Dickson told me.

"One Saulteaux community wanted to honor her by giving her an Indigenous name, and my understanding is that they had a sweat lodge in which they did some exploration about what they might name her. The white bear in Indigenous culture has great significance because it's so rare, and then the sparkling applies to her creativity.")

Back in Maidstone, young Joan's spell couldn't be broken—not even by the prospect of three flavors of ice cream. She walked home empty-handed. Whereupon Myrtle tried to convince her that Joan had been too scared to enter the store.

Mitchell has long understood the way that clothing can pull focus. Her own wardrobe has seen her embracing the flower child aesthetic (peasant blouses, turquoise jewelry, bare feet); berets; and, later in life, the tenty, unstructured robes of designer Issey Miyake. But the woman who wrote the lyric "Everything comes and goes / Marked by lovers and styles of clothes" has also loved mixing it up, using wardrobe to subvert expectations and to reveal parts of her personality. "The lights went up revealing her dressed in a grey suit and hat," one William and Mary student wrote about a show Mitchell gave on campus in 1976, "looking more like a thirties gangster than a popular music star." To a student reporter for the University of Pittsburgh's paper that same year, Mitchell's wide-brimmed black hat, high-cut black jacket, and scarlet blouse made her look "more like someone who was ready to perform a flamenco than sing songs from *Blue*." When, in 2015, Mitchell became one of the faces of Yves St. Laurent in a series of stark black-and-white photos shot by the fashion house's creative director, it was Mitchell's age, not her bespoke leather cape and wide-brimmed hat, that subverted expectations: she was seventy-one.

Let's enjoy one outfit from each decade of her life.

Her childhood.

What she wore to school on Halloween in the first grade: high-waisted pants; a dark, bolero-like blazer over a button-down dress shirt; her father's necktie; bunny ears; an air of glee.

Her teens.

What she wore to the first concert she ever attended (Ray Charles in 1956): her father's jacket; black pants called "Slim Jims" onto whose sides she glued rhinestones.

Her twenties.

What she wore to compete to be the queen of the Southern Alberta Institute of Technology in 1964 (for which she was sponsored by the school's Industrial Electrical Technology Department): a sleeveless, pale pink organza gown with shoulder ruffles; a black handbag; long white gloves.

Her (almost) thirties.

What she wore when she performed at the Berkeley Community Theater in March 1972: a tie-dyed, strawberry-colored, bishop-sleeved pantsuit.

Her (almost) forties.

What she wore to perform at Wembley Arena in London on April 23, 1983: a black jacket over a vividly printed red-and-black blouse, earrings in the shape of half-moons, a trilby. During that same show: a double-breasted, striped men's suit with shoulder pads, the pants cuffed to mid-calf; a tweed newsboy cap.

Her fifties.

What she wore when Herb Ritts photographed her for the June 1997 issue of *Vanity Fair*: cuffed white jeans; a knee-length, black shirt-dress, tied with a belt but unbuttoned almost to the navel; bare feet; a facial expression of petulant subjugation.

Her sixties.

What she wore to her sixtieth birthday at a funky trattoria near her house in British Columbia: a tailored, pin-striped jacket over a loose-fitting black blouse and skirt. Hanging from her waist on a four-inch leather lanyard was an elongated red triangle that looked like a cross between a Native American coin purse and a hot water bottle.

Her seventies.

What she wore to the opening of a David Hockney exhibition at Los Angeles's Louver Gallery in February 2019: a vivid-verging-on-cartoony navy-blue-and-yellow, tufted and fringed steam-stretch sweater from Yoshiyuki Miyamae's fall 2018 collection from Issey Miyake; a black cap; micro-pleated blue slacks; red nail polish; no lipstick. In her left hand: David Hockney's fingers. In her right hand: a wooden cane.

Her (almost) eighties.

What she wore to the tribute concert held at Washington, DC's Constitution Hall when she won the Gershwin Prize for Popular Song in March 2023: a calf-length, sapphire-blue, scoop-neck dress and matching robe, both appliquéd with leaf patterns; a gold beret; three necklaces, a pair of dangly earrings, and various rings and bracelets, all in gold; designer sunglasses; a cane (a gift from one of her health aides) whose handle was capped on one side with a metal bear that Joni has painted white and adorned with sparkles in celebration of her Indigenous name.

Mitchell's interest in fashion may have even helped spur her growth as a singer-songwriter. In a portion of an interview that Mitchell gave writer Matt Diehl for the *Los Angeles Times* in 2010, but that Diehl wasn't able to use, Mitchell alluded to the fact that adjusting her guitars' open tunings during performances has required her over the years to fill long stretches of airtime with patter, so Mitchell got in the habit of telling rambling stories. Early on in her career, Mitchell told Diehl, the stories were "more fanciful. I had more of a fantasy head, but I killed it pretty young and made a conscious effort to become a realist. So they became more personal, but they used to be the art of the prairie tall tale—they used to be kind of fish stories." One night in the mid-sixties when she showed up half an hour late for a gig at a Philadelphia club wearing knee-high black boots and a yellow, secondhand drum majorette's jacket with gold braid and fringe, she concocted a shaggy-dog story to explain her jaunty getup: "I said I was really sorry, I was marching with the most unmilitary marching band." Then, to the Philadelphia audience's delight, she launched into a tale involving both a train that almost ran someone over as well as a crop duster that gave Mitchell a ride. "I'd invent this whole saga and as it would get more far out, people would giggle and forgive me for being late," Mitchell told Diehl. "I developed a kind of compulsive intimacy where everyone in the world was my confidant."

13

Winter, 1967–68. We're at a party at a popular den of iniquity for the Laurel Canyon crowd, Peter Tork's house at 3615 Shady Oak Road.

Even though Peter Tork was a member of a manufactured boy band—the Monkees, whose eponymous sitcom ran on NBC from 1966 to 1968—the teenybopper idol had street cred: he'd come out of the Greenwich Village folk scene. His house was a white, gated, hilltop compound that had formerly belonged to character actor Wally Cox. In the tiny microcosm of Laurel Canyon, you'd go to Mama Cass Elliot's place to meet other groovy up-and-comers (e.g., Jimi Hendrix, Eric Clapton, Jack Nicholson) or maybe to be life-coached by an earth mother (Elliot), and you'd go to Joni's place to join a kind of songwriters' salon presided over by Good Empress Joni, but you went to Tork's to unwind, or possibly even to unleash your throbbing id.

"Someone would always be pushing the limits of public decency in the kitchen," as one Tork resident once put it; because there were no houses above Tork's, the nudity and the carousing could also spill out to the pool, like a Bruegel painting with more vitamin D. Tork's friend Augustus Owsley Stanley, the Grateful Dead's audio engineer, made regular visits from San Francisco with fresh batches of his homemade LSD; Tork's private chef whipped up delicious vegetarian fare for whoever was around. At one gathering, Jimi Hendrix played guitar in the pool house while Tork's girlfriend accompanied him on drums, naked. Some of the parties lasted for days.

Yikes, Laurel Canyon—just reading about you gives us a contact high. Centered around one of the deeper fissures in the only mountain range to bisect a major city, this neighborhood was both a literal and metaphorical refuge for the creative folk who moved there in the sixties—as it had been for the film industry folk who'd lived there previously. Imagine a Lite FM theme park populated by all your favorite peddlers of mellow—Carole King, Neil Young, James Taylor, Linda Ronstadt, Bonnie Raitt, Harry Nilsson, Glen Campbell, Paul Williams, and Jackson Browne lived in this enclave, as did members of the the Eagles, the Byrds, the Turtles, Three Dog Night, the Doors, and the Mamas & the Papas. The neighborhood smelled of eucalyptus and potential.

Up here at this higher elevation, overlooking the smoggy monster that was LA below, the twisty, serpentine roads—on a map, Laurel Canyon's roads, all loop the loop and whorl, look like a fingerprint—were littered with mature oaks and small, rentable houses built on stilts. It was rare that anyone locked their door. As the crow flies, you were only a couple of miles from the grit and neon of the Sunset Strip, where most of the rock clubs were, but ideologically, you were on another planet. Spring rains brought swaths of wildflowers; in the afternoon of any day of the year, the air was thick with the sound of young bands practicing. If, while stoned out of your mind, you could navigate the neighborhood's many rickety wooden staircases and vertiginous hills, you were in a kind of paradise; as the title track of Joni's 1970 album *Ladies of the Canyon* would attest, here was a place to get really serious about baking brownies and wearing wampum beads.

The gathering in question was probably more sedate than some of the wilder evenings chez Tork. At one point, Joni announced that she had a new song she'd like to play for everyone. Sharing music was more or less the lingua franca of Laurel Canyon ("Someone would always say, 'Get a load of this new song I'm working on,'" Graham Nash wrote in his memoir *Wild Tales*. "You could set your watch by it."), so no one was likely surprised by Joni's offer; but, then again, this was Joni talking, so, who knows, she might be trotting out the next "Both Sides Now" or "The Circle Game." The assembled let out a little cheer: a new Joni song!

Joni looked over at the guy she'd most recently been seeing—David Crosby, he of the walrus mustache and the fringed buckskin and the signature purple velvet cape, the blustery Yosemite Sam with the surprisingly lovely tenor who'd been kicked out of the folk-rock group the Byrds for his motor mouth and intransigence, and who decades later would be the sperm donor for two of Melissa Etheridge's four kids. He'd grown up in Southern California, the chubby and insecure son of an Oscar-winning cinematographer father who'd shot *High Noon* and *The Old Man and the Sea* but who never told David that he loved him. Depictions of Laurel Canyon often have a goofy, stoned-at-breakfast shagginess to them, and none more so than the ones featuring Crosby, even though he lived ten miles west of the Canyon, in Beverly Glen: the sight of Crosby tooling around on his Triumph motorcycle with his cape thrashing in the air behind him caused one onlooker to comment, "It's Lawrence of Laurel Canyon!" Others talked about Crosby's "pullover pot"—marijuana so powerful that, if you were in a car while under its influence, you'd pull over to the side of the road to try to remember where you were headed.

It had been an intense couple of months for Crosby and Mitchell. Crosby had stumbled onto her when she was performing at a club called the Gaslight in Coconut Grove, Florida, in the autumn of 1967. He had been blown away by her talent and her beauty (Crosby: "After I peeled myself off the back of the room, I realized I had just fallen in love"). The two of them had started hanging out and swapping songs and talking about making Joni's first record. Mitchell was a little cooler on the brash-but-enthusiastic Crosby than he was on her—and indeed, she'll later deny their couplehood, downshifting it to a brief summer romance—but she was clearly impressed at the time by having the attention of a star: the Byrds, sometimes referred to at the time as "America's Beatles," had more or less put folk rock on the map with their hit covers of Pete Seeger's "Turn! Turn! Turn!" and Dylan's "Mr. Tambourine Man." At some point during her and Crosby's fling, Mitchell excitedly called up her manager, Elliot Roberts, and told him "I'm fucking a Byrd!" (Roberts responded, "Excuse me?")

Weeks after meeting her, Crosby brought Mitchell out to LA and started introducing her to people in the business. Though Mitchell's first big commercial break hadn't happened yet—Judy Collins's single of "Both Sides Now," which would sell a million copies and win a Grammy, would come out in October of 1968—but industry folks knew other Joni songs, like "Urge for Going" and "The Circle Game" and "Michael from Mountains," because already established singers like Tom Rush, Buffy Sainte-Marie, and Dave Van Ronk had started covering them.

Los Angeles, with all its gas-guzzling cars, was initially off-putting to eco-conscious Joni, who sometimes broke into tears at the sight of motorboats. But soon she and her music were getting a lot of attention. When introducing Mitchell to industry folk, Crosby liked to get them staggeringly stoned on his pullover pot—sinsemilla, fairly rare at the time, but Croz had the hookup—and then have Mitchell play a few songs for them. Mitchell found these mini-concerts a little dog-and-pony. It probably didn't help that, along the way, Crosby had also encouraged her to lose the false eyelashes and the mascara and the man-made fibers, as if to put her in lockstep with bohemia. (Joni had been in the habit of wearing false eyelashes because she thought she looked plain without them. But, once she abandoned them, she found it was "a great liberation" to wake up, wash her face, and not have to do anything else.) "I was outside the uniform of rock & roll, and it was annoying to some people," she'll later say, recounting how, when she wore a pair of Yves St. Laurent pants and a nice blouse to a Carole King concert once, she felt "really uncomfortable." In 2014 she told the *Sunday Times* of London that she was never a hippie, "I was in it for the costume show."

One of the people Crosby introduced Mitchell to was Mo Ostin, the head of Hollywood's hippest record label, Warner-Reprise, which had been founded by Frank Sinatra in 1960 in order to allow more artistic freedom for his own recordings. Ostin agreed to sign Joni and offered—under the condition that Crosby produce the record—full creative control. Shazam.

At the Tork party, Mitchell launched into her new song, much of which she addressed to Crosby. A slow ballad, "That Song About the Midway" addresses a male, guitar-playing singer who has a striking appearance and who is a devil disguised as an angel; according to the singer of the song—who says she has lost her romantic ardor over time—the guitar-playing devil/angel is a cheat. (Crosby will later telegraph his reputation as a libertine—at one point he'll go on tour with two female lovers—by writing a song, "Guinnevere," in which he refers to Guinnevere three times as "m'lady.")

As many of the people in the room knew, Mitchell and Crosby had grown apart during the intense process these past few months of recording Mitchell's first record. Moreover, Mitchell knew that Crosby had reacquainted himself with his former flame Christine Hinton, the founder of the Byrds' fan club. Crosby and Mitchell would have been working on, or would soon work on, "Cactus Tree," the final song on the record. If there's any song that Mitchell has ever written that captures a woman's prerogative, it's this one: though three men long for our narrator, she is too busy with her own life—too busy, in the song's parlance, being free—to be tied down. The narrator will love these men, the lyrics tell us, when she chooses to; but if they try to follow her, they'll lose her.

The party grew deeply awkward as Mitchell finished up what everyone realized was her breakup song with Crosby. It was difficult to know how to respond—Great nail in the coffin, Joni?

And then Joni did something interesting.

She sang the song again.

The money from her first record deal allowed Mitchell to buy a house in Laurel Canyon for $36,000 in the spring of 1968. (She's making between $3,000 and $5,000 per concert at this point; by the time she records *Blue* in 1970, she'll have netted half a million dollars—more than $4 million in today's money—in songwriting publishing royalties.) Home ownership is always a powerful marker of independence, but let's add to it the fact that in 1968, women wouldn't have their own credit cards for another six years. Joni had a house, a car, and creative control over her record. Hear her roar.

Built into the side of a hill by a Black jazz musician in the 1930s, Mitchell's cozy one-bedroom bungalow on Laurel Canyon's Lookout Mountain Avenue was a charming accumulation of knotty pine and ripple-paned windows and creaky floors. Mitchell kitted it out with her artwork, Victorian shadowboxes, quilts, a Tiffany lamp, a wooden pig from a carousel, a grandfather clock Leonard Cohen gave her, cloisonné tchotchkes, old dolls, and other boho frippery. Looking out the bungalow's windows, she could see the homes of neighbors Frank Zappa and Chaka Khan (when Myrtle, who would continue to have a psychological hold on Joni until Myrtle's death in 2007, came to California to nurse an ill Joni once, Myrtle saw naked women floating on a raft in Zappa's pond and was horrified. But probably not as horrified as the night when cops climbed up on Joni's roof in order to spy on her next-door neighbors, the band Canned Heat.)

But while Mitchell was waiting to move in, she was living at Crosby's house in Beverly Glen. (This was probably less awkward than it sounds, given that Mitchell hadn't fallen in love. Also, she will enjoy a long history of working with, and remaining friends with, her exes.)

Graham Nash had gotten divorced, left his group the Hollies, and moved to LA. A self-called "poor man's son," Nash had grown up in Blackpool, England, and worshipped the Everly Brothers, the American rock duo known for their close harmony singing. A year older than Joni, he had warm but penetrating eyes, a sculpted mane of hair, and a Manchester brogue that turned "touch" into "tooch." He dressed with a neo-Edwardian flair that incorporated vests, floral print shirts, and ankle-length, black velvet coats. His band the Hollies had had a hit in the States with "Bus Stop," and, back home, had shared bills with their friends the Rolling Stones and the Beatles (you can hear Graham whistling at the end of the Beatles' "All You Need Is Love"). He calls Joni "Joan" or "luv." Most people call him Willy—a nickname that, despite his claim that at a Hollies show in Glasgow once, some seventy-five women fainted and had to be passed hand-over-head, mosh pit–style, to safety, was not a reference to his todger (his full name is Graham William Nash).

Mitchell knew Nash because they'd hooked up in Ottawa in the summer of '67 when they'd both been performing there. "After the show the promoter throws the usual party where you're standing there with a plastic glass of awful wine, and you're trying to, you know, smile at everybody," Nash, whose marriage was crumbling at the time, has said. "And I was—I saw this blonde in the corner, and she was incredibly attractive. And my manager was nattering in my ear about whatever it was—you know, promoter and his wife's name, and say hello to Georgie, and all that kind of stuff. And I say, Stop talking to me, I'm just trying to attract this woman. And he said, Well, if you'll just listen, I'm about—I was trying to tell you that her name is Joni Mitchell and she wants to meet you."

Nash walked over and introduced himself; "Yes, I know who you are. That's why I'm here," Mitchell said. She was wearing a pale blue silk dress. Seeing the thick, book-like object in Mitchell's hands, Nash said, "Tell me about the Bible."

"It's not a Bible, it's a music box," she said, activating the music, whose final, off-key note caused them both to laugh and then to start talking in earnest.

Joni invited Graham to her hotel room at the Château Laurier, where the combination of a wood-burning fireplace, incense burning in ashtrays, and scarves draped over lamps further beguiled him. She played him twenty or so of her songs. So heady and intoxicating was his evening with Mitchell that when Nash woke up the next morning, he realized that when he'd called the front desk the evening before and asked for a wake-up call, he'd forgotten to hang the phone up properly; now he'd have to get himself 938 miles away to his band's next show in Winnipeg, toot sweet. Blimey!

But he also found a note in the room that read, "I will find you once again."

The next summer, when Nash flew to New York, he discovered that Leonard Cohen was staying at Joni's Chelsea apartment. Joni had met the Chekhovian, deadpan Cohen, one of the greatest lyricists of all time, at the Newport Folk Festival; though Cohen hadn't put out a record yet, he had published fiction and poetry, and Judy Collins had covered his timeless "Suzanne." An oft-told story runs that Cohen went to a Dylan concert in Montreal and exclaimed, "This guy is so fucking bad! If that son of a bitch can make a living singing, then so can I!"

Cohen will later say of Mitchell, "It was already current at that time that Joni was some kind of musical monster. There was a certain ferocity associated with her gift." The incantatory and sexually frank nature of Cohen's songs was not a disconnect from his in-the-flesh persona: his collaborator Sharon Robinson has said of the famous ladies' man, "Leonard had a way of putting women on a pedestal. He saw women as part of the path to some kind of righteousness or enlightenment." (After reading a book on hypnotism at age thirteen, Cohen had tried out his new powers of persuasion on his family's housekeeper, who proceeded to remove all her clothing.)

At some point in their friendship, college dropout Mitchell asked Cohen, who was nine years older and a published author, to recommend some books for her to read. To his credit, Cohen frontloaded his pedagogy by telling Joni, "For someone who hasn't read anything, you're writing very well." Cohen turned her on to Lorca, Camus, and the *I Ching*, the third of which launched her interest in Eastern spirituality. The Mitchell/Cohen romance lasted barely four months, and they were never exclusive, but their friendship and influence on each other endured. At one point he wrote her a poem in which he called her "Master Poet. Master Painter. Most Subtle Technician of the Deep"—someone who "Changed the Way Women Sing, and the Way Men Listen."

Nash annealed his disappointment by writing two songs he grouped together with the title "Letter to a Cactus Tree," a reference to the aforementioned "Cactus Tree."

Shortly thereafter, in Los Angeles, "Graham ended up at David's place," as Joni has put it, "where I was staying until my house was ready. He came down sick and I took him to my new house to play Florence Nightingale." (According to Nash, she took him by the arm during a wild party at Crosby's and said, "Come to my house and I'll take care of you.")

Joni and Graham's relationship in LA was a slow burn. "I fell in love with Graham, not initially, because initially he was not a warm person at all," Joni has said. "There was always a thin, icy barrier between him and anybody. Charming, genteel, and gentlemanly and all, but very withholding. Withholding of his heart. English reserve, perhaps."

But if Nash's lack of initial warmth is an obstacle for Joni at first, it's his experience with caretaking that will serve him well over the long haul. When Nash was eleven, his father was jailed for a year in a high-security prison called Strangeways after refusing to divulge where he'd gotten the camera that he'd given Graham (his father had bought it from a work colleague but, for some reason, didn't want to name the colleague). His father's imprisonment forced young Graham to take a more protective attitude toward his mother and his two younger sisters; meanwhile, his father's heart was broken by the experience, and he died at forty-six.

Both Graham's English reserve and his caretaking prowess will be assets in the band that he's about to form—Crosby, Stills & Nash, or later, once they add Neil Young to the mix, Crosby, Stills,

Nash & Young. In contradistinction to David Crosby and Stephen Stills, who'll have, respectively, a touch of the blowhard and the showboat to them, particularly when these gents are enlivened by cocaine—a drug that Crosby, Stills & Nash will be so enamored of that the group's nickname will be the Frozen Noses—Nash is a peacemaker. Crosby and Stills called him "Daddy." Maybe he was the Paul McCartney of CSN—mild-mannered, shaggily cute, and prone to writing the kind of song (e.g., "Marrakesh Express") that would not alarm your mother. (Later, he'll get spikier, with songs like "Military Madness" and "Chicago/We Can Change the World," about the Chicago Seven.)

Soon enough, English Reserve and Reckless Daughter are cooing and warbling in her Lookout Mountain Avenue aerie, the unofficial prince and princess of Laurel Canyon (a distinction that would eventually be usurped by Linda Ronstadt and JD Souther, the singer-songwriter and inveterate ladies' man who will cowrite some of the Eagles' biggest hits.)

Given that one of Mitchell's main themes as a songwriter is the dynamic between wanting true love and having personal freedom ("Caught in their struggle for higher positions / And their search for love that sticks around"), it's not surprising, and is maybe reassuring, to learn that, as a lover or partner, she embodies this essential push/pull tension; Nash will later say that Joni exhibited "an interesting clash of 'I want to get as close to you as possible'/'Leave me alone to create.'" Mitchell often has a laser-like focus when she's songwriting: Estrella Berosini, a singer-songwriter friend of Mitchell's from this period whom Mitchell immortalized as "Estrella, circus girl" in the song "Ladies of the Canyon," told me that her and Mitchell's song-swapping sessions could be intense: "Joni and I would sometimes go so deep into the right side of our brains, we'd speak in prose poetry and iambic pentameter. Hours would pass, it'd get dark, and still we were completely immersed in each other's creative process."

Graham learned to leave Joni alone when she entered what he calls "the Joni Zone." He later described this state with "She was gone for hours. She was physically right there. But she wasn't right there. She was gone."

What would Joni have been like as a roommate in her heyday? Sculptor Nathan Joseph, who rented half of his Soho loft on Varick Street in New York City to Joni from 1978 to 1987, told me that on some mornings Joni would visit him on his side of the loft, whereupon she would sing to Androcles, Joseph's African gray parrot, whatever song Joni had been up all night working on. Then, when Androcles sang the melody back to Joni, Joni would harmonize with the parrot.

Alas, living with Mitchell can't be all Snow White and her musical creatures. Nevertheless, when she's neither in a music- or painting-derived "Joni zone" (she once told a friend who'd called her on the phone, "I can't speak with you. I have to stay angry because I'm writing about the recording industry") nor ill (Joni's illnesses as an adult have included hepatitis, hypoglycemia, dengue, abscessed ovaries, double pneumonia, acid reflux, bronchitis, a bleeding lesion on her larynx, vocal nodes, three kinds of measles, post-polio syndrome, and the strange, possibly psychosomatic skin disease known as Morgellons), she sounds like a lot of fun. She has spent most of her adult life—due both to her metabolism and to early run-ins with stalkers—going to bed around 7:00 a.m. and then waking at 1:00 pm—so no fighting for the bathroom in the morning. Prior to her 2015 aneurysm, she preferred hanging with men ("I like men's humor. I like locker room talk") rather than women ("In my observation, what passes for feminine camaraderie is conspiracy"). She lerrrves her cats: she likes to make up songs for them, and she sometimes turns into a kitten when playing with them. She loves to shoot pool and play poker and pinball (at one point she'll acquire a pinball machine themed to the band KISS). She has tended to eat a lot of salad, lentil soup, and whole grain oats. She gets invited to a lot of killer Hollywood parties. She does yoga. She listens to NPR. It's no surprise that she listens to Steely Dan and Stevie Wonder ("a musical genius"), but it turns out she's also into Aerosmith and Journey. She's a gardener (which is fitting, given that her song "Woodstock," in lamenting lost innocence, urges us all to return to the Terrestrial Paradise). She is, according to one longtime colleague, a terrible driver. If you have an appointment with her, she might be as much as two hours late. She enjoys television and a bottle of Château Margaux. Could you hand me that ashtray, sweetheart?

Graham started painting when he lived with her; they took up photography together. Joni and Graham's cohabitation will achieve a kind of mythic status after Nash immortalizes it with his song "Our House," a sugar-sweet celebration of domesticity, complete with two cats and a flower-filled vase. (Nash once admitted that he was "bored with 'Our House' the day after [he] recorded it," but will play it occasionally "because it does mean so much to so many people.") Decades later, the song will show up on episodes of *This Is Us, The Simpsons, Cheers, The Blacklist,* and *How I Met Your Mother*; in commercials, the song has been used to sell sausages and throw pillows. So potent is the collective unconscious circling around Joni and Graham's union that in 1980 when Joni's fan Stevie Nicks records *Bella Donna*, her first solo album, Nicks will say of her musicians, "We were like Joni Mitchell and Crosby, Stills & Nash, living in this great house and making music"—despite the fact that only three of the four people she has named ever lived in one house at the same time.

Two years into their relationship, Joni and Graham went to Saskatoon. They were staying at Joni's parents' house, where they were required to sleep in separate rooms. "I can't describe what Joan's room looked like because I wasn't allowed within 20 feet of it," Nash writes. "Bill and Myrtle were a very straight, religious couple, and they weren't about to let a long-haired hippie sleep with their daughter under their roof, that was for sure . . . they put me in a downstairs bedroom, separating us by a floor, and made it clear I'd need an army behind me if I intended to sneak up there."

At one point during the visit, while Nash's hand was on the door to the downstairs bedroom, he asked Mitchell to give him more details about her mother.

"I'll tell you what my mother's like," Mitchell said. "Run your finger on top of the door."

Nash ran his finger across the top of the door. Uncovering nary a speck of dust, he said, "Wow!"

"Myrtle."

Nash's description of the time he lived with Mitchell—whom he calls a musical genius—bears one overriding similarity to the descriptions offered by her other boyfriends and her two husbands, almost all of whom have been musicians: Joni is spectacularly talented—but, damningly, Joni is also spectacularly prodigious. Every time you think you've had a creative breakthrough and *finally* written a song that might stand the test of time, Joni has written three songs that are better—their lyrics are more acute, their musicianship is more sophisticated and surprising, their overall effect is more memorable. Nash will say he felt "unworthy."

Estrella Berosini, the aforementioned lady of the canyon, told me, "Joni's house was so tiny. And they were both such monster talents. There wasn't enough room for both of them. I was a marriage counselor for so many years!" Adopting a woe-is-me voice, Berosini continued, "'My boyfriend! Oh my God, Willy!' I wanted to smack her on the face and say 'Snap out of it!' I was like, He's so wonderful, how could she do this to him? But other times it was like, Yeah, sure, get rid of him."

But ultimately, it's not envy or inadequacy that spells Nash and Mitchell's demise two years into their union. In March 1969, en route to the photo shoot for what will be Crosby, Stills & Nash's debut album—the record will hit #6 on *Billboard* and stay on the charts for a whopping 107 weeks before going quadruple platinum and winning a Grammy for Best New Artist—Mitchell wrote "Willy," her haunting song about Nash that will appear on *Ladies of the Canyon,* from which we deduce that it's Nash who didn't want to tie the knot because he wasn't ready. But, with time, Nash will change his mind and propose.

Mitchell initially said yes. But then, the more she thought about another marriage—her short-lived and largely practical one to fellow musician Chuck Mitchell a few years earlier had slightly tainted the institution for her—the more she decided it wasn't a good idea. To her mind, Nash was looking for, or would be best suited by, a more traditional wife, one who would stay home and raise the children. Nash denies this; as he'll write in his song inspired by the breakup, "Simple Man," he just wanted to hold Joni, he didn't want to hold Joni *down*. (In an interesting bit of parallelism, the first time that Nash performed the song, at the Fillmore East in June 1970, Mitchell was sitting in the third row. Mercifully, Nash didn't play it twice.) When Joni contemplated marriage to Graham, she thought, "I'm gonna end up like my grandmother, kicking the door off the hinges."

Nash—who'll go on to date singers Rita Coolidge and, sharp intake of breath, Barbra Streisand—was the first person with whom Mitchell ever thought she could pair-bond. A self-described serial monogamist, she'll have, over the years, three other serious relationships (with drummer John Guerin in the mid-seventies; with drummer Don Alias in the late seventies; and with bassist and producer Larry Klein, whom she'll be married to from 1982 to 1994), as well as various intense, shorter-lived ones. But Nash was the first of the sustainable ones, and thus the rupture seemed all the more dismaying, particularly to those who had internalized the goldeny glow that seemed to seep from the Lookout Mountain Avenue house like so much honey from a comb.

"Sometimes I get sensitive or worried, and it might bother the man I was with," Mitchell said in 2021. "But not Graham. He just said, 'Come over here to the couch; you need a 15-minute cool-out.' And then we would snuggle."

But, as Neil Young would title a song he wrote about Mitchell and Nash's troubles, only love can break your heart. Nash's next serious girlfriend, singer Rita Coolidge, will write in her memoir, "He had such a great love and respect not only for Joni but for her music." Three years after he and Mitchell broke up, Nash was still slightly depressed about it—and skeletally thin, down to 120 pounds. He and Mitchell have remained friends over the decades, and in 1996 he showed her how she could hook up a customized Stratocaster guitar to a Roland VG-8 computer processor that allowed her to preprogram all her artisanal guitar tunings, thus saving audiences from enduring long stretches of guitar hygiene. When Nash performs in Minneapolis in 2023, that city's *Star Tribune* will report that anytime Nash mentioned or referenced Mitchell, "a new intensity, a profound emotionalism, a heartfelt something—be it a loving warmth or an unrequited ache—surfaced in his singing." He sends her a dozen roses for her birthday every year.

Nash realized the relationship was over when, while installing new floors in Mitchell's Laurel Canyon house one day in the spring of 1970, he got a telegram that she had sent from Greece. The telegram read: "If you hold sand too tightly, it will run through your fingers"—which must have resonated when Nash reached for the sander.

Worse, *Déjà Vu,* CSNY's album with "Our House" on it, had just been released.

Joni's lyric from "Blue" was more right than ever: songs are *exactly* like tattoos.

In 1966, when the *Detroit News* visited Joni and her then-husband Chuck at their apartment in Detroit, the male reporter ended the article with the sentence "Joni nodded her approval, as any dutiful wife would." But we get a much different ending to an article that a *New York Times* reporter wrote three years later when she came to visit Joni and Graham in Laurel Canyon. The *Times* article captures Nash's openness, and hints at what made the Mitchell/Nash union work when it did.

Joni and Graham are at a recording studio where Joni is trying to record "Chelsea Morning," the song that will later inspire Bill and Hillary Clinton to name their daughter Chelsea. CSN's debut album is still a month away from being released.

In the article, Joni is struggling with "Chelsea Morning" while Graham is cheerleading on the sidelines. "I can't make it cook," Joni says, at which point the *Times* article adds, "Working, she looked very serious and womanly, an artist intent on creating perfection from visual images made into words, guitar chords providing a vessel to hold them and a voice to carry them as deep and as far as they'll go. She is essentially alone with her music."

When Joni stops in the middle of her eighth take of "Chelsea Morning," Nash asks, "Do you want to pack it in, luv?"

Joni smiles at him and, prior to launching into Take #9, tells him, "Just sit there and look groovy."

14

Queen Elizabeth School in Saskatoon. Fall 1956.

Joan had Mr. Kratzmann for English. Arthur Kratzmann was the tall, good-looking, middle-aged Australian teacher with a gold cap on one of his front teeth who, the previous year, had seen Joan hanging up some of the paintings she'd made for a PTA meeting. "Like to paint, eh?" he'd asked. "Yes," Joan had answered.

"If you can paint with a brush, you can paint with words. I'll see you next year."

Mitchell's longtime friend Sharolyn Dickson said of Kratzmann, "He really contributed to her fascination with putting words together." More tellingly, Kratzmann would help Joan figure out *what* to write about.

"This was a time of *Rebel Without a Cause* and *Blackboard Jungle* and the era of the deadly teenager," Joni said on CBC Radio in 1983. "Being a teenager was like being a punk. And he was the perfect teacher for a class with that feeling rising in them." *Rebel Without a Cause* opened less than a month after its star, James Dean, died, at age twenty-four, on September 30, 1955; by the next April, Elvis Presley's "Heartbreak Hotel" had reached #1 on *Bill-*

board's charts. "It was so animal, so sexual, the first musical arousal I ever had," Led Zeppelin's Robert Plant would later say of Presley's hit. "You could see a twitch in everybody my age."

The lesson Joan learned from Arthur Kratzmann started when, for her first assignment for him, she wrote a poem about a stallion. She'd done a little bit of riding at the time and had seen *Black Beauty*. Eager to impress, she used some words that she had looked up in *Reader's Digest*.

When Kratzmann handed the poem back to Joan, he'd made a lot of circles with his red pencil and written "cliché" next to the circles. He'd given Joan a B; at the bottom of the piece of paper he wrote, "Write about what you know, it's more interesting."

"Competitive" is a word that sometimes comes up in discussions of Mitchell. "We were on the bowling team together," Vancouver-based entrepreneur Tony Simon, who has been close friends with her since the ninth grade, told me. "It'd be her turn to bowl and it'd be like, Don't get in her way, or say anything, because she'll bash you with the bowling ball."

Back in Kratzmann's class, Joan read the poem written by the kid who sat next to her. It was terrible. But Kratzmann had given it an A+.

So Joan stayed after school and approached Kratzmann. He asked her how many times she'd seen *Black Beauty* and how much riding she'd done. They talked for a bit. When she told him what she'd done over the weekend, he said that her account of what she'd done over the weekend was more interesting than her poem. He'd been reading Nietzsche, so he even trotted out some of the thorny nineteenth-century philosopher and cultural critic for her: "You must write in your own blood."

The quote would stay with Joni; when she is on the cover of *Time* in December 1974, her first quote in the article is "The most important thing is to write in your own blood." Her interest in the philosopher will later lead her to name a cat after him; at times her life will seem to illustrate the philosopher's most famous aphorism, "What doesn't kill me, makes me stronger."

But the burning question for young Joan, of course, was her classmate's grade. "Excuse me, but how do you give an A+ to that when you give me a B?" she asked.

Kratzmann told her, "Because that's as good as he's ever going to write."

Of course, Joni *would* go on to write in her own blood. In early 1971, while recording *Blue*, her most personally revealing album, the album that allowed many of us to honor the fact that sometimes we're "selfish and sad," Joni appeared to be in the midst of a nervous breakdown or, as she called it, a "shamanistic breakthrough," that was fueled largely by her increasing celebrity and idolization. Joni once explained the ailment thusly: "Fame does cause you to get very unnatural responses from people. Somebody will call you an asshole in a public place, then someone tells that person who you are and they light up like a Christmas tree. I receive an inordinate amount of affection, which is a lovely thing, but sometimes, depending on your own undulating patterns of self-esteem, it can be terrifying. If your self-esteem is at a low ebb and you're being showered with affection it seems out of whack. It's like someone you feel nothing for telling you they love you. It's a weird feeling." (A variation on this phenomenon is also tricky: Mitchell told the *Calgary Herald* in 2007, "I was at a cafe somewhere, smoking, and a girl came up to me and said, 'I'm a manic depressive. I love your music but I hate pictures of you. Every time I see you, you're smiling and it makes me so mad!'")

Mitchell first experienced the disconnect at the Newport Folk Festival in 1969, when she and a friend tried to get into a party but were turned down by a bouncer. When the friend said "Do you know who she is?" some kids standing in line sucked their breath in at the mention of Joni's name. Joni's heart started beating rapidly. So she started running, as she has put it, "like some crazed animal. I ran, and I ran and I ran. I must've run about five blocks before I realized how strange my reaction was."

Ever since Rimbaud wrote the sentiment "I is another," artists have been grappling with the weird disconnect between the "I" in their work and the "I" of the meatspace. As Dylan once said after reading a newspaper article about him, "God, I'm glad I'm not me." Because keeping tabs on "me" is exhausting. The history of popular musicians trying to be, or trying to appear to be, authentic is long and storied, touching as it does on urban-dwelling singers on the Grand Ole Opry in the 1920s pretending to be poor white trash, to Dylan trying to emulate Woody Guthrie's hobo street cred by, say, starting two "Blowin' in the Wind" verses off with "Yes'n"; from Kurt Cobain writing a suicide note stating "The worst crime I can think of would be to rip people off by faking it," to various rap and hip-hop artists avowing, despite their embrace of Bentleys and bling, to "keep it real." Some of these impulses would be consonant with the anti-corporate, DIY ethos of the folk music scene from which Mitchell emerged.

In its mildest form—say, when a concertgoer yells out "I love you, Joni!" at a show—Mitchell has tried to deflect the moment with humor; when an audience member yelled out that very statement at a show in St. Paul in July 1974, Mitchell responded, "I never know what to say to that. Maybe you don't squeeze your toothpaste tube in the right place. I mean things like that can ruin a perfect relationship." But in more severe cases, Mitchell has, over the years, in an effort to maintain equilibrium amid an onslaught of expectation, literally run from fans, canceled appearances, shied away from the press, disguised herself with wigs, become flustered and embarrassed by her inability to remember the names of people flooding into her life, told photographers "please put a silence on your trigger," and hired private security. Sometimes she'll defy expectations by choosing to perform few or none of her hits at shows ("I kind of put a set together to please myself," she told an audience at the Gorge in Washington State in 1998). Crowds, as mentioned earlier, can freak her out.

If her fans were going to put her on a pedestal and see her as an icon rather than a living, breathing human, then, Joni thought at the beginning of the 1970s, it behooved her to give these fans a strong dose of the living and the breathing: the album *Blue*, whereon Joni cops to being lonely and flawed, baldly asking "Will you take me as I am?" If enough people "could listen to me saying 'I' and make it their own 'I,' then I wasn't just a nude up there, you know, jumping around for some kind of crazy pleasure," as she put it to a radio host in 1980. (When she made her subsequent album, *For the Roses*, she meant "a nude" literally: she had wanted the nude portrait of herself that ended up on the album's inner sleeve to be on the album's cover instead, but her manager Elliot Roberts dissuaded her by asking "Joan, how would you like to see $5.98 plastered across your ass?") As St. Augustine had put it in his *Confessions* in 397, when the bishop craved a monastic life rather than a life of service, "Why then do I put before you in order the stories of so many things? . . . I have become an enigma to myself, and herein lies my sickness and inner struggle."

By the time she was recording *Blue*, she was so beset with emotion that she had to have the studio doors at A&M locked; if anyone managed to wiggle in—Carole King was in an adjacent room of A&M, making *Tapestry*, and the Carpenters were simultaneously at A&M recording *Carpenters*—Joni would burst into tears. During these turbulent months, she felt like people were literally transparent to her—that she could see inside them and know too much about them. She could not go to the supermarket. She had a dream in which she was a transparent bag of organs that was sitting in a theater, sobbing. "I had no defenses," she would later explain. "I found myself in the public eye, and I felt transparent. I could see through myself and through everybody else, and it was too much information for my nervous system to take. I cleared out the psychology and religious departments of several bookstores, searching for some explanation for what I was going through."

15

February 4, 1991. The Wiltern Theater in Los Angeles.

Joni had gone to see Sting at the Wiltern. Joni loves Sting—ever since the night she and her ex James Taylor had dinner at their mutual manager's house and found out how much Sting admired them, Mitchell has always thought of Sting as their son. In the early eighties, she tried to get his band, the Police, to be her backup band for her album *Wild Things Run Fast*. By 1988, probably referencing Sting's increasing pull toward jazz, she'll say, "Sting is going over my territory."

Mitchell was really at the show at the Wiltern to see Sting's drummer, Vinnie Colaiuta, whom she'd worked with and admires. Already in an irritable mood—the show saw her alternately yelling "Give Vinnie a solo!" and smoking ciggies in the theater's wings—Mitchell went to the after-party, where she saw the former Eagles member Don Henley, Mr. Hotel California himself, sitting alone at a long booth. Mitchell and Henley were both on Geffen Records; Mitchell's last three albums for the label (*Wild Things Run Fast, Dog Eat Dog,* and *Chalk Mark in a Rain Storm*) hadn't made a lot of noise, and were part of her estrangement from Geffen and his companies, while Henley's most recent solo album, 1989's *The End of the Innocence*, had yielded three Top 40 singles and moved 6 million copies.

Joni walked over to Henley as if to sit down and said, "Hi, Henley," whereupon Henley looked left and right with a worried look on his face. Computing that this meant Henley was saving the booth for Sting, Mitchell mumbled something noncommittal, and went and sat at another table with Colaiuta and Bruce Springsteen and his girlfriend, Patti Scialfa.

A short while thereafter, Sting entered the room and went and sat with Henley.

Moments later, Henley sent an emissary over to Mitchell; the young woman said to Mitchell, "You can come and sit with Sting and Henley now."

Rising up on her haunches, Mitchell looked over at Henley and yelled, "Never!"

16

Late at night on February 10, 2019. An Italian restaurant in Los Angeles. Joni, who had not made many public appearances since her 2015 aneurysm, was having a quiet dinner with the singer-songwriter Brandi Carlile and a few others the night after the Grammys. Carlile, who'd won three Grammys the evening before, will, over the next few months, emerge as a dear friend and colleague of Joni's—Joni will call Brandi her "ambassador"—as well as the organizer of the "Joni Jams," the informal singalongs at Mitchell's house that will include participants like Dolly Parton, Paul McCartney, Elton John, Herbie Hancock, Meryl Streep, Bette Midler, and Bonnie Raitt. Also in attendance at the dinner in question were Joni's close friend and assistant Marcy Gensic and Carlile's partner, Catherine Shepherd.

Brandi and Catherine had taken an Uber to the restaurant, and then sat in their Uber and waited until Joni and Marcy pulled up in a small, dark car. Joni slowly emerged with her cane.

Brandi, unexpectedly, had not been a longtime Joni fan. When Brandi was recording her 2007 album *The Story*, her producer, T Bone Burnett, had played her "All I Want," the first song on *Blue*, and Brandi had not been all that impressed. Then, the first fight she'd had with Cath had been early on in their relationship when Cath put the CD of *Blue* on in the car during a road trip to Michigan, and Brandi told her she wasn't a fan; Cath responded with a sentiment that is not uncommon among Joni fans when they are considering people as potential life partners: "I'm not sure I even know what this is if you can't get your head around Joni Mitchell." Brandi took particular exception to the lyric in "All I Want" wherein Joni sings that she wants to shampoo and renew her lover; Brandi thought it sounded "really heterosexual" and that Joni wasn't "tough." ("I was like, nope! Not tough. Very heterosexual. Turn it off," Carlile has said.)

"Do you know what 'Little Green' is about?" Cath asked, referring to another of the songs on *Blue*.

"No," Brandi replied laughing.

"This isn't funny. Believe me, Joni is tough."

A few more careful listenings to *Blue* later, Brandi was a convert, convinced that what she was listening to was "the greatest album ever made and that 'Little Green' is the toughest song in rock 'n' roll history." When Brandi heard that a celebration of Joni's seventy-fifth birthday was being prepared—it would be held at the Dorothy Chandler Pavilion in LA, and would air on PBS—she sent letters and made phone calls to whomever she could think might secure her a spot in the lineup of performers. Brandi's dream came true: she got to sing "Down to You" by herself, and "A Case of You" and "Big Yellow Taxi" with others. She met Joni after the show but was too nervous and starstruck to fully steady her fangirl jitters and make much of an impression.

But soon Brandi was hatching another Joni-centric dream: a concert where Brandi would cover all of *Blue*'s songs in order. Would Joni ever approve of such a thing?

At the restaurant, Joni told the waiter, "Pinot Grigio for the table." Brandi, anxious not to go all fangirl on Joni, waited for the right moment to make her big ask: Would Joni ever consider letting her do a *Blue* concert at Los Angeles's Disney Hall?

Joni put her hand on Brandi's arm and said she'd be honored. Brandi was deeply thrilled; hours ago she'd won three Grammys, and now this.

Then Joni asked Brandi, "You know I'm a painter now, right?"

"Of course. One of the greatest."

Mitchell has long described herself as a painter "derailed by circumstances." Whenever she faces writer's block as a songwriter, she redirects her energies toward painting; she calls this "crop rotation."

Mitchell continued, "It doesn't bother me to not sing anymore, but there is music in my house and a lot of great instruments, too . . . sometimes that does bother me."

Brandi wasn't sure where this was going. Which is understandable. Joni, after all, has said that her own aura is so expansive—"it's almost like autism"—that a shaman once taught her how to tuck it in—an "auric tuck"—to keep Joni's "antennae" from pulling in too much information. (Similarly, Joni once told a colleague that every letter of the alphabet has a different "color.") So was the woman who sometimes needs to tuck in her aura suggesting to Brandi that her unplayed musical instruments . . . had feelings of abandonment?

Before this question could emerge in conversation, Joni's friend Marcy interjected: "Maybe we could get some fun folks together."

Joni added, "Maybe we could have a jam."

Then, finally, Joni asked Brandi, "Are you in?"

Brandi struggled not to shake.

17

1973. Mitchell was being interviewed by her friend Malka Marom, a Canadian folk singer turned journalist who had known Mitchell since her coffeehouse days. The two women were in a posh Beverly Hills house—swimming pool, manicured garden, terraces that stretch on into nowhere like an M. C. Escher illustration.

The house belonged to film director Blake Edwards and his wife, Julie Andrews, but was being rented by David Geffen, Mitchell's agent and the head of the label she recorded for. At the time Mitchell was Geffen's platonic roommate, which sounds like an odd arrangement, but was not unusual for Geffen—previously, Stephen Stills had lived in Geffen's Central Park South duplex, and Jackson Browne in Geffen's house on Alto Cedro Drive in LA; after Geffen broke up with Cher in 1975 he stayed for a while at Warren Beatty's on Mulholland Drive.

Joni and Malka were talking shop. Malka asked, "What happens to you when you go on stage, Joni? What happens inside your body, inside your head, when you perform?"

Joni replied that it can be pretty intense—sometimes the audience gives you almost *too* much. "It can be almost like eating too much chocolate cake," Joni explained. "I've come to a point in a concert where I've had so much applause and been fed so much enthusiasm and so much love that I've suddenly felt like I was . . . um . . . I don't know how to say this delicately—full of shit."

A perfect opportunity for auric tucking.

18

Carnegie Hall. February 1, 1969.

About a year after her debut album, *Song to a Seagull,* had been released, Joni flew her parents to New York for her sold-out performance at the illustrious Carnegie Hall. The audience included Bob Dylan and many, many enthusiastic New Yorkers who would give her a standing ovation.

As a marker of mainstream legitimacy, performing at Carnegie Hall was probably rivaled only by being on the cover of *Time.* But it also—for Joni and her peers, at least—has sometimes inadvertently presaged a "gotcha" moment or a tiny burst of debasement. The day after Dylan's 1963 show at the hall, *Newsweek* published an article that outed Dylan as a Jewish kid from the suburbs who'd flown his parents in for his Carnegie Hall appearance, and not a part–Native American hobo who'd lost contact with his family for years, as he'd led some to believe. When Graham Nash and David Crosby played the venue in 1973, there were later media reports that Crosby asked their manager David Geffen to escort Crosby's drug stash across the country to him, and it did not go well. In 2011, when James Taylor was being interviewed by the *New Yorker* about the series of concerts he would start giving a few days later to celebrate Carnegie Hall's 120th year, a nervous waiter spilled a full glass of water on him.

Joni's "gotcha" came minutes before the show. To get to the venue, Joni, Graham, and Joni's parents walked the three blocks from the Plaza Hotel. Graham was wearing a floor-length, black velvet coat with a pink-and-white chiffon tie-dye scarf; Joni was wearing a green-and-white plaid maxi coat. Myrtle and Bill, embarrassed by the prospect of standing out in a crowd, followed behind from a distance of six feet.

Fifteen minutes before showtime, Joni, whose hair was waist-length and featured bangs, removed her coat to reveal her colorful outfit—two necklaces, a bishop-sleeved blouse under a many-buttoned waistcoat, and a long skirt appliquéd with colorful sequins depicting a large eagle (on the front) and a large artichoke (on the back).

Myrtle looked at her daughter and said, "Oh, Joan, you're not going on in those rags."

19

Saskatoon, Calgary, Toronto, Detroit. 1956 and onward.

Teenaged Joni, whom childhood friends describe as slightly aloof and prissy but with a wild streak, liked to draw and paint; she was amassing a collection of trophies she'd won for five-pin bowling (Joni will continue bowling as an adult, with an average score of 179 in 1973). But her true passion at this moment of time was dancing. Joni lived for the YMCA dances on the weekend. She and her girlfriends would get their hair done, sometimes at a local beauty school where Joni liked to get a beehive with sparkles; someone's mom would drive them to the Y where they and the boys would jitterbug to Chuck Berry and Elvis Presley. "We called it jiving, not jitterbugging," Joni's friend Sharolyn Dickson told me in 2023 when I visited Saskatoon. "It was a little different. I was chuckling with Joan on Zoom the other day because we were talking about the movie that Cameron Crowe is making about her, and what would be in it, and I said, Joan if there's dancing you're gonna have to teach them the Canadian way of jiving. Because it's a little different." (The Canadian version was slightly more relaxed and less prone to aerials.)

The Y dances were bereft of alcohol or drugs. But as high school dragged on, Joni was increasingly a drinker and good time Charley (in fact, Good Time Charley, along with Boney Maronie, was one of her nicknames). Maybe the husky laugh she'd developed even before she started smoking presaged an affinity for mischief: the standoffish girl who often showed up in a hairband and a color-coordinated outfit, it turned out, could chug a beer, put her fist down her throat, and do swan dives off of beds. Polio schmolio.

"There was a close-knit group of us. It was all guys, we called ourselves The Boys," Tony Simon, the Vancouver-based entrepreneur who was Joni's prom date, told me. "Joan ended up as part of that group. The reason was that you could say 'fuck' in front of her and she didn't care. She'd say it right back. She had, even at an early age, more of a guy's sense of humor than a girl's."

Most of the partying happened at weenie roasts. Thereat, a bunch of kids would drive their cars into "the bush" and, angling a few cars at one another, train the cars' headlights into a campfire at the center. These gatherings, fueled by alcohol and whatever hormone causes teenagers to repeat the punchline of a joke seven thousand times in the course of an evening, would often result in singalongs of dirty drinking songs—which, in her junior year, inspired Joni to buy a $38 baritone ukulele and a Pete Seeger instruction booklet, so she could accompany the singing. She'd wanted a guitar, but Myrtle wouldn't spring for one because Joni had quit piano lessons after her piano teacher rapped her on the knuckles; Myrtle had said of a guitar, "You'll buy it and you'll just quit. You're a quitter."

"She carried that fucking thing with her all the time," longtime friend Simon told me. "It drove me crazy. She was totally interested in it. She wouldn't be singing, she would just be practicing the same thing over and over. You'd go someplace and she'd be playing it, playing it—you'd have to tell her, You gotta stop. She got her hands on this thing and nothing was the same again."

Toward the end of high school, Joni ran into her friend D'Arcy Case—a weenie roast friend who one night had listened intently as Joni recited poetry to the evening sky. Joni had been accepted into the Alberta College of Art in Calgary and was working at a local department store and doing freelance modeling in an effort to raise the $800 tuition. The beatnik D'Arcy now comanaged, with her boyfriend, Saskatoon's only folk club, the Louis Riel. She'd seen Joni around during the previous year, wearing, as she told biographer Sheila Weller, "little Jackie Kennedy, princess-line coats. She had a model-y, tight-assed persona, but I *knew* she wasn't that."

Originally, Joan was going to be the club's resident artist, who would draw customers' pictures. Instead, she ended up working as a waitress at the Louis Riel, where, amid both the twangy earnestness of the emerging folk scene and the hashish vapors emanating from the club's performers lounge, she started to grow her hair long and straight. Folk music had taken off, and, after the payola scandals of the late 1950s, wherein disc jockeys were found taking bribes to play certain records, was seen as a refreshingly homespun antidote to the commercialism of the now-tainted music industry.

The Kingston Trio had had a surprise #1 hit in 1958 with "Tom Dooley," their entry in the Appalachian "murder ballad" genre. In the midst of her run of gold records in 1961, 1962, and 1963, Joan Baez would grace the cover of *Time* in November of 1962. So numerous will Baez's imitators in Japan be in 1967 that one folk music fan, referring to a high school–aged Baez wannabe, told an American reporter, "I was so surprised at Joan Baez's concert the other night. She sounded exactly like Maki Nishimura."

One Sunday night at a Louis Riel "hoot"—hootenannies are informal music sessions where anyone can join in—Joni walked up to the mic and let loose with a combination of warbling and pitch changes that resulted in some head-scratching among the club's denizens. Ditto Joni's subsequent audition for a spot on the club's lineup: some people loved her singing, and some found it operatic and shrill. But it was good enough that she was asked to start subbing when acts canceled. She bought a guitar.

D'Arcy got pregnant. To be unmarried and pregnant in 1963 was a huge taboo; as Joni has put it, "A daughter could do nothing more disgraceful. It ruined you in a social sense. It was like you murdered somebody." D'Arcy started wearing a series of girdles to hide her bump, including at her wedding to her boyfriend in May 1963. That fall, unhappy in the marriage, the still-pregnant D'Arcy tried to commit suicide by jumping off a building.

By this point, Joni had moved to Calgary to attend art college. She started booking $15 gigs at a coffeehouse called the Depression, where, as one folkie puts it, she "came with her uke and tormented us with a shrill 'Sloop John B.' and 'I Wish I Was an Apple on a Tree.'" Vocally, she was trying at this point to imitate Baez or

Judy Collins. She performed mostly so that she would have money to buy cigarettes.

In her second semester, she started dating a tall fellow freshman with high cheekbones named Brad MacMath. Brad's nickname was Moochie because he always showed up around dinnertime; Joni gave him a glass-bottomed pewter mug emblazoned THE MOOCH.

And then came The Incident: after Joni and Brad had been romancing for a while, Joni found out that she was pregnant (she'll later blame her high school's health class and its assertions about the rhythm method). Abortion was out of the question—it would not be legal in Canada until 1988; and though the Pill was obtainable in Canada as early as 1957 for "menstrual irregularities," it was illegal for use as birth control until 1969. A common route for young women in her situation was to disappear into a big city during the pregnancy; Joni figured that, given Myrtle already thought she was a quitter (not just the piano lessons: Myrtle had also predicted that Joni wouldn't last at art college), it would be believable to Myrtle if Joni told her she was quitting art school in order to move to Toronto to become a folk singer. "I had to get out of my hometown," Mitchell will tell the *Irish Times* in 1999, "to protect my mother, protect her reputation."

Joni and Brad bought one-way tickets to Toronto; on the train ride there, Joni wrote her first song with lyrics, "Day After Day," whose narrator relates how lonely she has become ever since she got on an eastbound train.

Joni and Brad moved into a boardinghouse in Toronto. Joni got a job at Simpsons Department Store to start saving up $150 to join the musicians' union so she wouldn't have to play only at scab clubs. She kept writing songs and discovered that her singing voice changed the more she wrote—she sounded less like Baez or Collins, and the shift between her lower and upper registers became smoother. (At the very end of "Big Yellow Taxi" when Joni drops her voice down low and then laughs, is she making fun of this vocal tic? Is it a coded goodbye to her folk-singing younger self? In this TED talk I will . . .)

In early autumn of 1964, Brad left the three-months-pregnant Joni and headed off for Regina, Saskatchewan, and later San Francisco. Joni was denied admission to the Salvation Army she visited. It's at this point, presumably, that she ended up in the attic of a Chinese landlord who was suspected of being a human trafficker, whom Joni would mention decades later; soon, a friend will warn her, "Get out of there, he's just waiting for you to give birth."

Joni was fortunate to fall in with a group of loving comrades, including an Indigenous poet from the Ojibway tribe named Duke Redbird, who lived at the boardinghouse, and whose brother, on determining one day that the pregnant and poor Joni was not eating well, gave her a gift of a bag of apples. Joni also befriended Vicky Taylor, the vivacious den mother of Yorkville, the neighborhood where most of the clubs that Joni was performing in were located. Vicky introduced Joni to fellow Canadian and polio survivor Neil Young, who struck Joni as a kindred spirit: they had both gotten polio from the same outbreak and had started making music around the same time; they'll both decry the corporatization of rock and will remove their music from Spotify in 2022 (and return it in 2024).

Among the songs that Joni played at clubs was "Crow on the Cradle," a modern version of a Child Ballad—the collection of 305 bleak English and Scottish songs anthologized in the second half of the nineteenth century, often chronicling murders and adultery, and much in favor with the young folkies of the late fifties and early sixties. "Crow on the Cradle" features a crow who sits on a baby's cradle and makes dire prognostications about the baby's future.

By December, Joni was still living in the $15-a-week attic room; only one out of every four spindles on the staircase banister was left because tenants had used the other ones as firewood. She subsisted on Ingersoll cheese spread, rice pudding, tomato juice, and Hovis high-wheat-germ whole-meal bread. Joni was too pregnant to play a guitar anymore, so she started playing a smaller, lighter stringed instrument called a tiple. Around Christmas, unable to perform and thus make any money, she moved in with Vicky, over a restaurant called the Lickin' Chicken. Vicky played Joni a song that Neil Young had written—"Sugar Mountain," which details how once you're old enough to do the things you've been waiting to be old enough to do, you find yourself wanting to be a kid again. Intrigued, Joni started writing a response song that she would finish months later.

The third week of February, Joni checked into the charity ward of Toronto General Hospital and gave birth to a healthy girl. She wrote "Kelly Dale Anderson" on the birth certificate. As was the practice then, Joni's breasts were bound to stop her breast milk supply. Complications with the birth required Joni to stay in the hospital an extra ten days, which meant she met and held Kelly.

Joni put the baby into foster care so she could figure out how to proceed. “I couldn’t leave her too long in a foster home,” Joni has explained. “I had to find a job so that I could support her, or give her up for adoption before she got too old.” Two weeks after giving birth, she was looking for gigs again. The owner of one club told her “So, Miss Anderson, I see you’re going for the Baez sound,” and offered her a job in the kitchen (he subsequently claimed he was joking). She opted to keep performing.

A month later, Joni met Chuck Mitchell, a folk singer who was much more established than her, and eight years older. They met when they were both playing at a club called the Penny Farthing—he was the headliner downstairs, and she was the minor act upstairs. As Chuck told an interviewer from Temple University’s radio station in 1966, “Joni was working the same club as I was working. I’ll let her finish the story.”

“There’s nothing really to finish,” Joni responded with a laugh.

“It’s a great story,” Chuck countered.

“Well, Chuck was working at that time in a duo with a fellow named Loring James, and they walked into the club, and I was singing. I had sung there the previous week. And Loring James was a classical guitar teacher at the time and was very impressed by the fact that I play with a perfect, almost classical guitar position. And he said, ‘Oh, look at that hand,’ and Charlie said, ‘Oh, look at those legs.’” Joni laughed here. “And that’s the story. That’s why the big pause. I didn’t know whether I should tell it.”

Chuck responded, “I was very interested in her style and her technique and her class.”

Joni’s come-on was correcting Chuck’s version of Dylan’s

"Mr. Tambourine Man." ("He'd rewritten some of it, and badly, too," Joni has said, "so we immediately got kind of into a conflict." But when I got in touch with Chuck in 2023, he emailed me that he didn't remember Joni taking him to task on this front, though he admitted, "After decades of reflection, I like to think I am selectively forgetful. What's left is more forgiving than what's gone.")

Chuck proposed thirty-six hours after meeting Joni. Even though D'Arcy's suicide attempt had been a vivid example of the consequences of a bad marriage, Joni decided to marry Chuck despite her reservations about their compatibility. Chuck and Joni's versions of their relationship with respect to the baby—whom they referred to as "it," for distance—vary. Joni says that Chuck "agreed to take us both" and that the plan was to save up money while living in Detroit and then "get the baby out of hock," but that Chuck reneged and declared "I'm not raising another man's child." Chuck has said that he doesn't remember agreeing to take on Kelly. He has said that, while, yes, he didn't really want to raise a child, he figured that if he simply left the decision up to Joni, that Joni, who talked incessantly about her music and art and whom Chuck has called "feral," would simply realize that child-rearing would slow her career. But Joni has pointed out that she didn't really *have* a career then—at least, not one as a songwriter, which, distinct from performing, is what would bring in enough money to support her.

According to Joni, Chuck was late for the ceremony because he was putting down $500—the money was a wedding gift—on a Porsche Speedster. Joni walked down the aisle thinking, "I can get out of this." She had sewn her own dress; she performed for the assembled.

To each other's mild irritation, Joni and Chuck subsequently appeared at clubs and coffeehouses as a duo. A November 10, 1966, *Toronto Daily Star* review stated, "Where she cloaks absurd humour beneath smiley wholesomeness, he hides neat irony beneath clean-cut deadpan." Chuck's sensibility was more cabaretish than Joni's, and saw Joni playing a kazoo in one song and putting a pillow under her dress to play a hippopotamus for British comedy duo Flanders and Swann's "The Hippopotamus Song." (The audience traditionally accompanies the performers for the last verse of "The Hippopotamus Song," which extolls the virtues of "glorious mud." Chuck Mitchell told me that, to incite the audience to participate, Joni would often ad-lib, "Come on, hippies!") Baez has said that she saw them perform together one night at the Gaslight in New York City: "I remember thinking, 'You gotta drop this guy.'"

Though Chuck would ultimately do two very important things for Joni—he encouraged her to start a publishing company so she would retain her music's publishing rights, and he gave her the Saul Bellow novel *Henderson the Rain King*, part of which she would read before writing "Both Sides Now"—the marriage was a bust. Chuck, according to Joni, had no problem reminding his art-college-dropout wife that he was more educated than her. Meanwhile, Joni, according to Chuck, was increasingly obsessive and monomaniacal about her music, often staying up till dawn to work on it.

Joni signed the adoption papers in the second month of the

marriage. "Although I was kind of stoic about it," Joni will tell California's Commonwealth Club in 2005, "I guess I must have made some kind of terrific emotional display in there because it said in the papers that it was very hard for me to sign that day. I don't remember. I blocked it." As she'll put it in "Little Green," her song on *Blue* inspired by the baby:

You sign all the papers in the family name
You're sad and you're sorry but you're not ashamed

It's unclear when exactly Joni wrote this song and started sharing it (the publication date is October 16, 1967), but we know that she waited till her fourth album to commit it to posterity.

We also know that, when singing that she hopes that Little Green will have a happy ending, she sometimes heartbreakingly swapped out "Little Green" for "Kelly Green."

Joni will later say, "Bad fortune changed the course of my destiny. I became a musician." As a confidante of hers will put it to biographer Sheila Weller, ever since Joni realized she was giving her child up, "she's never really been able to live with herself." Or, as Charles Dickens put it in *Bleak House*, "Oh, baby, baby!"

Over the next forty-eight months or so, Joni will write four songs that will permanently secure her a place in the songwriting pantheon, arguably putting her on an equal footing with American songbook greats like Irving Berlin, Bob Dylan, and Stephen Sondheim. She'll finish her response song to Neil Young's tune, writing an ode to the permanence of time that she'll call "The Circle Game"; her reading of the Saul Bellow novel on an airplane will yield the bittersweet ballad of ambivalence and acquired wisdom that we know as "Both Sides Now"; she'll urge a return to innocence and to the garden of Eden in the generation-defining anthem "Woodstock"; and her "Big Yellow Taxi" will imprint on the American consciousness the idea that we don't know what we have until it's gone.

Each will emerge a classic.

Each can be read as instructions from an older, wiser friend or parent.

The AFTERMATH

20

It's 1945 in Fort Macleod, a tiny town on the edge of the prairie in Western Canada. It would not be eccentric to apply the word "blighted" here—the town declared bankruptcy in 1924 and saw no growth for fifty years; the exteriors of many of the houses have been stuccoed with broken glass and chicken feed. The war is on, so you'll need to use the same soap to wash your hair, clothes, and dishes. There's been a recent and long-standing drought, so maybe don't go looking for fountains or gardens. There's a library you could check out, though—if you can hack the stench of gas issuing from the potbellied gas stove next to the librarian's desk.

In her parents' modest apartment—a single room, shared by two couples, and bisected by a sagging curtain—a blond toddler, not yet two years old, places three oranges on a purple scarf. She gathers her mother and father round and exclaims "Pretty!"

1978. The A&M Studios in Los Angeles. The little blond girl has morphed into the legendary recording artist Joni Mitchell, who has appeared on the cover of *Time* and been hailed as the voice of her generation.

She is recording *Mingus*. "The Wolf That Lives in Lindsey," the song on *Mingus* that Mitchell is working on today with her lover, the drummer Don Alias, is not quite taking off in the way she hoped it would.

But Mitchell has a brainstorm.

She turns to her drummer/lover and announces, "We need to get sounds of wolf choirs and water chimes."

2009. A stage in a New York City park. Performance artist John Kelly, wearing a long blond wig and playing a guitar, is treating an audience to his uncanny impersonation of a twentysomething Joni, all dazed enchantment and beatific serenity and flower-child rapture.

In the middle of Kelly's show, one of New York City's estimated 9 million pigeons happens to land on the stage. Kelly-as-Mitchell gazes at the pigeon and starts to brim with rhapsody.

"Oh, wow," he ad-libs. "A dove."

21

Toronto, Ontario. Early August 1968. Joni was at the Mariposa Folk Festival, where some of the festival's performers have been corralled inside a storm fence for privacy. She was chatting with singer-songwriter Kris Kristofferson, who will write "Me and Bobby McGee" and "Help Me Make It Through the Night" and go on to star opposite Barbra Streisand in the 1976 remake of *A Star Is Born*.

Mitchell and Kristofferson's tête-à-tête was interrupted when someone from the festival told Joni, "There are some people at the fence that would like to talk to you." Joni looked over at the fence and saw a young, fair-haired man and woman—hippies, but more kempt—and two children. Sitting on the man's shoulder's was a boy of about two years; the three-year-old girl, who had curly, blond hair, clutched the fence with her fingers.

Joni looked at the family. The family looked at Joni. No one said anything.

Finally, the little girl spoke. She said to Joni, "Hello, Kelly."

"Oh, my name's not Kelly. My name's Joni."

"Nooo. No, you're Kelly."

"No, I'm Joni."

The mother looked at Joni warmly and said, "She's Kelly."

"Oh, you're Kelly," Joni said to the girl.

"Nooo, *you're* Kelly."

Joni and the girl made another pass or two at their game before Joni stopped and gave the family a look that conveyed, Well, do you have anything to say?

They didn't, so Joni walked off. "When I turned my back," she would later say, "all of a sudden this shiver went up my spine—all my chakras rang, if you'll pardon the term. I turned around and they were gone. So I've always suspected that that was her and that the mother had said something to her in the course of the concert out of, you know, some kind of pride or, you know, about—I don't know but it was a strange little game."

But the real Kelly, Joni would later learn, did not attend a folk or rock concert during the first three years of her life. Though Joni's close friends knew about the baby at the time, no one else did; it had taken two years after Kelly's birth for Joni to tell her parents, who vowed not to talk about Kelly, even to relatives.

Then, a month later at the Big Sur Folk Festival in Northern California, according to *Girls Like Us,* something similarly weird happened. Joni and Graham had lined up for a communal dinner being served buffet-style, when an eight- or nine-year-old girl who was also standing in line said to Joni, "Who are you?"

"I'm Joni Mitchell."

"No, you're not. *I'm* Joni Mitchell."

22

Summer 1999. London's Air Studios, the recording complex owned by the Beatles' longtime producer, Sir George Martin. Joni, whose voice was now a cigarette-deepened mezzo, was recording her album *Both Sides Now*—a collection of standards, along with her own "Both Sides Now" and "A Case of You"—with an orchestra that included members of the London Symphony Orchestra. Some of the players, on finishing a take of the song "Both Sides Now"—these seasoned vets only needed three takes, and no postproduction will be required—could, unexpectedly, be seen crying. "Also, they were looking at each other during the take, which is very unusual," composer and arranger Vince Mendoza, who won a Grammy for arranging and conducting the song, told me. "Usually they're laser beam–focused on their parts." At one point a security guard walked up to one of the players and said, "I don't know what you folks are doing in there, but I've never seen musicians act like this during a session—all serious and respectful like, and concentrating and all." After recording, some of the musicians huddled excitedly in the playback booth to hear the take, like little kids in a photo booth. That faint sound of tiny inbursts of air? British snuffling.

One common refrain from Joni fans is that we think Joni is singing directly to us—perhaps even that she does it because she knows us better than we know ourselves. Like the two female fans who once told Joni, "Before Prozac, there was you," or like the fan who once camped outside of Joni's house because he thought the song "This Flight Tonight" from *Blue* contained messages from his dead sister, many of us feel like we are receiving Joni's musical transmissions subcutaneously, or like she's tapping into some vestigial life force deep within us.

I will confess that, during one of the more self-involved eras of my life—when I was twenty-four—I had a "Free Man in Paris" moment while vacationing in France's capital. One evening, I walked along the banks of the Seine, singing "Free Man" aloud, even giving voice to its blasts of crescendoing flute hysteria (bup bup BAAAAH). I was bowled over by how accurately the song described my life: at the time, I was working for a casting director in the film industry, and thus all the song's references to people schmoozing you and asking you for favors and screaming at you on the phone seemed ripped from my subconscious. My revery was probably aided by the fact that, in the pre-internet, pre-cellphone mid-eighties, "free" was a very apt description of a trip abroad, constituting as it did a virtual telecommunications eclipse.

Mitchell has said that one of the best fan letters she ever got was from a criminal lawyer in New Jersey who told her he was sorry that she had to endure such difficulties in order to be her fans' "salve." He talked about how grueling his job was—he was about to send someone to prison. He wrote that he sometimes felt like he was going down, down into the abyss, but that he would rebound whenever he thought of a lyric from "The Last Time I Saw Richard," the devastating last song on *Blue*: "before I get my gorgeous wings and fly away." As Joni has said of the lawyer's letter, "So he's able to take out of my music that it's okay to go down, and you don't have to stay there."

Similarly, Joni once received a letter from a girl who had grown up in Northern Ireland during the Troubles. Someone had given the girl an old, wonky cassette recorder with "The Circle Game" on it, saying "This is a good song for a child like you to learn." At 8:00 each night in the girl's town, helicopters would shine floodlights on the houses as a scare tactic. The girl preserved her sanity by clinging to a neighbor's extra pillow, and by softly playing "The Circle Game" while pressing the tape recorder into her chest.

What causes fans to bond so hard? The phenomenon might be chalked up to the warmth of Joni's voice, not to mention her emotional candor and the specificity of her lyrics. She's been known to spend as much as a month on two words in a song, and it shows: what other lovelorn poets or songwriters have noticed that their frying pan is now too wide or that the sound inside a seashell is both a sigh and a foggy lullaby? Who else has noted that chimneys in winter look like white flags that are entreating the moon for truce? Who else has ever rhymed "tourniquet" with "mouthpiece spit," or glamorized that most humble entity, pawn shops ("Pawn shops glitter like gold tooth caps / In the grey decay")?

Mitchell gains immediacy, too, by having her singing voice resemble speech, sometimes elongating or clipping phrases, sometimes jammingwordstogetherlikewedowhenwetalk.

But there are other things going on as well.

It's counterintuitive that we like to listen to sad music, particularly if we are already sad, but Joni's music, particularly *Blue,* has long been a go-to for ugly-crying. ("When I first started drinking—when I was like 21—I used to cry about Joni Mitchell all the time after a few glasses of wine," Taylor Swift said in 2014. "All my friends would know, once I started crying about Joni Mitchell, it was time for me to go to bed.")

Daniel Levitin, a neuroscientist who has interviewed Mitchell and studied her music and become her friend, has written, "Prolactin, a tranquilizing hormone, is released when we're sad. Sorrow does have an evolutionary purpose, which is to help us conserve energy and reorient our priorities for the future after a traumatic event. Prolactin is released after orgasm, after birth, and during lactation in females. A chemical analysis of tears reveals that prolactin is not always present in tears—it is not released in tears of lubrication of the eye, or when the eye is irritated, or in tears of joy; it is only released in tears of sorrow." According to David Huron, a scholar of music cognition and the psychology of music, sad music is able to trick our brain into releasing prolactin in response to a safe and fictional source of sadness, which then lifts our mood.

Joni's open tunings play a part here, too. By superimposing chords on top of chords, she creates tiny amounts of dissonance that our brain tries to resolve. "Chords are depictions of emotions," Joni has said. The ones that she creates "feel like my feelings. . . . They have a question mark in them." Speaking of the period when she started using open tuning, she added, "There were so many unresolved things [in my life]. I'd stay in unresolved emotionality for days." This lack of resolution reverberated throughout her life: "Will I survive this disease? Will I ever walk again? Where is my daughter? Is she alright? Will we nuke them? Will they nuke us? Is there a mate for me?"

In a song like *Hejira*'s exquisite "Amelia," Mitchell ups the ante by having the song alternate back and forth between two keys, F and C, without decisively settling into either, thus creating a slightly hovering, up-in-the-air quality—which is wildly appropriate because the song is about aviator Amelia Earhart. Similarly, in the title track of *Blue,* when Mitchell sings that she wants to sail away, the lyric is set atop rising intervals in a major key, creating the sensation of forward movement. The song is the only one on the album that doesn't follow a regular pattern of verses and choruses, almost as if its raw emotion can't be party to formal constraints.

Sometimes the means toward Mitchell's musical onomatopoeia are more direct. Joni loves to "blue" a note—the practice, common in jazz or blues, whereby you sing or play a seemingly off-pitch note for dramatic effect; the first word Joni sings in the song "Blue" sounds sort of like a saxophone falling down a flight of stairs. On *Court and Spark*'s "Car on a Hill," Mitchell had the horn passages carefully altered and panned, thus creating a Doppler effect of a car (and its honking horn) whooshing by.

On *Blue*'s "All I Want," Mitchell repeats various words and phrases—"traveling," "do you want"—to convey her breathless excitement; when she skaaaaaaaaaaates away in "River," we slide across the ice with her. On her duet with Peter Gabriel on *Chalk Mark in a Rain Storm*'s "My Secret Place," the sound sometimes cuts between Mitchell and Gabriel while they're in the middle of a word—creating the sensation of a couple's mind meld rather than a series of isolated, he-said-she-said statements. When a cricket got trapped in her home studio in 1990, Joni has said, "We sampled him. I made him the drummer on 'Night Ride Home.'"

In short, Mitchell is messing with us. And most of us are so happy—er, sad—that she is doing so. She has been called a genius by many music luminaries, including Herbie Hancock, Leonard Cohen, and David Geffen.

But occasionally, of course, the rawness and candor of some of her songs elicits strange reactions, much as the searingly frank poetry of Robert Lowell, Anne Sexton, and Sylvia Plath has done since the early sixties. When Joni played the album *Blue* for Kris Kristofferson, he famously told her, "Oh, Joni—save something for yourself." It's been said that the punk group the Sex Pistols fired their original bass player because he listened to Joni. Many of us who have tried to share Mitchell's music with others have met with similar responses: if you play at full volume the end of Joni's "Woodstock" on *Ladies of the Canyon* when she goes into her high-pitched, incantatory wailing, it is possible to clear a room of pets and heterosexual men.

Other listeners stumble over the sophistication on display. When Joni played parts of the just-finished *Court and Spark* for a drunk John Lennon—he was recording in a studio down the hall at A&M Studios—he accused her of being "the product of your own over-education," an odd comment to level at an art college dropout, even if he was one himself. (The rhythms of *Court and Spark*'s "Car on a Hill" are so complex that notating its bridge has been used as a final exam question in theory classes at the Berklee College of Music. The hugely influential musician and producer Brian Eno has said of *Court and Spark*, one of his all-time favorite records, that "it is the best engineered album you've ever heard.") When Joni played Dolly Parton her 1975 album *The Hissing of Summer Lawns*, Dolly shyly commented, "My God, if I thought that deep I'd scare myself to death." When Joni played her 1977 album *Don Juan's Reckless Daughter* for the Sex Pistols' lead singer, Johnny Rotten, and a Rastafarian friend of his, Rotten's friend—presumably because of all the drumming on the record—commented, "It makes me want to eat white people."

But for the most part, of course, Joni's fans are moved to tears by the poignancy and honesty being extended to them. "Sometimes I have to hug people if they get emotional," Joni has said. "I've had amazing experiences. A young mother with a baby came up to me, and she was very emotional. She was trying to express gratitude, I guess, but she couldn't articulate it. I'm always curious—like, what song? But she didn't get a chance because her mother came out of the drugstore and sees her daughter kind of emotional. And mother says, 'For God's sake, get yourself together.' Girl looked like she was going to cry, so I grabbed her hand and said, 'No, she's entirely appropriate, the music has been very moving to her.' And then the mother, who was hard as nails, started to quiver. So I had to jump up and hug them both."

But if anyone's reaction to Joni's music was revelatory, it was Myrtle's. When, at age nineteen, Joni made her television debut—she sang and played her baritone ukulele on a hunting and fishing show called *For Men Only*—her parents watched the show in a showroom on a top floor of Saskatoon's Bessborough Hotel, one of the few venues in town that could pull in the signal, and the place where Joni's high school prom was held. (It's the turreted castle in the background of Joni's terrific self-portrait on the cover of *Clouds*.) Myrtle's jocular response was not what one might have expected: "It was very tastefully done," she said. "But I think they cancelled a moose to put her on!"

Myrtle, it turns out, grew increasingly proud of her daughter as Joni made her way in the music business. "She had, like, forty different scrapbooks of what Joni was doing," longtime friend Sharolyn Dickson told me, "and she was in touch with someone on Joni's staff who would send her information about every coffeehouse she was playing at." Longtime friend Tony Simon concurs: "I think to this day Joan doesn't realize how much Myrtle supported what she was doing."

23

1994. A hotel suite in Midtown Manhattan, wherein Jancee Dunn, a writer and editor at *Rolling Stone*, was interviewing Mitchell.

"I *had* to meet Joni," Dunn told me, recounting how *Blue* had helped Dunn get through a difficult breakup with a boyfriend. She said she fought to get the assignment.

Before meeting Mitchell, Dunn threw herself into her Joni research, as Dunn's editor had encouraged her to do, and listened copiously to *Turbulent Indigo*, the album Mitchell was promoting at the time; nevertheless, Dunn's stomach was in knots at the prospect of meeting the great and rarely sighted Joni. Joni's publicist told Dunn that Joni likes to talk about art and literature; a *Rolling Stone* colleague told Dunn that if Joni was a little standoffish, Dunn should ask, "Why won't MTV play you?"

Joni was not standoffish with Dunn; as she chatted away, she chain-smoked and, charmingly, served tea from a teapot. Dunn asked her how she liked to relax on the weekends, and Joni reported that, for the past several years at her cottage in British Columbia, she had started hosting a weekly potluck for friends.

MITCHELL: [I]t was usually outside with candles and two strings of Camel lights.
DUNN: Pardon?
MITCHELL: I smoked 150 packages of Camels and sent away for two strings of Camel lights. (*She laughs.*)
DUNN: Wait. You collected Camel Cash, those coupons in packs of Camels, and sent away for camel-shaped lights?
MITCHELL: Yeah. (*She laughs.*) You wouldn't believe how cheap the plastic on them is. The paint peeled off of it, and I'm really pissed off. Because that was a lot of smoking, and why couldn't they have sprung for real yellow plastic?

Dunn told me, "So often the vision you have of someone famous does not match up with reality. In this case, when she had a teapot and we had tea? I almost wanted to die. Normally I can keep it buttoned up but at one point I thought, I'm so happy that I'm sober and this is a daytime interview because otherwise I might start crying. Also, I didn't put it in the piece because I didn't want to seem disrespectful, or make the piece about me, but the entire time that we talked, or for at least ten minutes of it, *our knees were touching.* I'm not intimating anything. It was just this delightful, we're-having-tea-together-and-our-knees-are-touching thing. I started thinking, We're having tea and our knees are touching, and I just floated away. I had to call myself back, you know? Something's happening/It isn't happening/Knees/Tea/Knees/Tea. It was too much."

24

October 29, 1970. At the Paris Theater in London, where Mitchell and the guy she was seeing, James Taylor, were performing together. Taylor introduced the next song, Mitchell's haunting ballad about a street musician, "For Free," from *Ladies in the Canyon*; in his typically self-deprecating fashion, Taylor confessed "I've never played it with her, but I play a little, too—maybe we can make it work." Given that "For Free" is a song that Mitchell plays on piano, she didn't need to launch into her usual hairball of guitar tuning, so she gently replied, "Ready when you are, James." But Taylor, it turned out, was still tuning *his* guitar, so he offered in mock anguish, "I *know* . . ."

Break Shot, Taylor's 2020 audio memoir, opens with "I'm James Taylor and I'm a professional autobiographer." Taylor goes on to say, "I have a running joke that I keep writing the same six or seven songs over and over again. I think many of us keep trying to work out exactly what happened in our early years. We want to go back and fix something that has already vanished and can never be corrected. But we can correct it in a song . . ."

Taylor first heard Mitchell's music in 1968 in Paul McCartney's office at Apple Records during a meeting with McCartney and George Harrison. But kindred spirits James and Joni wouldn't meet until March 1969 when he opened for her at the Unicorn coffeehouse in Boston. She was four years older than him. "I'm sure Joan was *most* interested," Graham Nash, who was still Joni's "old man" at the time, has said; Nash attended the show and even took a photo of Joni and James meeting. But, given that they were both in relationships at the time of the Unicorn gig, Joni and James wouldn't hook up until the following summer at the Mariposa Folk Festival in Toronto, whereupon they were together for about a year. (Was Graham jealous that Joni took up with James so hard on the heels of his own relationship with her? He has said, "Why would you *not* want to hang out with James Taylor, for God's sake. Look at him.")

Joni had heard through the grapevine that James was a ladies' man with a drug problem. But Taylor had so much else going on for him that it's easy to imagine falling for him. Six-foot-three, spaniel-eyed, and winningly droll—Taylor liked to coarsely fingerpick a few notes during his song "Steamroller" and then deadpan, "Pick it, Big Jim"—the diffident and patrician Taylor was a child of privilege who had studied cello for four years and could speak French. His mother and four siblings were all musical; at their home in Chapel Hill, North Carolina, they'd pick cans off kitchen shelves and improvise advertising jingles for them. Like Joni, James was something of an acoustic guitar virtuoso; he liked to run counterpoints across his bass strings, and he subverted traditional folk forms with his pulled-string fingerpicking of higher inversion chords. The Beatles had given him his first record deal (Paul

McCartney: "Peter [Asher] says your songs are very good." Taylor: "Well, uh, I don't know. I hope they are.") McCartney played bass and sang harmonies on one song on Taylor's eponymous debut; George Harrison lifted the title of one of its songs, "Something in the Way She Moves," for a lyric in Harrison's song "Something." Taylor's next record, *Sweet Baby James*, his popular and critical breakthrough, had come out in February 1970; buoyed by the single "Fire and Rain," it would go triple platinum and land him on the cover of *Time* in March of '71.

In a word, lady bait.

It probably didn't hurt, either, that Taylor, who could sometimes be eerily silent and shoe-gazing in conversation, and who got in enough motorcycle crashes and swung from enough fire escapes to constitute a seeming death wish, was very open about having spent time at a psychiatric facility. In a press release accompanying *Sweet Baby James*, he'd stated "In the fall of 1965 I entered a state of what must have been intense adolescence . . . and spent 9 months at McLean Psychiatric Hospital in Massachusetts." At shows, Taylor sometimes referred to McLean, the infirmary in the suburbs of Boston whose former patients include many writers (Sylvia Plath and David Foster Wallace among them) and which inspired his song "Knockin' Around the Zoo," as "the nuthouse."

All the delight of living with a wildly talented heartthrob like Taylor aside, daily life with a recovering junkie—during most of the year or so that James and Joni were together, he was on methadone—would be a different matter. James was known for sometimes wearing ripped clothes days at a time; sometimes he would rend the air with the smell of burning flesh when he put cigarettes out on his arm. Drug withdrawal turns its subject into a kind of prisoner: think long, doomy silences, and bouts of sitting in the corner of a darkened room. When a *Rolling Stone* reporter visited James on Martha's Vineyard at the end of 1970, he recounted how James, after helping a small group of people kill a fifth of Glenlivet, went to a bar for a nightcap: three beers, three Scotches on the rocks, and a tequila. "I can get high on alcohol," James told the reporter, but then admitted, "I'm a druggie." We learn that "He still uses pot, hash, uppers, downers, opium, cocaine, acid, and mescaline."

Taylor's busy schedule of ingestion notwithstanding, Joni and James found plenty of time to act like a couple of teenagers in love—they would giggle and neck in the backseat of cars, or sit in fields with their guitars and play for each other. They went up the Wailua River in Hawaii with Buffy Sainte-Marie on a rubber boat. James wrote Joni poems and love letters. She knit him a sweater, one of whose arms was eight inches longer than Taylor's. They discussed feeling guilty about using friends and acquaintances as the inspiration of songs. He watched her sit at her piano and compose "River," her gorgeous and poignant anti-Christmas tune that opens with "Jingle Bells" in a minor key. At Christmas they went caroling with James's dad and others in the Morgan Creek neighborhood of Chapel Hill. And O the sexytimes: Taylor told a journalist that Joni was the best lover he ever had ("She's so sensual and free with her body. She's like a goddess: a goddess of love").

During one of the lovebirds' conversations, Joni likened songs to tattoos and explained, "They follow you forever, even when the relationship is over." This sentiment certainly rings true in her and

James's narrative: the echt moment in their relationship—their "Our House," if you will—is probably when she goes to visit him on a movie set in Arizona in the summer of 1970; as she falls asleep in their shared motel room, he sits on the edge of the bed and writes one of his most beloved songs, "You Can Close Your Eyes."

Swoon.

But this same cocktail of pretty boy looks and moody introspection was capable of setting others afire in another way: grumbly rock critic and punk apologist Lester Bangs—he's the mentor played by Philip Seymour Hoffman in *Almost Famous*—would in 1971 excoriate Taylor's "bardic auteur crap," writing in his essay "James Taylor Marked for Death" that "If I hear one more Jesus-walking-the-boys-and-girls-down-a-Carolina-path-while-the-dilemma-of-existence-crashes-like-a-slab-of-hod-on-J.T.'s-shoulders song," he would smash a bottle of cheap wine and twist it into Taylor's guts "until he expires in a spasm of adenoidal poesy." (Bangs's touch was not light.) Mitchell, to be sure, occasionally elicited this kind of allergic reaction from listeners, too—they'll think she's too navel-gazing or too twee, too likely to name one of her songs "The Silky Veils of Ardor" or to saddle her eighth album, *The Hissing of Summer Lawns*, with the proviso "This record is a total work conceived graphically, musically, lyrically and accidentally—as a whole. The performances were guided by the given compositional structures and the audibly inspired beauty of every player. The whole unfolded like a mystery. It is not my intention to unravel that mystery for anyone . . ."

Much of the anti-troubadour response, even when directed at Taylor, rings of sexism, as if the new class of sensitive longhairs were an affront to the rebellious, class-clown machismo that had been fueling rock and roll since the fifties. But in his book *How the Beatles Destroyed Rock 'n' Roll: An Alternative History of American Popular Music*, Elijah Wald points out that women, despite not holding the top jobs in the recording industry, were largely responsible for the course of American pop music. Before recorded music became widely available, as Wald puts it, pop music was performed live, mostly for people to dance to. "As a general thing, American women dance because they want to dance, while American men dance because they want to be around women," Wald writes. "The result is that the most popular dance music will be whatever style the most women prefer."

Sure, singer-songwriters could get precious with their evocations of morning dew and sunshine and feeeeeeeelings—but for many of us, these tropes were a refreshing antidote to rockers' need to be bad, bad, bad to the *boooone*. Moreover, most singer-songwriters have lovely, or at least unobjectionable, singing voices, whereas many rock singers sound like they are trying to open a jar. Some music critics, however, saw the singer-songwriter movement of the 1970s as a sign of how the Beatles' and Dylan's revolutionizing of the music industry—from an industry in which labels had hired singers and musicians to perform songs that other people had written, to an industry wherein singers and musicians mostly wrote their own stuff—had waxed increasingly Caucasian and mushy. To be sure, some Lite FM songs describe emotional states that border on the effete; outside of cross-country truckers, has the sound of one's own wheels *ever* actually threatened to drive anyone crazy?

In Mitchell's case, her angelic looks and demeanor presumably only heightened the stakes for skepticism from listeners like Bangs; why else would Texan singer-songwriter Kinky Friedman delight in telling the world that, when he threw a party at the Sunset Tower in Los Angeles once, the tone that Mitchell and Bob Dylan created when they holed up in a room during the party and gave a mini concert was so reverent that Friedman took it upon himself to fart during one of Joni's songs? ("It was like they were in church and I farted," Friedman has said. "It's not something I do now, but back then it was my thing.")

We don't know at what point, or even if, Taylor unveiled his family's story to Joni, but it, too, would make a sensitive heart like hers fibrillate. Either way, she certainly got snatches of it in song: "You could make a case that most of the songs I've written have been a way of trying to work out just what happened to us," Taylor says in *Break Shot*. "It's like that movie *Groundhog Day*: I'm assigned to keep going over and over it until I figure it out."

James's father, Dr. Isaac Taylor, or Ike, was delivered by his own grandfather in a home birth that the grandfather, although a physician, slightly botched. Baby Ike was fine—but, a week later, his mother (James's grandmother) died, and within two months Ike's grandfather, wracked with guilt, had drunk himself to death. Ike was then raised by his aunt and uncle. Being raised by your aunt and uncle after your mom has died might feel odd to begin with, but the fact that the aunt and uncle lived across a lawn from where Ike's widowed father lived sealed the deal: it was like Ike was a neighbor to his own life. Meanwhile, his aunt constantly told Ike that his father was a failure and an alcoholic.

Scarred by these events, Ike turned into an overachiever, becoming a physician and the dean of the University of North Carolina Medical School. He also became a problem drinker and a bit of a womanizer. When, years later, James's marriage counselor encouraged James to bring Ike to a session because so many of James's problems seemed to stem from him, Ike agreed; when the counselor asked Ike why, if his marriage was so flawed, he and his wife had had five kids, Ike sarcastically responded, "I figured childbirth killed my mother, maybe it'll kill my wife."

James's troubles began in his senior year at the boarding school Milton Academy. He fell into a heavy depression and checked into McLean.

Taylor first tried heroin as a struggling musician in New York City in 1966. "My family has a history of addiction," he has said, "and I'm probably genetically predisposed to substance abuse. So I didn't stand a chance. Those drugs, powerful drugs, were as available as a beer at the bar." Taylor tried to stop using but resorted to drinking several bottles of cough syrup a day, including in London during the recording sessions of his first album. Then he discovered that he could buy heroin from legal junkies who were registered users with London's maintenance program. "I'd shoot speedballs of smack and meth, all pure stuff over there," James has said. "But pure stuff is just pure poison."

This time he checked into Austen Riggs, a treatment facility in Stockbridge, Massachusetts.

In the end, it didn't work out for Mitchell and Taylor as a couple. "There were some very likable things about James," Mitchell tells biographer David Yaffe in *Reckless Daughter*, "but for the most part, he was incapable of affection. He was just a mess. If somebody's dark and brooding, you're better off brood[ing] beside them. Don't go acting cheerful. You're just a reminder of what they're not. They'll hate you for it. . . . That's when I learned that lesson." (For Taylor's future wife Carly Simon, who has suffered from low self-esteem all her life, Taylor's brooding had a different effect: Simon writes in her memoir *Boys in the Trees* that "his pain diverted my attention away from myself, the result being that I agonized about myself less.")

Remember how Graham Nash had witnessed Mitchell meeting Taylor for the first time? In a seeming act of karmic retribution, Mitchell witnessed Taylor meeting Carly Simon when Mitchell and Taylor went to a concert that Simon gave at the Troubadour in 1971. As we know from Simon's memoir, a barefoot Taylor, who was nodding out—the term for an opiate user's sleepy, wobbling head—lay on the floor of Simon's Troubadour dressing room. Mitchell burst into the room and, without looking at Simon, said, "James, we have to go now."

Taylor told the *Guardian* in 2021, "When I was taking her to meet my family in North Carolina, between flights she suddenly said she had to return to California and left me at the airport—at the altar, so to speak. Maybe she sensed the wreckage of my next fifteen years and didn't want to be tied down."

Sometime after Mitchell and Taylor had broken up and he'd taken up with Simon (Taylor and Simon would be married from 1972 to 1983), Mitchell called Taylor at the Martha's Vineyard house that Taylor and Simon would spend years building. In her memoir, Simon laments Taylor's bouts of "coldness," and recounts how, on the day of Mitchell's phone call, she heard Taylor bluntly tell Mitchell, "You shouldn't call here anymore." Simon writes, "Yes, I was relieved that his relationship with Joni, his most recent lover before me, was over, but at the same time, how could anyone ever be 'over' Joni Mitchell? Joni was brilliant and enchanting, and her love for James, I always imagined, was original and deep. When James hung up the phone and came down the stairs from the loft, he looked steely and furious. As a woman who loved him, the last thing in the world I wanted to say was 'Don't ever speak to someone you have loved, or told that you loved, or made love to, in such a way,' and I didn't."

By the early 1970s the woman who wrote "Woodstock" and "Big Yellow Taxi" and who inspired Graham Nash's "Our House" had emerged as an icon of back-to-the-land, flower child sensitivity, and it became possible to see her amorous tribulations, and the depictions thereof on her albums, as emblems of failed utopian idealism. Graham and Leonard and James weren't going to last the duration—and neither were the optimism and youthful idealism that their generation had tried to put into the water supply.

As happens at the end of "The Last Time I Saw Richard," the last song on *Blue*, people were starting to hide behind bottles in ill-lit cafes. The dark and brutal tail end of the sixties, when the horror of the Manson murders and the violence at Altamont only made the death tolls coming out of Vietnam that much more palpable, sent a strong message that the world, despite all the peace protests and the campfire songs, was falling apart. The tie-dye had gone brown in the wash.

Exposed to so many forms of violence, many Americans, as the seventies rolled in, were anxious to take stock and to heal. Hello, the self-help boom. Hello, the singer-songwriter movement, wherein sensitive souls make delicious meals of their sorrows.

From rusty pipes can grow mansions. Taylor cleaned up in the early eighties and has gone on to be a Kennedy Center honoree and win a Presidential Medal of Freedom, to sell more than 100 million records, and to rival the PBS tote bag as a symbol of the wholesome appeal of public television. His air of mellow self-effacement continues to charm and to hold others in its sway, even if it sometimes gives Taylor the vibe of the world's most beloved mortician.

As collaborators and muses for each other, not to mention friends, he and Mitchell have a rich history that lasts to this day. As she has often stated, Joni doesn't want us to think about her life when we listen to her songs, she wants us to think about our own so that we can accrue wisdom or achieve catharsis—or "take you through a kind of heavy place and then lift some weight off of you, just as it did off of me as the creator," as she put it in 1980—and thus she has always been cagey about pegging specific songs to the specific people who may have inspired them. One exception is the bittersweet "See You Sometime" from *For the Roses,* which she has acknowledged is about James. (After Mitchell encouraged the unnamed "you" in the lyrics of "See You Sometime" to pack his suspenders and visit her, Taylor, she has pointed out, more or less outed himself by wearing suspenders on the cover of his next album, *Mud Slide Slim and the Blue Horizon.*) In Mitchell's song, she's wondering where he is—if he's in a nice hotel room, or in the arms of some young lovely he met on the road. What the two of them shared, the song suggests, was painful, but, nevertheless, her affection for him keeps on keeping on.

The other Joni songs that are thought to be inspired by Taylor are "All I Want" (Joni wants to shampoo and renew James), "This Flight Tonight" (parting at Logan is such sweet sorrow), "Blue" (heroin is a bitch), "Cold Blue Steel and Sweet Fire" (heroin is *really* a bitch), "For the Roses" (fame is a bitch), "Woman of Heart and Mind" (love is bittersweet), and "Blonde in the Bleachers" (groupies are *putanas*). These are some of the darkest and most affecting works in Mitchell's oeuvre. Taylor, whose first songs played on guitar were hymns from the hymnal at Milton Academy, has described his work as "spirituals for agnostics," and that tag would apply to most of these songs of Mitchell's, too. (Which might help explain why, in 1994, a pregnant Rosanna Arquette played Mitchell's music to her unborn daughter, Zoë. "Zoë is a poet and I like to think that playing Joni Mitchell when she was inside my womb had a lot to do with it," Arquette told me.)

On Taylor's side, his guitar contributions enliven and flesh out *Blue*'s "All I Want," "California," and "A Case of You" (the liner notes of Mitchell's 2021 *Archives: Volume 2* found her writing "He really locked up to my dulcimer," which sounds like graffiti in a public bathroom in Laurel Canyon). You can also hear Taylor playing on the title tracks of 1975's *The Hissing of Summer Lawns* and 2007's *Shine*.

After they'd broken up, James and Joni sang background vocals together on Carole King's "Will You Love Me Tomorrow?," for which they're credited as "The Mitchell/Taylor Boy-and-Girl Choir." To see the most widely circulated photo of them doing this recording—Taylor is wearing the sweater that Mitchell knitted him—is to witness an atom bomb of adorable. As King writes in her memoir, "Though James and Joni are singing on separate mics, their closeness is almost a physical presence." Joni also sang backup on James's version of King's "You've Got a Friend," which hit #1 on the *Billboard* charts on July 31, 1971—a first and only #1 song for both of them. In 1975, long after they've broken up, Mitchell and Taylor—joined by two of Mitchell's other exes, Crosby and Nash—will all sing backup on Mitchell's "In France They Kiss on Main Street" while Mitchell's ex John Guerin plays drums. Patrick Milligan, the coproducer of Mitchell's three *Archives* collections, has said that in 2021 when he sent Mitchell a recording of her 1970 BBC concert with James Taylor, "She heard it and said something to the effect of 'That's the best thing I ever did. My intonation is so good here and James and I sound great together. Maybe James and I should have been an act!'"

That, of all the sensitive singer-songwriters in the world, two of the most prominent (and good-looking) ones would not only find each other but also fall in love was deeply satisfying for many fans. Mitchell and Taylor's brief union yielded the same by-products that romantic comedies and Lifetime movies do: hope, relief, the assurance that, when a high-powered executive quits her job in the cruel city and moves back to her dopey Iowa hometown, she will meet a sad, handsome carpenter whose wife just fell into an industrial meat grinder. Additionally, the fact that Taylor is one of Mitchell's very few exes that she has never subsequently bad-mouthed in public keeps the nostalgia surrounding their union pristine. Indeed, for those of us who were emotionally invested in the Joni and James narrative—two soulmates who, had they met at another time in their lives, might have been able to attend to each other's gaping wound—there's probably no more moving moment than when Taylor covers *Blue*'s heartrending "River." After Taylor sings that he has become difficult to handle as a result of his selfishness and his sadness, he delivers a couplet that suggests that his and Joni's bruises exist in synchronicity:

Now I've gone and lost the best baby
That I ever had.

25

1950. In the first few weeks of first grade in North Battleford, Saskatchewan, the town that Joni and her parents lived in before they moved to Saskatoon, Joan's teacher quizzed her students on various subjects. In one version of the story that Joni has told, the teacher reconfigured the seating in the classroom such that the A students sat in the outer row, against the wall. The teacher dubbed this group the Bluebirds. Then the B students sat in the next row, and were called the Wrens. And finally, the C students, the Crows.

Joan, designated a Wren, looked at the Bluebirds and thought, "I don't like any of them. I like the Crows." And from there on in, she decided, she didn't care about letter grades.

She'd later experience a disconnect with Sunday school, too. One day she asked her teacher, "OK, Adam and Eve meet, they're the first man and woman, and they have two sons: Cain and Abel. Cain killed Abel, then Cain got married. Who did he marry? Eve?"

Such precociousness was not looked on kindly; the teacher winced, making Joni feel "shabby." So Joni refused to go to church for a while.

Maybe it should come as no surprise that this same child would grow up to be someone who would confound the type of critic or fan who wants their artists to stay within tidy lines. Musically, Joni has always been difficult to categorize (which is her wont: as early as 1967 she was saying "That's what I've been striving for for a long time, is not to be categorized"). She started out as a folk singer who sang other people's songs, but as soon as she started writing her own stuff, the music sometimes sounded more like art songs—e.g., "Both Sides Now" or "Michael from Mountains" would seem to have more in common with Stephen Sondheim or Jacques Brel (or, as Mitchell would put it, Franz Schubert) than with Woody Guthrie. Next she embraced pop and light rock (*Ladies of the Canyon, Blue*), and then slowly injected it with jazz (*For the Roses, Court and Spark, Miles of Aisles, The Hissing of Summer Lawns, Hejira*). More overt experiments with jazz followed (*Don Juan's Reckless Daughter, Shadows and Light*) as did a full embrace of the idiom (*Mingus*). After *Mingus*, she had a two-album run-in with synthesizer-heavy pop and rock (*Wild Things Run Fast, Dog Eat Dog*) before making a duets album (*Chalk Mark in a Rain Storm*) and then returning to the less electronic, sensitive singer-songwriter fare that her fan base craved (*Night Ride Home, Turbulent Indigo, Taming the Tiger*). Subsequent albums saw her toying with fully orchestrated versions of both jazz standards and her own work (*Both Sides Now, Travelogue*) as well as the unlikely axis of classical and easy listening (*Shine*).

Folkie? Jazzer? Pop star? She's too polyrhythmic for the first, too pop for the second, and too multivarious for the third. As Mitchell would tell a reporter who asked her in 2013 about musical influences, "I'm a mutt. I belong to nothing."

In a larger sense, too, Mitchell is someone who resists categorization and received wisdom. She once called free love "a ruse for guys." She's a feminist role model who doesn't consider herself a feminist ("I don't want to get a posse against men. I'd rather go toe to toe myself. Work it out"). Biographer David Yaffe told me that when he toured Mitchell's alma mater, the Alberta College of Art, with her once, he asked, "Joni, did they have a humanities requirement here?"

"What's that?"

"You know, literature, philosophy, history, religion."

"Really," Joni responded, "you call that humanity?"

Mitchell's monolithic nature is also in evidence whenever the conversation turns to the radical idealism of the 1960s. Having wrongly designated Mitchell as a fragile hippie princess, the world has long assumed that she embodies a certain ethos and politics. After all, folk, the idiom she started out in, had a long history of political protest—back in the 1940s, Woody Guthrie had put on his guitar a sign reading "This machine kills fascists," and Dylan had made his name by championing the little man and taking on the voice of the oppressed. Protest songs were so popular among folkies that in the program book for 1964's Newport Folk Festival, singer-songwriter Phil Ochs wrote "I wouldn't be surprised to see an album called *Elvis Presley Sings Songs of the Spanish Civil War*, or the Beatles with *The Best of the Chinese-Indian Border Dispute Songs*."

But that wasn't Joni's way. During the Vietnam War, she gave a concert at Fort Bragg because she had uncles who had died in World War II and she thought it would be a shame to blame the young men who'd been drafted. When Joni appeared on the radio show *Innerview* in 1980—after having turned them down for six years—she said, "I didn't feel a part of the sixties even though that's the part I'm accredited. Mine was an internal revolution. In the sixties I was going through more what people were going through in the seventies in a certain way. You know what I mean? I was going through more of a personal revolution. I didn't find a lot of the leadership in the sixties particularly inspiring in government or within our own peer group. I always felt that we were rather fleas on an elephant's leg and much more powerless than we would want to trump one another up to believe. . . . I'm not a political person. My interest has always been in the spiritual, and they stand in direct opposition in a certain way. Mine has been a freeing of my own bigotry, you know. You need to be a bigot from time to time in order to have confines on your art. You have to prefer, which immediately makes you a bigot. So for me it's been lack of identification with groups. I mean I have no religious affiliation, I have no national affiliation. I'm a Canadian living in America, but I don't feel any more like a Canadian or an American or—you see what I mean? . . . It's been a very kind of subjective, I guess you'd say, journey. Subjective but hopefully universal. That was always my optimism that if I described my own changes through whatever the decade was throwing at us, that there were others like me. And it turns out that there were."

The great irony of refusing the easy consolations of group affiliation is that it often causes us to forge stronger one-on-one relationships with other individuals. One of the most surprising "others like me" that Joni found was her own mother. Referring to the emotional crisis that she was going through when she recorded *Blue*, Mitchell told her friend Malka Marom in 1973, "I got this illness—crying all the time. My mother thought I was being a wimp, and she was giving me buck-up advice. Later in life, she was walking through the supermarket and started crying for no reason. She also had it, milder than this. She called me up and apologized."

Mitchell would elaborate in an Irish newspaper seven years later. "Papa was just proud," she'd say to *Western People* of her fame. "For myself and my mother, it became almost like Joni Mitchell was an external creation, with all this attention being paid to 'Joni Mitchell'—but what about the person? Is there room for the person or is there only this fascination with the phenomenon of success?" Joni had been thinking such thoughts since the age of sixteen, when, sympathetic to the plight of actress Sandra Dee, who was hounded by paparazzi while breaking up with her husband, Joan had written a poem called "The Fishbowl."

Mitchell contends that the fans most likely to project ideas onto famous people are the ones who lack self-knowledge: once, at Studio 54, she met the fan who years earlier had yelled out during a performance the bizarre comment, "Joni, you have more class than Mick Jagger, Richard Nixon, and Gomer Pyle—combined!" (For the young people: Gomer Pyle was a wide-eyed, naive, Southern character on *The Andy Griffith Show* and *Gomer Pyle, U.S.M.C.*) So at Studio 54 Joni said to the fan, "I've always wanted to ask you: Are *you* just like Mick Jagger, Gomer Pyle, and Richard Nixon rolled into one?" The man replied yes, and Joni said, "I thought so."

But it's the media, of course, that is the prime engine of mythos and generalization. Try to follow, if you can, this 1974 *Toronto Star* description of Mitchell and her career: "In swirling soprano self-portraits and worshipful press clippings, all cornsilk flashes and free-spirit poetry . . . she has emerged unscathed in portraits of enchanted dewdrop vulnerability . . . immaculate, preserved forever as the elusive pastel prairie wildflower, the misty wispy moonbeam princess lushly chording in her castle of bittersweet sorrows and stained-glass dreams." Whuuuh?

In 2023, I interviewed performance artist John Kelly, who met Joni in 1996 when she came to one his performances in which he incarnates her. Kelly told me, "Maria Callas said, 'Glory terrifies me.' So much stuff was thrust upon Callas. But she was just trying to do the work. And do it well. She wasn't aiming for celebrity and glory. But you're nobody in this world unless you have some kind of identity."

"Yes," I said, "which is why we now have an entire generation of people who can't watch things: they go with their camera to watch their favorite performer but spend the whole time taking selfies of themselves *not* watching their favorite performer."

Kelly responded, "Joni calls it 'ego puke.'"

As a public figure, you can't fully control the narrative that people harbor about you—but you can limit people's access to it. Whereupon you discover that this tactic often only causes fans to obsess even more. "Ziggy for me was a very simplistic thing," David Bowie has said of Ziggy Stardust, the alter ego that he started developing during a trip to the U.S. in 1971. "What it seemed to be was an alien rock star. But other people reread him, and contributed more information about Ziggy than I'd put into him."

Given only a few details about a charismatic person or alter ego or place, it seems only natural that our brain sometimes builds up a network of associations and suppositions that are more vivid than the actual person or place might have been had we had time to study or interact with them. It's similar to how listening to the radio can be more intense than watching TV or a movie.

Or it's like Joni and the song "Woodstock." Though she made it to Woodstock to celebrate its twenty-ninth anniversary in 1998, Joni, famously, didn't get to go to the epochal concert in 1969 because she had a talk show appearance the next day and her agent and manager worried that she wouldn't be able to make it back in time. So she stayed away. And wrote the historic event's theme song.

26

9130 West Sunset Boulevard, Los Angeles. 1973 or thereabouts. David Geffen's office at Asylum Records. The music potentate is schmoozing Robbie Robertson, the guitarist who played for Bob Dylan before going on to help form The Band and then to find or create music for many of Martin Scorsese's films, from *Raging Bull* through *Killers of the Flower Moon* (which is dedicated to Robertson, who passed away in 2023). It is unclear to the casual observer whether Geffen is interested in signing the tall, faun-like, half-Jewish, half-Mohawk guitarist because Geffen likes (and thinks he can make money from) Robertson's work, or whether he sees Robertson as a stepping stone to Geffen's great white whale, client-wise: Dylan.

Geffen broke the ice by casually working into the conversation the fact that he was going to a therapist five days a week. Robertson was warmed by the admission's disarming candor.

Then Geffen deployed a second arrow from his quiver: a name drop. "Your fellow Canadian Joni Mitchell is living with me," he told Robertson. "We're housemates. She's a genius. It's not easy living with a genius, but I love her."

Geffen invited Robertson over for dinner that night—"I'll ask some friends over, and you can say hello to Joni."

Hours later, Robertson showed up at Geffen's place—the aforementioned Blake Edwards/Julie Andrews rental—where Robertson discovered that "some friends" translated to two of Hollywood's biggest players, Jack Nicholson and Warren Beatty ("Joni's trophies," as John Lennon will call them behind her back).

"I soon noticed that everyone here was on a mission," Robertson will later report of the gathering's business-minded, darty-eyed participants. "All eyes in the room were casting about for what might be right for their next project." (David Yaffe told an audience at the Leon Levy Center for Biography in 2017 that he once talked to Mitchell about being repeatedly hit on by Nicholson and Beatty over the years, asking her, "Was that fun?" Whereupon Mitchell took a drag of her cigarette and said, "Fun?! Celebrities are not fun. They're neurotic, sick people.")

After dinner, Joni announced that she had a new song. She picked up one of the acoustic guitars in the living room, tuned it up, and launched into her new offering. "I tried to follow her on guitar," Robertson, a legendary guitarist, later confessed, "but between her unusual tunings and obscure fingering, I was a man in search of the lost chords."

That Joni lived for a time with power broker David Geffen—her agent and the head of her record label—bespeaks either ambition or the ability to find the humanity in anyone, or some combination of the two. It's easy to see how the friendship worked when it did—for her, here was someone who not only loved her music, but had a financial and professional incentive in its propagation;

for him, here was a sensitive soul with whom he could talk about his closeted homosexuality (after dating Cher and Marlo Thomas, Geffen announced in 1992 that he is gay), as well as her own troubled love life. But given that Mitchell tends to be honest to a fault, it's surprising that she would find shelter with the man who gleefully admits that he once forged a letter in order to keep his job in the William Morris Agency's mail room.

Brash and fast-talking and witty in a way that feels earthy rather than haughty—in Geffen's Brooklyn tones, the word "song" always comes out "sawng"—the physically slight Geffen would come to have a stranglehold on the singer-songwriter movement of the 1970s by dint of his working relationships with Joni, Bob Dylan, Linda Ronstadt, Crosby, Stills & Nash, Tom Waits, Jackson Browne, and the Eagles. Though he dressed conservatively and hardly did drugs, he was seen at first as his clients' contemporary and protector; but by 1983, infamously, he'd sue his artist Neil Young for turning in "musically uncharacteristic" material, forever branding Geffen as uncool, if not The Man.

He'd grown up the son of a woman who, when buying a blouse at Bloomingdale's, would try to negotiate the price with the salesperson. She called her son King David. Geffen started his career in the William Morris mail room; as he has told it, when he found out that one of the other trainees at the agency had gotten fired for lying on his résumé, Geffen, nervous about having lied himself about going to UCLA, hawk-eyed the mail coming into William Morris daily, then steamed open a letter from UCLA to the talent agency, had a stationer duplicate the letterhead, and rewrote the letter saying he'd graduated. His ruthlessness as a negotiator will earn him enemies both in the music industry, where he starts, and in film and theater, where he ends up before becoming a philanthropist. A record executive once screamed at him, "You'd jump into a pool of pus to come up with a nickel between your teeth!"—decades before reality television made the exchange of dignity for cash a tinselly badge of honor.

But two qualities—besides his tenacity and his eye for talent—save Geffen from being the full monster. Firstly, his sense of humor. It's awful that on driving to the hospital to see his dying mother, whom he adored, Geffen had the thought "When your mother dies, you can sell the house—you'll get 1.3 million." But the fact that we know this about Geffen means that he told someone about it, which suggests . . . a touch of self-awareness? An ability to self-deprecate? Secondly, you expect Sammy Glick to have either horrible taste or highly situational taste. But Geffen (though, yes, he would later pony up a lot of money for Broadway's *Cats*) fought hard for great offbeat artists who weren't necessarily the easiest sells, like Joni and the filmmaker Albert Brooks. ("I only sell about 300,000 records. It takes about 600,000 to break even," Mitchell, who makes a living from songwriting royalties, not record deals or touring, explained in 1997.) Too, he spent the early part of his career devotedly representing one of the very few living (at the time) female singer-songwriters that Joni has acknowledged as an influence, the underappreciated Laura Nyro, who wrote "It's Gonna Take a Miracle" and "And When I Die" and made the heartbreaking record *Eli and the Thirteenth Confession.*

"David was always very ambitious for himself," David Crosby told the *New Yorker* when Geffen was profiled by the magazine in 1998, "but there was one interesting, unprotected place in him—he really loved Laura Nyro. That was a window into something in him that was not primarily about money." Geffen believed so strongly in Nyro—a Goth oddball who had hair down to her thighs and sometimes wore Christmas bulbs as earrings—that he even got her label to agree to her request that *Eli*'s lyrics be printed on the album's cover in lilac-scented ink.

But the tireless dynamo—one acquaintance called Geffen "the elf on roller skates"—also managed to get a half share of Nyro's publishing, an unusual, and perhaps unethical, arrangement for a manager or agent.

Which, by 1971, may have netted Geffen $2 million.

In February and March of 1972, Joni toured thirteen cities. Her opening act was Geffen's latest "find," Jackson Browne, a dashing-verging-on-beautiful singer-songwriter loaded down with hummable, fine-grained songs. (Browne will repay the favor of Geffen's devotion to him early on in his career by introducing Geffen to a group that will make Geffen another boatload of money, the Eagles.) Musician and songwriter Jimmy Webb writes about Jackson and Joni in one of his memoirs, saying that he watched Browne "fall in love with her. I remember him coming to me, very nervous, and saying, 'So, how should I talk to her?' And I smiled, moved yet deeply amused at the same time. 'You just talk to her like you would talk to . . . a really nice person,' I said."

Mitchell had probably first become aware of Browne in November 1971. Come with me now to a car that is rocketing from Los Angeles to Redwood City, en route to Thanksgiving dinner at the home of Neil Young and his girlfriend, actress Carrie Snodgress. In the car are Joni, Graham Nash, David Crosby, and photographer Joel Bernstein.

Nash noticed that Crosby was smiling mischievously.

"So what is it?" Nash asked.

"None of you have heard *this*," Crosby said, pulling a cassette out of his pocket. "This is the new Jackson Browne record." Crosby had provided backup vocals on Browne's debut album.

"Who's Jackson Browne?" Mitchell asked.

Crosby and Bernstein chimed in unison, "Only your next boyfriend!"

Jinx.

While touring together in 1972, Joni and Jackson, who was five years her junior, started seeing each other. "L.A.'s two newest lovebirds," a student reporter will call the duo in the University of Pittsburgh's daily paper when he sees them later that year at the Mariposa Folk Festival. "They each did their own sets, then ran around taking little Instamatic photos of the other, the audience, and people in general." As with Mitchell's, Browne's doe-eyed beauty seemed to crystallize or heighten his air of childlike wisdom. "He was a real soulmate," Bonnie Raitt has said of Browne, who would go on to become a tireless activist on behalf of the environment. "There was something so truthful and at the same time so heartbreaking about his songs." Case in point: his lovely "Fountain of Sorrow" from *Late for the Sky*, a song, probably inspired by Mitchell, about how a single photograph can open memory's floodgates.

Joni's take is less enraptured. "Jackson Browne was never attracted to me," she'll say to David Yaffe about the singer-songwriter who'll have three gold records in the early seventies before reaching even greater success with 1976's *The Pretender* and 1977's *Running on Empty*. "We got thrown out on the road together and traveled all around. We were companions, because we were playing in Amsterdam and playing from London to New Orleans. But when he spoke about old lovers, he leered. He was a leering narcissist." (Mitchell, as we're reminded in a lyric on 1991's *Night Ride Home*, has always been sensitive about freighted enthusiasm: "Does your smile's covert complicity / Debase as it admires?")

We don't have many details about the Joni-Jackson romance, other than that it ended very, very badly, probably because it was the rare instance of Joni being the dumpee. *Girls Like Us* is probably our best source here. One night Browne did a show at the Roxy, the Sunset Boulevard club that Geffen and others had opened to compete with the reigning Troubadour. Mitchell took exception with a comment Browne made about her onstage; after the show, they had a huge argument in a stairwell, causing Joni to run out of the club barefoot. Cut to: a different night at the Troubadour, Browne sees a gorgeous woman being screamed at by her boyfriend, so Browne rallies to her defense, causing the boyfriend to throw a punch at Browne, whereupon Browne and the woman, professional model Phyllis Major, end up going home together and eventually falling in love. (Tragically, she would later overdose on barbiturates. Browne's ruminative "Sleep's Dark and Silent Gate" on 1976's *The Pretender* captures some of his pain.)

Dark times for Joni. While at her West Hollywood apartment one subsequent night—Joni was still living part-time with Geffen but had now also rented a place on the hilly part of West Hollywood's Crescent Heights Boulevard—she waited for Jackson to show up, but he didn't (this will inspire her song "Car on a Hill" on *Court and Spark*). Whereupon Joni launched into what she would later tell confidants was a "suicide attempt." According to *Girls Like Us*, she took a lot of pills; smashed her head against a wall, breaking glass; then vomited the pills (Mitchell will deny this suicide attempt when Yaffe interviews her: "I'm crazy but not that crazy"). Geffen came to the rescue by getting her medical attention, and then encouraging her to come back to the Blake Edwards/Julie Andrews rental.

Geffen is also important to the Joni story, of course, because of Joni's songs "Woodstock" and "Free Man in Paris." On the former front, it was Geffen, along with manager Elliot Roberts, who convinced Joni *not* to go to Woodstock because of her *Dick Cavett Show* commitment. Joni watched the concert on TV—"I missed it," as she put it to an audience at Worcester Polytechnic Institute in December 1969—"and then felt sorry for myself"—and wrote her anthemic tribute to it at Geffen's hotel suite at the Pierre Hotel in New York. She has said that she probably wouldn't have written the song had she actually gone to the concert because she probably would have gotten caught up in backstage drama or performers' egos, which would have tainted the idyllic, utopian spell that Woodstock cast over her and her song. When the documentary of the concert was being put together, Geffen told the filmmakers that they couldn't use footage of his clients Crosby, Stills, Nash & Young unless the filmmakers made CSNY's cover of

Joni's "Woodstock," with Neil Young's blistering guitar intro, the movie's theme song.

Geffen was the inspiration for one of Mitchell's biggest hits—*Court and Spark*'s "Free Man in Paris." It had started when Geffen, still schmoozing guitarist Robbie Robertson, planned an all-expenses-paid trip to the City of Light that included Robertson, Robertson's wife Dominique, and Mitchell. The four flew first class, stayed in the Coco Chanel suite at the Ritz, gallivanted up and down the Champs-Élysées, and drank a bottle of 1928 Château Margaux at La Tour d'Argent (Geffen: "You only live once"). One member of the party ended up vomiting on the room service cart in the Ritz's hallway, but the origins of the regurgitative offering are murky: "Joni wasn't sure if it was her," Robertson writes in his memoir, "Dominique thought she had done it, and David was sure it was him." (As Joni once said, "Stardom is a glamorous misunderstanding.")

But the trip wasn't all fine wines and *vomir vomir*. Joni brought along a guitar, of course, and worked so copiously on "Free Man"—the account of a music mogul who finds huge liberty in being in Paris, away from his needy clients—that at one point Dominique said to her, "Can you *please* not sing and play right now? We just want to talk for a while." Whereupon all four broke into laughter, because telling Joni to stop making music is like giving Mother Nature "notes" on the weather. (That said, Mitchell apologized and stopped.)

Geffen begged Mitchell not to include "Free Man" on *Court and Spark*. The song recounts how the mogul is frequenting cafes and cabarets in Paris while relishing the thought of running into "that very good friend of mine"; the closeted Geffen thought the song might out him. (In 1973, gay liberation was still a fringe movement; gay men and women regularly lost jobs when their sexual orientation was discovered.) Also, given Geffen's high level of ambitiousness, it's possible that he thought the portrait of a blithe and carefree mogul made him look unprofessional. It's one thing for the world and your colleagues to know that you've done est, Lifespring, and *A Course in Miracles,* as Geffen has owned up to, and another for the world to think that, at any given moment during a workday, you'd rather be gallivanting up and down the Champs-Élysées, calling everyone *bébé.*

In either case, Joni prevailed, and the song charted on *Billboard* at #22 and stayed on the chart for fourteen weeks. Because the song is written in first person, it lends itself to you-go-girl interpretations—*Sex and the City* author Candace Bushnell said in 2015 that she listens to it when she's down and struggling; in 2017, the song was played in its entirety during episode 2 of the final season of *Girls.*

The topic of Geffen and "Free Man" came up when Joni appeared on *CBS This Morning* in 1995 to promote her album *Turbulent Indigo.*

> PAULA ZAHN: You sing about things a lot of us can't even talk about. In the process of writing these songs, does it sometimes become so invasive that it's difficult for you to face your own emotions or are you completely free?
>
> JONI: Well, it depends. I mean, sometimes—I guess I am in this sense a true artist, in that I feel it's better to sac-

rifice myself to the song than someone else. I can forgive myself for revealing myself; whereas, sometimes, very simple portraits that I don't think are—like David Geffen had a hard time with "Free Man in Paris" for a long time. He was offended by it initially and yet it doesn't reveal anything unattractive about him. . . . After we returned [from Paris]—David and I were roommates at that time—I can remember him lamenting, "Oh, I want to go back to Paris, I want to go back to Paris," and he was kind of drowning in business responsibility. That's how I recall it. The song contains a lot of feelings in his own words at that time. You know, I kind of scribed them. And initially he didn't really want to be—not that I put his name on it; everybody knows it now because the press always ferrets these things out, but . . .

PAULA: Because you were dealing with sexuality.

JONI: Was it? Was there sexuality in it? I don't know, it just seems to me like a longing to be back on the Champs-Élysées. It became a symbol, I think, of freedom as opposed to business responsibility. So it's easier to do a portrait of myself and my own foibles.

In the end, though, as often happens with comic depictions of people—cue those members of seventeenth-century Parisian society who would attend the debuts of Molière's plays and, on recognizing themselves caricatured onstage, stand up in their seats and announce, "Madame Pernelle, *c'est moi!*"—Geffen, years later, after he'd come out publicly, would proudly tell young male romantic prospects that he was the inspiration for the song. Or he'd even sing along: one evening in the mid-nineties, when Geffen and a thirty-year-old date were being chauffeured around Manhattan, Geffen expressed surprise that his young friend owned no Joni records, so he instructed his driver to put "Free Man in Paris" on. And then started warbling.

But Mitchell and Geffen's friendship wouldn't have the same staying power. In 2002, when Mitchell was asked about Geffen by writer James Reginato, she hesitated before offering "David is almost like my mother. With her, I'll always be a little girl. Geffen once said to me, 'I know you better than anyone.' That was several lives ago—I've changed a lot. I've been several people. David seems to have an inability to see me fresh."

Then, in the 2013 book *Gathered Light*—an anthology of Joni friends and fans musing on her work—one of the anthology's co-editors asked Geffen if Mitchell's creative process ever sparked his own or vice versa. Geffen told her that Mitchell made her albums entirely by herself from start to finish, "stating in no uncertain terms that it was 'like they were there to deliver her baby.'"

27

Los Angeles, 1979. Writer Cameron Crowe, who is interviewing Joni at her house in Bel Air, ventures the opinion that being Georgia O'Keeffe—in her nineties, living in the desert, and without any children—sounds a little lonely. Joni responds, "I don't know, really, what your choices are. Obviously, that's a constant battle with me. Is my maternity to amount to a lot of black plastic? Am I going to annually bear this litter of songs and send them out into the marketplace and have them crucified for this reason or that?"

April 1983. Mitchell tells the *Sunday Times* of London, "There is not a lot of room for children. My husband [Larry Klein] and I are not about to become John and Yoko, but we have a beautiful balanced relationship that would not be augmented by child-rearing. And I've already reproduced myself on the planet."

In 1988, Mitchell tells journalist Ben Fong-Torres, "The creative drive is a family in itself."

Three years later, David Wild interviews Mitchell on the eve of *Night Ride Home*'s release. Mitchell says that she has paid a price for shifting her music away from pop and toward jazz. "I lost my ability to broadcast, my public access. It was worth it. I would do it all over again in a minute for the musical education. But, of course, it hurt. Your records are like your kids. And you want to say, 'Don't bloody my baby's nose when I send him to school, because he's a nice kid. You just don't understand him. He's a little different, but if you try, you'll like him.'"

Three years later, 1994. Mitchell tells her *Mojo* interviewer Barney Hoskyns, "I've always been a couple of years ahead of people in my personal changes so that when records come out, people kind of dump on 'em and then two years later they go through the changes and something becomes their favorite but it's too late. It's already—it's got a bad tailwind on it, you know? It's too late for my child, you know? The child's been bloodied on the playground so to speak."

1995. Mitchell tells *Goldmine* magazine, "Of course, once I began to write my own songs, I was slightly ambitious for them. I was a stage door mother to them. I wanted to display them. I thought that this was a superior work to selling women's ware, which was all I was really trained for. I had a Grade 12 education."

In 1997, Mitchell told music journalist Bill Flanagan in *Vanity Fair*, "Until the mid-sixties, the technology hadn't developed to make a career like mine viable." When Flanagan expressed confusion, given that Mitchell had started out as a folk singer, Mitchell smilingly explained, "I had to be able to plug up my puppies. Before 1965, I would have had twelve kids. I'm very fertile."

1998. In a review of Mitchell's appearance with Van Morrison and Bob Dylan at the Pauley Pavilion in Los Angeles, a *Variety* writer offers, "The dichotomy of the two performers was reflected in the crowd: They bounced and clapped in time during Morrison's perf, but sat in rapt attention during Mitchell's, focusing on every lyric and nuance like kindergartners during story time."

2007. In a public interview, Mitchell tells singer-songwriter Amanda Ghost, "The place where I take pride in my songs is their utility. Are they good kids? Do they go out into the world and make nicey-nicey? You know, like, can they hold a job out there? You know, like, can they survive?"

Mitchell also talks in 2007 to the *Calgary Herald* about *Shine*, the album she's working on. "I've been reluctant to birth this album," she says. "You know, I cross my legs—but it's coming anyway. They all come out that way. It's like they're writing me."

28

2013. Joni was recording a new version of her 1994 song "Borderline" at her house in Bel Air with the trumpeter Ambrose Akinmusire. Akinmusire, who was recording in, yes, one of Joni's bathrooms, was having trouble laying down his part. "I know what you need," Joni told him. "You need an egg shaker." So Joni stood outside the bathroom and wildly shook an egg shaker out of the song's time signature; this freed up Akinmusire, who now played beautifully.

So many of the stories about Joni working as her own producer are shot through with a similar lushness. She never let the fact that she doesn't read music get in the way. When she was making *Court and Spark* at A&M in 1973, she sang every part to every member of the band. Working from her initial guitar or piano track, she would sometimes tell bandleader Tom Scott things like "OK, here's a pressure point in the music. It needs a tension line, a drone. It needs a horn line coming out of here and it should begin to break here, right?" Whereupon Scott would say something like "All right, that's bar sixteen." Then Mitchell would add, "OK, when it begins to bend right here, let's make it a three-part harmony." Then Mitchell would hum some chords and Scott might suggest adding a certain note—whereupon Mitchell would say, "Great, and what if we take it . . ." Back and forth.

When Mitchell hires the right collaborators—e.g., Scott, longtime engineer Henry Lewy, Wayne Shorter, brilliant bass player Jaco Pastorius, bass player and later husband Larry Klein—the results can be glorious. Lord knows it can't be easy: in the mid-eighties, while making her album *Dog Eat Dog,* she put a sign on the studio door reading, "NO BOYS ALLOWED." In 1998, she told *Rolling Stone,* "Music is like sex. It's difficult to give instruction to a man."

What she seems to crave in the studio is an environment in which she feels free to experiment. And to call the shots: "Yes, I am controlling and so it should be," she once told her friend Malka Marom. "I should be in control of my art. I'm within my rights to control my own art." Herbie Hancock and Wayne Shorter aren't the only musicians she has tried to inspire via unusual imagery: other sessions have seen her prompting, "Play high-heel shoes going down cobblestone," "Give me a dolphin jumping in the water," "Sound like someone's falling down the stairs," "Sound like a garbage can."

Her efforts to mastermind have led to interestingly unorthodox ends. On 1985's "Smokin' (Empty, Try Another)," Mitchell became entranced by the sounds emanating from a cigarette vending machine in the A&M parking lot, so she and Lewy ran a microphone up inside it. In 1988, initially unable to get the swish-like drum sound she wanted for her duet with Peter Gabriel, "My Secret Place," Mitchell stumbled onto using the sound of audiotape flipping at the end of the reel before it came to rest.

Her sixth sense has led to some astute choices: after the masters of *Blue* had been sent to the record pressing plant, she recalled them so that she could replace the first song with the gem "All I Want" and the last one with "The Last Time I Saw Richard."

By all accounts, Mitchell is not the tyrant or hothead that all this impulsive and headstrong activity might suggest. "Believe it or not," a studio assistant told *Circus* magazine in 1978, "she's always running around hugging and kissing everybody between takes. She's real affectionate, isn't temperamental because she surrounds herself with friends and pros."

Mitchell's talent-wrangling skills reached their apogee on her 1988 album *Chalk Mark in a Rain Storm*, a duets album that features not only Tom Petty, Peter Gabriel, Willie Nelson, and Benjamin Orr from the Cars, but also that most unlikely Joni Mitchell collaborator, post-punk towhead Billy Idol, who voices a character named Rowdy Yates, "all chide and snide and bluff." Encountering Billy Idol on a Joni record is like picking up a magazine in a pediatrician's waiting room and discovering it's *Soldier of Fortune*.

Some of Mitchell's talent-wrangling seems like the work of a guerrilla casting director. Visits to the coffee machine in the hallway of the studio she's working in have brought her in contact with musicians—José Feliciano, a whole horn section—whom she has inveigled into her session; she has said, "Often, I've put musicians on my albums simply because of their proximity."

There's a bonkers story she has recounted over the years about recording "Lakota" on 1988's *Chalk Mark*. To wit: during a break in a session, Joni leaves the studio to go to a Native American artifact show at the Santa Monica Civic Auditorium, where she meets Iron Eyes Cody—he played the Native American who's shedding a tear over pollution in Keep America Beautiful's ubiquitous TV ad from the seventies. Iron Eyes has gone bald; he's wearing a gray, braided wig that he's tied under his chin like a bonnet. Joni asks Iron Eyes if he knows any Native American songs, whereupon Iron Eyes, right there in the aisle of the Civic Auditorium, tilts back his head and starts Hey-ya-ho, Hey-ya-ho–ing. Joni loves it and asks "What are you doing right now?" and Iron Eyes says "Well I'm going to dinner with some people at nine o'clock."

"I'm recording nearby," Joni says. "It's a song about the Lakota and the Black Hills. Would you come and sing on it?"

"You want me to overdub?"

They go back to the studio, where Joni and Larry Klein play back "Lakota" for Iron Eyes, who says, "Oh, it's got the haunting! I think you're turning Indian! You want me to overdub?"

They want him to overdub. He overdubs. Just as Iron Eyes finishes taping his vocal, everyone in the studio hears a clap of thunder. Joni and Iron Eyes rush out the door to the studio's back steps, from where they see a golden ball of lightning zooming down the nearby telephone lines, headed straight for the studio. So Joni rushes back inside and screams, "Get the tapes off the heads!"

As I say, bonkers. But, better yet, the final fillip (which I've never read or seen Joni mention): in 1996, the New Orleans *Times-Picayune* discovered that Iron Eyes wasn't Native American after all. His parents were both Italian. A glamorous misunderstanding with under-chin wig braiding.

I can't get enough of these kinds of stories. They thrill me. They encapsulate James Thurber's definition of humor: emotional chaos remembered in tranquility. But they also make me wonder about context. When I talked to musician and songwriter Jimmy Webb, who worked a lot at A&M at the same time Mitchell was recording there, I asked him, "There's a story that Joni recorded Don Henley singing on one track of *Wild Things Run Fast* but then realized that his voice sounded too much like hers, so she goes out into the hallway and grabs Lionel Richie and replaces Henley's track with his. Was that kind of thing common?"

"I just don't think she had a rule book," Webb said. "She was primarily an artist, a creator. A furious young talent. It was contained explosion all the time."

29

When walking to school as a youngster, Joni and her schoolmates were sometimes able to see the skyline mirages of grain elevators twenty miles away because the arctic temperatures bent light rays over the curvature of the earth. These are auspicious beginnings for a girl who would grow up to be ever alert to the forces of coincidence and premonition. In the liner notes to *Mingus,* her 1979 collaboration with the jazz bassist and composer who was fighting ALS at the time, she wrote, "Charles Mingus, a musical mystic, died in Mexico, January 5, 1979, at the age of 56. He was cremated the next day. That same day 56 sperm whales beached themselves on the Mexican coastline and were removed by fire. These are the coincidences that thrill my imagination."

Similarly, Mitchell is often cited as an artist whose innovations have proven predictive. In 1968, she made her first record a concept album—Side One is subtitled "I came to the city," and Side Two, "Out of the city and down to the seaside"—a decade before concept albums would become a cliché of prog rock. On 1975's *The Hissing of Summer Lawns,* she sampled Burundi drumming a decade before sampling became standard fare in hip-hop, and long before Paul Simon and Peter Gabriel and Talking Heads used African drumming in their work. She used jazz musicians to play mainstream pop a decade before Sting did. When Herbie Hancock presented her with the Les Paul Innovation Award in 2020, he said, “She was multi-tracking guitar parts to get wide chorusing effects on *Hejira* in 1976 *way* before you heard the term ‘chorusing.’”

What other examples of prophecy and coincidence do Mitchell’s life and career hold?

FIRST: While recording her first album, Mitchell tells her manager, Elliot Roberts, “You’ve gotta meet Neil Young. You’re going to love this guy.”
THEN: Elliot Roberts serves as Young’s manager for more than fifty years.

FIRST: Joni writes in 1970’s “Big Yellow Taxi” about paradise being paved over to create a parking lot.
THEN: The Matador, a Toronto club Mitchell used to play at, is targeted by the Toronto Parking Authority in 2007 to become a twenty-spot parking lot.

FIRST: Mitchell idolizes Miles Davis and Pablo Picasso for their creative restlessness.
THEN: In one of the rare instances that Mitchell agrees to work with a producer, the producer (Paul Rothchild) literally tapes her ever-shifting feet to the studio floor.

FIRST: Mitchell cautions Leonard Cohen about working with producer Phil Spector.
THEN: While they are working on Cohen's 1977 album *Death of a Ladies' Man*, Spector holds a gun to Cohen's head, hijacks the master tape, and releases his version without Cohen's consent.

FIRST: Mitchell trains her gimlet eye at celebrity culture in *Court and Spark*'s "People's Parties."
THEN: Six weeks later, *People* magazine publishes its first issue.

FIRST: Joni records Annie Ross's comic ode to mental illness, "Twisted."
THEN: Joni deals with a recent heartbreak by driving across the country while wearing a red wig and calling herself Charlene Lattimer.

FIRST: Joni names her eighth album *Hejira*, meaning exodus or migration.
THEN: Joni's publicist tells *Vanity Fair* writer Bill Flanagan, "If you find her, will you tell us?"

FIRST: Mitchell says, "I guess people identify with songs that you write and think that you wrote them just for them."
THEN: Legendary singer Nina Simone walks up to Joni at the Beverly Center shopping mall and, without introducing herself, references Joni's song "Ethiopia" by putting

her hands over her head and yelling "Joni Mitchell! Joni Mitchell! 'Ethiopia'!" and then walking off.

FIRST: Joni puts an end to various fads at her high school. THEN: A secret 1975 memo from the U.S. Embassy in Moscow, discovered in 2013, recommends that Joni be sent on a tour of the Soviet Union in order to help stop Communism.

30

In 2000, Joni, appearing with a seventy-piece orchestra, performed an evening of standards at the Mars Music Amphitheatre in West Palm Beach. "I'm just a chick with a band this time," she told the audience. "I bought a bra and burned my guitar."

On one of the infrequent occasions when the direction of Joni's career followed, rather than preceded, the direction of her peers', Joni put out an album of standards, *Both Sides Now*, in 2000. Two months earlier, George Michael had put out a strange collection of standards in which "Brother, Can You Spare a Dime?" was followed by the well-known musical plea to a prostitute "Roxanne," as if to showcase first the pros and then the cons of the burgeoning gig economy. In 1999, Bryan Ferry had, according to *New Musical Express*, "crashed and burned" with his standards album *As Time Goes By*; in 1992, Sinéad O'Connor had put out the somewhat batty *Am I Not Your Girl?* featuring a kittenish "I Want to Be Loved by You," two versions of "Don't Cry for Me Argentina," and an impassioned hidden, spoken track titled "Personal message about pain (Jesus and the Money Changers)." More successfully, Linda Ronstadt had made three albums of standards with Nelson Riddle in the eighties, and Carly Simon had put out *Torch* in 1981 and *My Romance* in 1990.

But Mitchell, who coproduced her album of standards with her ex-husband Larry Klein, gave her version of the classics a fun twist by sequencing the songs to trace the arc of a love affair—as arguably happens in a much looser way on *Court and Spark*—this time going from flirtation ("You're My Thrill") to consummation ("At Last") to disillusionment ("You've Changed") to heartbreak ("Stormy Weather") to renewed longing ("I Wish I Were in Love Again"). With a certain amount of hubris, she also included terrific versions of two of her own songs, both arranged by Vince Mendoza—"A Case of You," which appears in the middle of the imagined affair, between "Answer Me, My Love" and "Don't Go to Strangers," thus suggesting love-lit resignation (Joni has referred to "A Case of You" as "my version of 'Hit Me With Your Best Shot'"), and also "Both Sides Now," which comes last on the record, suggesting hard-won acceptance and an ability to work with one's ex-husband.

But in real life, the stages in Joni's romantic relationships are sometimes even more specific.

Stage: Try to extract opinion or anecdote from him like a miner with a pickaxe

Example: Mitchell and Leonard Cohen, the bard of spiritual brokenness, the singer whose gravelly but weirdly lulling bass baritone can roofie you into submission, helped shape each other's music; "I think he's my strongest influence," Mitchell told the *Ann*

Arbor Argus in March 1969. When Cohen heard "A Case of You" the first time, according to David Yaffe, he told Mitchell "I'm glad I wrote that"—Cohen had quoted the *Julius Caesar* line "I am as constant as the northern star" to her and had read her a Rilke poem about how love is touching souls, both of which ended up in the song. Mitchell has said that she wouldn't have written her song "Marcie" had she not heard Cohen's "Suzanne." Each brought their own background to the table when writing somber songs that ripple with keen imagery and an investigation of the strange overlap between religiosity and lust (like when Joni sings in "A Case of You" that her lover is coursing through her veins like holy wine).

Lifelong depressive Cohen—the man who taught us that there's a crack in everything and that "that's how the light gets in," a seeming allusion to thirteenth-century Persian poet Rumi's assertion that "the wound is the place where the Light enters you"—grew up in Montreal, a Jew among many Catholics. He has said that the first time he used language in a sacramental way was when his father died when Cohen was nine: after the funeral, Cohen wrote a poem to his father, then slit open one of his father's neckties and placed the poem therein, and buried the necktie in the Cohens' backyard. An auspicious beginning for someone who would go on to write one beloved tune ("Who By Fire") based on a Yom Kippur poem, and another, "Hallelujah," which Cohen often performed while kneeling.

Mitchell has said that she picked up some religious imagery from Cohen, who would later spend a lot of time at a Buddhist monastery on Los Angeles's Mount Baldy, be ordained a Rinzai Buddhist monk in 1996, and pass in 2016 at age eighty-two. Her unreleased song "Wizard of Is" is essentially a cover of "Suzanne" but with new lyrics. Michelle Mercer has written that when Cohen sings about fourths and fifths and major lifts in "Hallelujah," the song's chords shift as described by the lyrics: "It's a Mitchell-inspired moment of musical onomatopoeia; she'd been matching music to lyrical meanings since her first record."

But what started as mild mutual infatuation between Mitchell and the alluring, sloe-eyed Cohen would gradually sour. "Young girls take him seriously," Mitchell will later say of Cohen. "I did. He seemed so worldly to me as a young woman. He gets funny as you get older."

The dissonance started early on in their friendship: "I'm unstable," he told Mitchell. "Maybe I'm more unstable than you," Mitchell replied.

Though he would take her to his childhood home in Montreal (that's likely him watching Joni sleep on his mother's bed in "Rainy Night House" on *Ladies of the Canyon*), and he would stay at the Laurel Canyon house, there was always between them a kind of chasm. "He was always hard to talk to," Joni told Malka Marom. "We were briefly romantically involved, but he was so distant, and so hard to communicate with. There wasn't much relationship other than the boudoir. I thought there had to be more than that. So I asked a lot of questions of him, trying to get to the heart of it. I remember him saying, 'Oh, Joni, you ask such beautiful questions,' but he evaded the questions. We still became friends and he would stop to see me in Laurel Canyon from time to time. But years went by and I saw him less and less, and one night we went out to dinner and he hardly spoke to me. I felt uncomfortable. It felt unfriendly for the first time and I said, 'Do you like me?' And he said, 'Well, what is there to say to an old lover?' I said, 'Well, that's kind of a shame. There should be many things.' He said, 'Well, you like ideas,' and I said, 'Well, you can hardly open your mouth without an idea popping out of it.' So after that, all he'd say to me was 'Joni, they'll never get us.' That's all he'd ever say, 'Joni, they'll never get us.'"

Stage: Return to something familiar in order to heal and grow

Example: In 1971, when Joni retreated from the music industry after making *Blue* and was spending a lot of time on the land she'd bought in British Columbia, she briefly and non-exclusively started seeing her old friend from grade school Tony Simon. Simon had not only been a longtime friend and Joni's prom date, he was a family friend: "Myrtle and Bill were like second parents to me," he told me. "I can't remember my own phone number from childhood but I remember theirs, 343-9689." (Simon would organize Myrtle's and Bill's funerals in 2007 and 2012.)

During the period she dated Simon, Mitchell was building her house on the Sunshine Coast. Simon grew to admire Mitchell's perfectionism and high standards as he watched her deal with her house builders. "I'd go up there on the weekends," he said. "She'd be watching these guys building her stone house. The fellows were from England, they're like artists with stone. They'd built a wall about knee high. Joan goes, 'Tony, this isn't big enough, they're gonna have to move this wall out.' She called the guy over, and tells him. You want to see a grown man cry? He was in shock. Then, at the end of the day, we're all having dinner, and he's like, 'This wall was put together with love, I can't tell my guys to move it.' I'm like, 'Well, you're gonna have to do it and bite the bullet.' Because there's no compromise with Joan. There never has been."

Simon, who would go on to become an entrepreneur—he has owned and/or run a construction business and several mineral exploration companies—added, "I ran a public company for a while and I remember saying that if people wouldn't see it as a blatant amount of bullshit, I'd put Joan on the board. Because she knows how to think. And she's not gonna get fucked around by anyone." (This appraisal was echoed in 1979 when, on the release of the commercial gamble *Mingus,* journalist Cameron Crowe asked Elektra/Asylum chairman of the board Joe Smith if he'd ever discussed "commercial direction" with Mitchell. Smith replied, "You don't tell Joni Mitchell what to do.")

Stage: Bask in his glow

Example: One of the seminal moments in Mitchell's career occurs in 1973 when, while noodling around on some of the songs that will form *Court and Spark,* Russ Kunkel, a highly regarded drummer who played on *Blue* and many of James Taylor's and Linda Ronstadt's records, tells Joni that, given these new songs' eccentric chords and mercurial time signatures, she should hire a jazz band. So Joni goes to the Baked Potato, a jazz club in Studio City, and finds a band called the L.A. Express.

John Guerin is the drummer for the L.A. Express. His and Joni's vibe is highly sexually charged and a little stormy; during the five years they'll see each other, they'll break up six or seven times. Mitchell thrived on Guerin's good vibes: during one recording session, she told her engineer Henry Lewy, "Set up the vocal booth facing the drummer." As she has explained it, Guerin "had this look in his eyes when he played. He gave me this fiery support and it pushed the music to a level that it wouldn't otherwise have achieved."

Guerin, who died of heart failure in 2004, enjoys several distinctions in the Joni universe. He's the first person she ever cowrote a song with (the title track to *Hissing of Summer Lawns*). Second, his romantic lapse (Joni stumbled onto him and another woman in Guerin's hotel room during a 1976 tour, a possible revenge ploy on Guerin's part after mistakenly assuming that Joni and Bob Dylan were fooling around) is the cause of one of the most ooey-wooey statements that Joni ever uttered: she'll later say about the hotel room scene, "My throat chakra opened up like a lotus, so much so that petals touched along my throat and it was hard to breathe." Third, Guerin is thought to be the inspiration for Joni's hit "Help Me," as well as three of the mesmerizing *Hejira*'s more beguiling songs: "Amelia," "Hejira," and "Blue Motel Room." Finally, it was Guerin who out-Jonied Joni in terms of candor: when he heard that she was going to collaborate with Mingus, about whom she didn't know much, Guerin told her, "You unconscious motherfucker. You don't even like his music. Why didn't he come for me?" (Guerin subsequently urged her to take on the project.)

Guerin was not especially tall. One day when he and Joni were visiting Saskatoon, they went over to Tony Simon's parents' house, where Tony was hanging out with his friend Butch, a light heavyweight boxing champion. Butch, unimpressed by Guerin, told Mitchell, "Joan, I got a suggestion for ya." Joni replied, "Oh, what's that?" Butch said, "Leave this little guy and come with me. With him, you can only make music; with me, we could rob the Bank of Montreal!" (Joni laughed.)

At Guerin's funeral in 2004, Mitchell thought that the speakers spoke too much about themselves. So she said to one of Guerin's other former lovers, "Let's get all John's girls and form a kick line. You know, 'We love you, John! We love you, John!'" But the idea was nixed out of deference to Guerin's wife, who was at the funeral.

Stage: Hold him at bay

Example: Most everything we know about Mitchell's friendship with Warren Beatty we know from David Yaffe's 2017 biography *Reckless Daughter*. When Mitchell called Beatty "Pussycat," she wasn't necessarily trying to be seductive: when she went out for dinner with Warren and Jack Nicholson—both of whom she has said were after her—she would drive her own car. But, at some point, Mitchell caved in to Beatty.

When Beatty saw how broken up Mitchell was after her relationships with James Taylor and Jackson Browne, he recommended the psychiatrist Martin Grotjahn. Lothario Beatty had told Grotjahn that Mitchell was the only woman who had beaten Beatty at his own game (Mitchell: "I don't know what the game is, but I don't feel like a victor. If I won something, what did I win?").

Dr. Grotjahn was as outspoken as Mitchell: "You call him the pussycat?" he asked her once in his thick, German accent. (Grotjahn and his family had fled Berlin when Grotjahn realized "there was no room for Hitler and me in the same town.")

Mitchell told him, "Yeah, for obvious reasons."

"What does a pussycat do? He's cute and fluffy and then one day you get scratched: Meow!"

"Warren is not my problem," Mitchell told him.

"But you are his!"

"That's indiscreet. Believe me, Warren is not my problem, nor will he be my problem. If he has a problem that I won't let him be my problem, then he's got a problem."

Is it Warren who inspired Joni in "The Same Situation" to pray for someone "somewhat sincere"? Joni doesn't want us to think this way. But some of us quietly wonder.

Stage: Have repeated squabbles, particularly with respect to domestic issues

Example: Mitchell met percussionist Don Alias (pronounced uh-LYE-us) while making *Hejira*; they were together for three and a half years. He's the guy who plays the almost four-minute-long drum solo on *Shadows and Light.* Previously, he'd played with Dizzy Gillespie and Miles Davis and had been Nina Simone's musical director; according to Sheila Weller, when Alias was first presented with the opportunity of working with Joni, he thought, "Oh, another one of those skinny-ass folk singers!" But soon he was singing a different tune: "What a genius of a musician Joni was! And intuitive! And eloquent!"

It was through Alias that Mitchell got to befriend her idol Miles Davis, the trumpeter, bandleader, and composer whose 1959 album *Kind of Blue* is often cited as the most influential album in the history of jazz, and who holds the rare distinction among artists and musicians of remaining cutting edge throughout his career. (Possible topic for study: given that Davis's most heralded album is called *Kind of Blue*, is Joni's naming her album *Blue* an act of homage or an act of one-upmanship?) Mitchell and Alias went to Davis's apartment so Mitchell could ask Davis to be in a TV special that never aired. But Davis, whose frustration with the music business found him in the middle of a drug-soaked six-year retreat, wanted a million dollars if he was going to come out of self-imposed exile. At one point in the visit, Davis asked Alias to leave the room, and then, according to Mitchell, Davis pledged his fiery troth: he lunged at her while she was sitting on a couch. Mitchell hurriedly stood up. Davis grabbed her ankles, but then passed out, whereupon Mitchell and Alias found themselves having to peel Davis's death-grip off of Mitchell's feet. (Davis sounds like the same drug-troubled virtuoso we encounter in his 1989 autobiography, *Miles*, wherein we learn that, while riding an elevator once, Davis thought he was in his Ferrari, so he turned to the elevator's other passenger and said, "Bitch, what are you doing in my goddamn car?," slapped her, and then ran out of the building.)

That Mitchell's conservative parents were taken aback by their daughters dating a six-foot-five Black man was, given Joni's essential rebelliousness, presumably only a further goad for her to try to keep her relationship with Alias going. Weller's *Girls Like Us* leads us to believe that, though Mitchell and Alias, who passed away in 2006, discussed marriage, their differences made that prospect dubious—he was a jealous type, and prone to physical abuse. Moreover, he, like others of Mitchell's lovers, suffered from the

Mr. Mitchell syndrome: when Joni asked Alias to move to her Bel Air house, he thought, "No way! That mansion was the princess's palace. I'd always be Mr. Mitchell if I lived there."

The weirdest part of this romance is undoubtedly the nude portrait that Mitchell painted of Alias and then hung in the living room of their Soho loft—not because it was nude, but because it depicted Alias with an erection. An embarrassed Alias pleaded with Mitchell to take it down or alter it; Mitchell pleaded that the portrait was a celebration. Finally, after many arguments, she was persuaded to repaint Alias's member, downgrading it to flaccidity.

Stage: Find your mid-career doldrums so doldrummy that you appeal to a higher power

Example: While making her 1982 album *Wild Things Run Fast,* Joni felt lonely. And while her religious inclinations run more toward Buddhism and Château Margaux, she found herself praying this time: "I said, 'Look God, I know I don't write, I don't call. However, I don't need that much. All I need is a real good kisser who likes to play pinball.'"

One of the musicians working on *Wild Things* was a thirteen-years-younger, mustachioed bass player named Larry Klein who, unaware of Joni's prayer, walked up to her two days later and asked, "How would you like to go to the Santa Monica Pier and play video games?" Whereupon Joni looked up at the sky and said, "Close enough." (Though Klein's come-on line is arresting, it can't compete with the one uttered by Cary Raditz, the itinerant bohemian Mitchell took up with on the island of Crete in the summer of 1970, and who was the inspiration for *Blue*'s "Carey" and is the redneck goat dancer she references in "California". Raditz and other hippies were living in the cliffs above the beach in Matala at the time, so he propositioned Mitchell with the Neanderthal-hot "Come to my cave.")

Mitchell and Klein would last twelve years. Once they married (in 1982, in a Buddhist ceremony), he stopped taking any payments for his musical contributions, concerned that it might lead to confusion (or maybe it's just his thing: he also didn't want any money for playing bass on Peter Gabriel's *So*). The DNA of the Klein/Mitchell union shared some of the Nash/Mitchell DNA: Larry and Joni had a nourishing home life (e.g., they did at-home yoga sessions three times a week, they built a studio in their house wherein they made the excellent album *Turbulent Indigo*), and he was not afraid to take on some caretaking duties (he tried to help her quit smoking, he helped produce eleven of her albums). Intriguingly, Klein, like Nash, had had some of his caretaking capacity built into his childhood: Klein's aerospace engineer father had been the gentle soother to Klein's more complicated, stay-at-home mother. During this time, a female psychotherapist had been a kind of second mother to him.

Joni was surprised to find herself, in her early forties, pregnant; though both she and Larry wanted to keep the baby, Joni miscarried in her first trimester. Larry delayed a recording commitment he had in England, and then asked Joni if it was OK for him to go. Joni assented, and he went—but a certain amount of trust was lost in the exchange. "I didn't know very much about what happens to women when they miscarry—the potential psychological problems, the depression," Klein tells Weller in *Girls Like Us*. "Knowing what I know now, I wouldn't have gone. It really damaged our relationship."

In the eighth year of their union, Klein fell into a serious depression, no longer able to be Mitchell's ever-consoling helpmeet. Mitchell was exercised about all the young, female musicians that Klein was producing in the home studio. Klein wanted to do couples counseling, but Mitchell was distrustful of Western psychology.

In *Gathered Light*, Klein wrote about "one of the many gifts that Joni gave" to him during their years together. The gift will sound familiar to anyone who knows about Buddhism: "the recognition of the fact that there are really no givens in life, any idea that we cling to must be continuously re-examined and must evolve throughout our life if it is not to become a simple blindfold or crutch that we can lean on. The only real stability upon which we can rely is the fact that there is no real stability or static permanence in life."

Post-divorce, Klein, in addition to going on to produce lots of high-profile musicians, has become a kind of dramaturg or *répétiteur* of Mitchell's music, bringing his deep knowledge of Mitchell's sensibility and practices to producing projects such as Herbie Hancock's Album of the Year Grammy–winning *River* and the Joni tribute concert at the Hammerstein Ballroom in 2000.

Stage: Put it on layaway

Example: "When I turned fifty," Mitchell has said, "I fell in love with a home boy." Given the types of men that Mitchell is attracted to, there wasn't much surprise to her aligning herself, for about six years starting in 1994, with fellow Saskatchewanian Donald Freed: he's a half-Indigenous poet and musician who teaches songwriting to Indigenous kids. ("He's a prairie mutt like me—Scottish, French, and Scandinavian," Mitchell said in 1994. "He has three Indian bloods, opposed to the one my parents say I'm a liar for saying I have.") Rather, the surprise was related to his provenance: Joni met him through Myrtle. ("He's kind of sexy," Myrtle had told her. Whereupon Joni responded, "Well, I'll pay to see your idea of sexy.")

On meeting Mitchell, Freed asked her how she was doing; Mitchell replied, "Undervalued."

Like many of Joni's other partners, Freed got to collaborate with her—they cowrote "The Crazy Cries of Love" on *Taming the Tiger*. That same record's "Face Lift" recounts Myrtle's embarrassment over Mitchell running around with Freed before Mitchell's divorce from Larry Klein had gone through. ("As far as she was concerned I was living in sin, flaunting my Hollywood ways in their faces, in their town," Mitchell once said. "Humiliating them. I said, 'Who am I humiliating you in front of? Your generation is all dead. There are no witnesses as far as I can see.' My mother thinks I'm immoral. I've searched diligently for a morality that applied to the times that I lived in. I keep saying to my mother, 'Think of me as a Catholic priest that drinks a little with the dock workers.' I just don't want to get that *clean*.")

We don't know why Mitchell ended things with Freed, but we do know that he struggled with something that Don Alias had struggled with, too: middle-of-the-night phone calls from the night owl. (When Mitchell hired Chaka Khan to sing on *Don Juan's Reck-*

less Daughter, she called Khan at 3:00 a.m.; when Mitchell conscripted Police guitarist Andy Summers to play with her on a 1989 TV special, she told him to come to a rehearsal at 1:00 a.m.)

People magazine caught up with Joni in 2000 while she and Freed were still chugging along, and she characterized the relationship in a way that sparkles especially brightly for anyone who has ever successfully conducted a long-distance relationship or been married to the same person for more than thirty years.

"It's great," she said. "We meet a couple of times a year."

Love needs oxygen.

31

"I started the 80's by going to a party—at ["On and On" and "It Might Be You" singer-songwriter] Stephen Bishop's—with the theme 'Be nice to the 80s and the 80s will be nice to you,'" Mitchell told *Q* magazine in 1988. "I had this car, my beloved '69 Bluebird, and I was on my way, driving past Tower Records on Sunset [Boulevard], it was that royal blue time of night, just before it goes black. I stopped and ran into the store because I just had to listen to a Jimmy Cliff record, *The Bongo Man Has Come.* But when I came out there was the empty slot where my car had been. Never saw it again. I loved that Bluebird. Anyway, that's how the 80's were ushered in for me, and it was all downhill from there."

The 1980s were Joni's decade *horribilis.* The directness of emotion that had been such a hallmark of her music was out of favor in a decade whose offerings (Talking Heads, the Police, the Pretenders, Madonna) tended to traffic in ironic cool. Radio stations, having already copiously avoided her 1979 jazz album, *Mingus,* now followed suit with her synthesizer-heavy albums *Wild Things Run Fast* and *Dog Eat Dog.* She aged out of her falsetto. Her housekeeper sued her after Joni kicked her in the shins during a disagreement. A dentist "butchered" her. She fired her longtime manager Elliot Roberts because he wasn't paying enough attention to her and because he'd encouraged her to work with a producer. She'd been having a glorious professional run with the bass player Jaco Pastorius—who, starting with 1976's *Hejira*, had changed Joni's sound by lifting the bass out of the rhythm section and making it burble and moan gloriously, most notably on *Hejira* but most astonishingly on the song "Talk to Me," where his bass seems to "talk" to Joni. But in 1987 the mentally unstable Pastorius was beaten to death after he kicked in a glass door at a club in Florida. She stopped working with her longtime recording engineer Henry Lewy. David Crosby—who would go on to receive a liver transplant with the financial help of his friend Phil Collins—spent five months in a Texas state prison in 1985 on narcotics and weapons charges. An audience member threw ice cubes in Mitchell's face when she played an obscure song at an Amnesty International concert. A storm that incurred twelve-foot ocean waves damaged a Malibu beach house that Mitchell was trying to sell for $3 million. Her income got tied up in an experimental tax levy. She had a huge falling out with David Geffen, whose company almost dropped *Wild Things Run Fast* and *Dog Eat Dog* due to poor sales. (She will eventually return to Reprise. Geffen will sell Geffen Records to MCA Music Entertainment in 1990, earning him an estimated $800 million in stock—which will look like chump change when the cash acquisition of MCA by Matsushita in 1991 makes Geffen a billionaire.)

The best way to get a sense of all this tumult's fallout is to look at the punctuation in Mitchell's lyrics. Here, in order, are all the punctuation marks from the lyrics in her first three records:

Song to a Seagull (1968)

- - - - : : : ( ) : ( ) : ( ) : ( ) : ( ) : : : : :

Clouds (1969)

, , , , , , , , , , ! - ! , , , , , , , , “ , “ “ ” “ , , ” “ ” “ , , ” , , , , , , , , ,

Ladies of the Canyon (1970)

, , , , , , . . . , - , , , , - - , , , , - - - , “ ” “ , ”

And here are all the punctuation marks from the three records she made in the eighties:

Wild Things Run Fast (1982)

, - “” - - “” - (- - . . .) . . . , - “!” - - - - - - . . . . . . ! - - ( ) - ? “” “!” ? “”
“” ? (, , , , , , , ,) - - - - - - - - - - - - - (, - ! ! ! . . . - ! ! ! - . . . - ! ! ! . . . - !
! - , - - ! - - ! - - - - - - - - - - - - - - - - - - , ,

Dog Eat Dog (1985)

- - . . . - - - - - - “!” “!” - - - - ? ? ? ? ? ( ) ? “ , ” “ , ” “” ? ? ? ? ? - ! ? ?
? ? . . . “ , ” “ ! ” , “ ! ” : “ ! ” ! ” “ ! ” “ . . . ” “” “ ! ” “ ! ” “ ! - ! “ ! ” “”
“” “” “” “” “” “ ! ” ! ! , ,) - - - , , , , , , , , , , - “” “” ( ) ( ) ( ) “” “” “” “”
( ) ( ) ( ) - , . . . “” . . .

Chalk Mark in a Rain Storm (1988)

- - ? - - - ? - - ? - ! ! ! ! - - - ? ! ! ? ! ! ! ? ? ? ! ! ! ! ! - - - ! ! ? - - - - !
! - ! - - - - - ! ! ! - ? - - - “ ! - ! “ - - “ - ! ” - “” “ ! ! ? , , “” “” “ ! ” - -
“ , ” - - “ ! ” “ ! ” “ ? ” “ , ” “ - - - - ” “ - ! - ! - ” “ - - - - - - - ” “ - ”
- ! ! ! - - ! - ? - - - ? - ? - ! - !
? - - ! ? ! ? ? ? !

32

December 1996. The Westin Hotel, in Ottawa. Mitchell, cigarette in hand, was talking to a reporter for the Toronto *Globe and Mail* about the flurry of recognition that she had started receiving earlier that year (the Polar Music Prize; two more Grammys, including Best Pop Album for *Turbulent Indigo*; induction into the Rock & Roll Hall of Fame; Ottawa's Governor-General's Performing Arts Award; being impersonated by performance artist John Kelly).

"I'm getting used to being honored," Mitchell told the writer between puffs. "I can really get into this."

This professional sea change was long in the making. Just two years earlier, on *Turbulent Indigo*, she'd put out the song "The Sire of Sorrow (Job's Sad Song)," a beautifully moody diatribe leveled at a "tireless watcher" who tortures the singer with his "visions." Throughout the song, the singer asks what she has done to deserve her punishment. The singer contends that the tireless watcher has caused all of the things that the singer both dreads and fears to come true; but the singer doesn't make this point once or twice, she makes it five times.

Even more tellingly, at some point in the mid-nineties Mitchell got in touch with the producers of a TV show that she loved—the warm and goofy *Northern Exposure*, set in the fictional town of Cicely, Alaska—and pitched the idea of her being on the show as a refugee of the music industry. (Mitchell has said that, during her marriage to Larry Klein, the couple watched so much television that she thought about giving her 1985 album, *Dog Eat Dog*, the title *Songs from a Couch Potato*.)

Alas, *Northern Exposure*, which ran on CBS from 1990 to 1995, had already stopped filming when she got in touch. The sadness inherent to not getting to see Joni deliver witty dialogue while wearing a coonskin hat and mukluks is only magnified by the fact that she would have found herself among kindred spirits. Meet Adam (Adam Arkin), an arrogant hermit who lives deep in the woods and believes that trees have voices. Meet Eve (Valerie Mahaffey), a hypochondriac who left the big city to get away from all the toxins and who at one point clobbers her doctor with a cast-iron skillet. Meet Ed (Darren E. Burrows), a half–Native Alaskan film buff who receives guidance from a 256-year-old Native American spirit guide named One-Who-Waits. Meet Chris (John Corbett), a philosophical, Caucasian disc jockey and conceptual sculptor who declares himself a "person of color" and is convinced he should go to Africa.

But most tellingly, meet Shelly (Cynthia Geary), a sweet, young, blond beauty pageant winner who hails from, yes, Saskatoon. Shelly has a lot of man troubles—one episode chronicling them is titled "Dreams and Schemes and Putting Greens," which sounds like an opener to one of the verses of "Both Sides Now"—and becomes addicted to television. She has a unique fashion sense, she sometimes sings rather than speaks, and she has recurring visions of dancers. In Season Five, a pregnant Shelly repeatedly sees the same blond girl at the laundromat one day, but each time she sees her, the girl has aged years; Shelly becomes convinced that the girl—a rebellious, headstrong musician named Randi—is her daughter.

I wrote to Joshua Brand, the show's co-creator—as well as the co-creator of *St. Elsewhere* and *I'll Fly Away*—to ask him about this last character. Brand wrote back, "I wish I could say Shelly was inspired by Joni Mitchell because I'm a HUGE fan. Since I'm a big believer in your unconscious knows more than your conscious-self knows, it's quite possible that my unconscious-self outsmarted my dumber conscious-self. In any case, since you bring up all the similarities, I will from now on insist on it."

The *Northern Exposure* character with whom Joni seems to share the fewest similarities is its main one, Dr. Joel Fleischman (Rob Morrow), an uptight New York City doctor contractually bound to hang up his shingle in remote Alaska in order to pay off a student loan. Descriptions of Fleischman invariably imply the phrase "fish out of water." But Joni, given her prairie origins—and, in the 1980s and early '90s, her languishing record sales—would not have inspired the descriptor "fish out of water." She was more like coral then: difficult to classify, and rapidly vanishing.

33

In 2002, shortly before the release of her album *Travelogue*, Joni met a reporter from *W* magazine for an interview at the Hotel Bel Air. Dressed in an understated, black Ann Demeulemeester dress and smoking American Spirits, Joni told the writer, "I'm quitting after this, because the business has made itself so repugnant to me." The record business, she said, was "the most corrupt one of all." She added, "They're not looking for talent. They're looking for a look and a willingness to cooperate."

That the lyrics Mitchell wrote after her 1980s travails took on a more hectoring tone toward her targets—televangelism, corporate greed, ecological disaster—is nothing compared to the inflammatory comments she made in subsequent interviews. In a 2002 *Rolling Stone* article, she called the music industry "a cesspool." In 2013, she told an audience at the Luminato Festival in Toronto that she squelched a film adaptation of Sheila Weller's *Girls Like Us*: "I called the producer and I said, 'If you're gonna make this movie, it's gonna be a piece of shit, you know. If you wanna do this, you can show me the dailies, and while it's going down, I'll tell you *why* it's going to be a piece of shit.'" In 2015, when explaining to *New York* magazine why she had painted and hung in her vestibule a portrait of David Geffen with a banana lodged in his mouth, she said that her former roommate had been using her as a "beard."

Perhaps most famously, Mitchell took exception to a 2010 interview she gave to a freelance music writer for the *Los Angeles Times*, Matt Diehl. In the article—a Q&A with both Mitchell and performance artist John Kelly, conducted to promote one of Kelly's live shows in which he impersonates Mitchell—Mitchell went off on Bob Dylan, as she has done on various occasions over the years, like the time she called him a "perverse little brat." This time, when Diehl said, "The folk scene you came out of had fun creating personas. You were born Roberta Joan Anderson, and someone named Bobby Zimmerman became Bob Dylan," Mitchell replied, "Bob is not authentic at all. He's a plagiarist, and his name and voice are fake. Everything about Bob is a deception. We are like night and day, he and I." (According to Robert Shelton's biography *No Direction Home*, Dylan, originally from Minnesota, adopted an Oklahoma twang after reading Woody Guthrie's autobiography, *Bound for Glory*, in 1960; Dylan has acknowledged that "Blowin' in the Wind" borrows from the spiritual "No More Auction Block.")

When, three years after Diehl interviewed Mitchell and Kelly, a subsequent interviewer—this one for Canada's CBC—brought up Mitchell's earlier quote about Dylan, Mitchell responded that her comment had been taken out of context, and called the original interviewer, Diehl, an "asshole," a "dolt," and "a moron whose IQ is somewhere between his shoe size and his knees." Then Mitchell clarified for this second interviewer her take on Dylan, which, to many ears, sounded even harsher than her previous one: "I like a lot of Bob's songs. Musically he's not very gifted. He's borrowed his voice from old hillbillies. He's got a lot of borrowed things. He's not a great guitar player. He's invented a character to deliver his songs. Sometimes I wish that I could have that character. Because you can do things with that character. It's a mask of sorts."

When I called the first interviewer, Matt Diehl, to ask him how it had made him feel to have Mitchell blast him in a public forum, I thoroughly expected to hear about his singed ego. But he told me, "It's better to be called an asshole by Joni Mitchell than not to be on her radar at all. You know what I mean? I think Joni Mitchell is a fucking genius, and if my name leaves her lips by *any* means . . . I mean, it might even be better to be bitched out by her than to be praised. I don't go into an interview with someone who's a visionary with an incredible body of work and expect them to like me. I just want them to be *them*—and I'd say, Joni Mitchell was very Joni Mitchell at that moment!"

Calling Mitchell an iconoclast, Diehl added, "But I came out of punk rock, and the punk rockers—Johnny Rotten, Patti Smith—*those* people are fucking i-*cono*-clasts. They challenge every single thing you say. It's pure intellectual combat. And thank God."

The aforementioned aren't the only entities that have elicited Joni's invective over the years. She has also mouthed off about Judy Collins ("there's something la-di-da about her"), CSN ("always out of tune"), Joan Baez ("would have broken my leg if she could"), Madonna ("what's the difference between her and a hard hooker?"), producer Thomas Dolby ("slimy little bugger"), ex-husband Chuck Mitchell ("my first major exploiter, a complete asshole"), ex-husband Larry Klein ("tyrannical, insecure" . . . a "puffed-up dwarf"), Jackson Browne ("a mini-talent," "a phony"), the curriculum of her twelfth-grade math, physics, and chemistry classes ("Everything I was memorizing was fucking wrong"), her fellow performers at the 1990 concert of Pink Floyd's *The Wall* on top of a recently demolished Berlin Wall ("Not one single adult in the whole pack"), *Time* magazine ("unbelievable"), record labels ("criminally insane"), the audiences at charity benefits ("when I go on, they use the time to talk"), Saskatoon ("an extremely bigoted community"), having her work called "confessional" ("makes what I do seem cheap and gimmicky"), "confessional" writers like Saint Augustine, Sylvia Plath, and Anne Sexton ("all three make me sick," "Plath is morbid and Sexton is a liar"), Shakespeare's sonnets ("I can smell the commerce"), her generation ("the greediest generation in the history of America"), her father ("a tremendous sense of entitlement and squashing").

For us fans, these blasts of vitriol are confounding. On the one hand, it's possible, when Joni's slams are amusing and well grounded, to admire her wit and candor, and to rally around a woman of a certain age who has no fucks left to give. Joni has always said that her greatest curse is sincerity—a sentiment echoed by the rapper Q-Tip, who rapped on Janet Jackson's 1997 "Got 'til It's Gone" that Joni "never lies"—and here is living, palpitating, bloody evidence of same.

It should also be pointed out that Mitchell will occasionally temper her biliousness with self-deprecation: in 1998, in "Come In from the Cold" on *Night Ride Home*, she'll take a little dig at her habit of speaking out in self-important tones; in 2010, she'll tell an interviewer, "I have a tremendous will to live. And a tremendous joie de vivre. Alternating with irritability." All this helps. A little.

But it's also possible to view Mitchell's persecution complex as self-serving and arrogant, a kind of victim porn that is doubly disturbing given that it hails from someone whose songs have accompanied us through the emotional terrain of our lives—and who, in these same songs, has often attacked arrogance and pettiness ("Big Yellow Taxi," "Hejira," "The Magdalene Laundries," "Borderline" et al.). To my mind, the only unforgivable thing that Mitchell has ever done was to write the lyrics to *Turbulent Indigo*'s "Not to Blame," a song about domestic abuse: after a celebrity drives his wife to suicide and beats up his girlfriend, the celebrity's three-year-old son, bizarrely, suggests that he and his father go pick up some girls; we learn that there hadn't been a single wet eye around the suicided mother's grave. Though Mitchell has denied it ("It's not about anyone specific," she told *Time* in 1994. "It's about the phenomenon of the battered woman at this time"), the song seems to me that it could be laying siege to Jackson Browne (understandable), his three-year-old son (deeply inappropriate), and Browne's suicided wife (unspeakable).

It would make sense if Mitchell's fiery comments over the years were purely the result of her seeing in print the stark reality of her highly candid interviews; you'd have to possess an iron constitution *not* to regret some of the stuff she's dished out. But that's not what's usually happening when she takes issue with writers like Matt Diehl or Ratso Sloman or Graham Nash (she has said that everything he wrote about her in his memoir is false)—her point more often seems to be that she's being misinterpreted or misjudged in some way.

Mitchell's reputation as a fire-breather has trickled down into the culture. In the 2020 fantasy novel *The City We Became* by N. K. Jemisin—whose Broken Earth trilogy has sold more than 2 million copies—the book's shape-shifting antagonist, the Enemy, sometimes takes the form of the Woman in White, an alien force that weaponizes white privilege by possessing the bodies of white women. At one point author Jemisin, who is Black, writes that the Woman in White has long, raggedly straight hair that is "very Seventies chic, which matches the pointed, narrow, sloe-eyed face that she currently wears. She looks like an evil midcareer Joni Mitchell." (I wrote Jemisin and asked if she cared to elaborate, but she did not respond.)

What are us fans to do with Mitchell's ire? At the risk of sounding patronizing, maybe the proper response is pity. Maybe we didn't realize how bad Mitchell's tough times had been for her. Or maybe we didn't realize the damage we'd done when we took a little break from Joni during her jazz period or during the *Wild Things Run Fast/Dog Eat Dog/Chalk Mark in a Rain Storm* period. Remember how, in 2022, when Brandi Carlile was asked what she had been hoping to achieve by bringing a post-aneurysm Joni back to the Newport Folk Festival for the first time since 1969—a highly emotional experience for many of us, only redoubled when we found out that Joni had had to relearn how to play guitar by watching videos of herself on YouTube—Carlile responded, "Joni hasn't always felt the appreciation that exists amongst humanity for her. I wanted her to feel that." Carlile's comment seemed strange—Joni had recently been honored at the Kennedy Center, accepted to the Rock & Roll Hall of Fame, won the Polar Music Prize, and been named the MusiCares Person of the Year, in addition to being the honoree of various star-studded tribute concerts, winning a Lifetime Achievement Award at the 2002 Grammys, and having *Blue* hit #1 on iTunes five decades after its release.

But a long-lasting commercial and critical drubbing, as Mitchell perceives the reaction to her work post–*Court and Spark* to have been, is not an easy thing to forget or overcome. Current celebration doesn't always erase past wounds—sometimes it simply provides distraction.

Which is all to say: maybe we fans didn't realize the repercussions of our neglect.

Maybe we didn't realize that we'd abandoned our girl.

34

The other night I lay in bed and couldn't stop thinking about the aforementioned night at the Joni tribute concert at the Hammerstein Ballroom in 2000 when Mitchell, seated in the audience watching colleagues perform her work, ate a banana. I started wondering why the image haunted me. My first thought was, Because it surprises. You'd expect someone who writes spectacularly sensitive lyrics to be sensitive to performers' feelings, or to other audience members' level of concentration, or to whatever keeps us from launching publicly into any of that array of slightly unattractive habits—putting gum on the undersides of tables, say, or clipping nails—that we typically reserve for the confines of our home.

My second thought was, Maybe I'm fixating on the incident because it's so entirely and purely Joni: Mitchell has made a career out of being private in public, and what advertises your grasp of the concept "You do you" quite like a peel-and-nosh in a former opera house packed with your colleagues? Given that the respect that Mitchell elicits from her colleagues has always bordered on terror—Elton John has said that performing for her is more intimidating than performing for the Queen; Brandi Carlile had to be hypnotized the first time she performed *Blue* in concert; biographer David Yaffe snapped a wineglass into shards while waiting to interview Mitchell for the first time—maybe Mitchell's banana-eating is the very *height* of sensitivity: maybe she's signaling to the performers that, hey, we're all just normies here, hanging out and scarfing down whatever snack foods we happen to have at hand, so let's all take a chill pill.

My third thought was, Maybe she just really likes bananas.

At which point I realized that the author of "Both Sides Now" had totally "Both Sides Now"-ed me.

35

Early spring 1997. Joni was sitting at an outdoor table at a restaurant in the Brentwood neighborhood of Los Angeles. She was smoking American Spirit cigarettes (duh).

Joni told her lunch mate that during the first few years after she'd put Kelly up for adoption, she "worried constantly" about Kelly's health because Joni's diet during her pregnancy had been "atrocious" and thus Joni wondered if Kelly's "bones were all right."

Joni said that the memory of her baby "comes to you at funny times. Like when a friend's child falls off a bike."

The REUNION

36

St. Paul's Hospital, Saskatoon. December 1952.

One afternoon while Joan lay in her bed, a young doctor in a wheelchair—he'd gotten polio, too—wheeled himself into her room. Joan told him, "I wanna go home for Christmas." The doctor said she couldn't because she couldn't walk.

"What if I walked?" Joan said.

"You can't even stand up."

"What if I stood and walked?"

The doctor looked at the ceiling. He sighed heavily, looked at his knees, and then rolled himself out of the room as if to say, I am not gonna argue with this kid. Would the doctor ever walk again himself? Probably not.

The hospital continued giving Joan her treatments—scalding hot rags were pinned to her and then a doctor or nurse would say "Touch your toes." But Joan's hands couldn't even reach her knees, let alone her toes. The trailer Joan was in had a down ramp that led to an up ramp to a scarier trailer, a trailer filled with the worst cases: the iron-lung patients.

Joan felt like the medical staff didn't spend enough time

with her on her exercises, either because they didn't have the patience, or because they didn't believe in the methodology of the cure. So, at night, after lights-out, during the hour when the hospital staff would let Joan keep her Christmas tree lit, Joan would exercise her legs on her own. By day, when the therapists would visit, she tried to let them bend her more than she had done previously.

When she started to notice improvement, she told the medical staff "I want to try to walk."

They wheeled Joan out into the hallway. Several patients in wheelchairs lined the hall, to cheer Joan on.

Joan got out of the chair, put her hands on the double chrome bars that ran along the corridor, and painstakingly pulled herself to the corridor's end. Then she turned herself around, and pulled herself back to her starting point.

"Now can I go home?"

She was home by Christmas.

In July 2021, Brandi Carlile, whom Joni had started calling her "ambassador," told Jay Sweet, the head of the Newport Folk Festival, "One year from now, I bet you we can get Joni Mitchell to this stage."

It seemed wholly unlikely to Sweet. In the two decades prior, Mitchell had suffered two medical crises. By 2010, she was at the height of her suffering from Morgellons, the self-diagnosed, medically unsubstantiated skin condition in which people get sores that they think are the product of bacterial infection or parasites.

Mitchell has claimed that "fibers in a variety of colors protrude out of my skin like mushrooms after a rainstorm." Which sounds altogether bizarre—though, if *anyone* is growing colorful, mushroomlike fibers on their skin, it's Joni Mitchell. But, wow, it's no fun being a human Chia Pet: "I couldn't even wear clothing. I had to have alkalized soft cotton, and even then it felt like barbed wire. I couldn't leave my house for several years. Sometimes it got so I'd have to crawl across the floor. My legs would cramp up, just like the polio spasms. It hit all of the places where I had polio. When it's severe, I can't walk. I had one attack where I had to crawl to the bathroom. And I had to turn around and back down the stairs. I started laughing. . . . I'm so glad I don't have a man to be repulsed by this. I thought I must look pretty funny."

Even more dramatically, in 2015 Mitchell had been found lying on her kitchen floor, where she'd been for three days after having had an aneurysm and incurring significant brain trauma. (Aneurysms occur when the wall of a blood vessel, bulging and weakened, balloons the vessel to more than 50 percent its normal diameter. Their cause is high blood pressure. Does cigarette smoking cause a temporary rise in blood pressure? It does.) She was rushed to the hospital for emergency brain surgery—though Mitchell doesn't believe in Western medicine, her care at the time was determined by the state of California because she was not conscious—prior to being put in an intensive care unit. Joni fans worldwide were on tenterhooks that night—*New York Times* music critic Lindsay Zoladz was put on obituary watch; NPR prepared its Mitchell obit; *People* magazine accidentally ran an obit on its website.

Once moved back to her house in Bel Air, Mitchell eventually started talking. She spoke almost daily with Graham Nash, telling him at one point that she'd forgotten that she smoked; her ex Larry Klein came by and showed her their wedding pictures, and Joni was able to identify nearly everyone. Childhood friend Sharolyn Dickson brought photos of Joni's childhood home in Saskatoon. Occasionally, there were glitches: Nathan Joseph, the former Soho flatmate with the singing parrot, visited with his wife; while sitting at the kitchen table, Joni looked at the assembled, including Joseph, and asked, "What ever happened to Nathan?"

But on the whole, Joni's short-term memory was patchier than her long-term memory, as is often the case with people who suffer brain trauma. She worked assiduously with physical therapists. Her doctors had told her that if she could walk, she could do whatever she wanted: shades of the polio ward.

Post-aneurysm, Mitchell had hosted a series of informal Joni Jams in her living room, but she had not returned to performing.

"I gotta be honest with you," Jay Sweet told Carlile. "You are the manifester of miracles, but you may have overshot on this one."

Indeed, when Brandi presented Joni with the idea, Joni was uncertain. Joni would only want to go on if she could be good; could she still be good?

"So I FaceTimed her. And we had one of the best conversations we've ever had," Carlile has said. Carlile pitched Joni's possible appearance at the waterside festival as an extension of Joni's living room jams. "I said, 'Joni, since we all met you, we've all started working together, we've become a family. You've created a community around you. All we want to do is just sit there in a circle and sing to show you what you've done for us. And if you sing along, fucking awesome; if you don't, we're just so happy to be with you. This is our way of thanking you. We don't want you to feel like there's something that you have to do.' And she said, 'I get the spirit of it now. We will just sit there and look at the water and sing.'"

Joni was in.

37

1965 or 1966. Joni is playing at the Sipping Lizard in Flint, Michigan. In the audience are a family of five—two parents and their three daughters, aged five, and seven, and nine. One of the girls walks up to Joni and says, "Would you play 'Urge for Going'?"

Joni asks her "How do you know that song?"

The girl says she's learning it on guitar.

Mid-1960s. Joni has been performing at the Flick coffeehouse in Coral Gables, Florida, where she has befriended one of the other performers, fifteen-year-old singer-songwriter Estrella Berosini, whom Joni name-checked in "Ladies of the Canyon." Having already complimented the younger singer's performance, Mitchell tells her, "I think some of my songs would be really good for you." She tells Berosini that her songs are not difficult to play, then leads Berosini to the club's pantry, where they sit on boxes and Mitchell teaches Berosini to play "Night in the City." After the next show, Mitchell teaches her to play "Play Little David" and to harmonize on "The Circle Game."

On October 19, 1968, Joni performed in the gym at SUNY Stony Brook, and received a standing ovation from a group of college students, some of whom had sauntered in during the performance. Then, retiring to the gym's bleachers, she watched the other billed act, folk singer Tim Hardin of "If I Were a Carpenter" fame, perform.

During Hardin's set, the college students grew increasingly restless, some of them wandering among the aisles, others collecting their coats and leaving. Hardin, irritated by the commotion, shortened his set and asked the audience, "How would you like it if somebody pissed in your canteen?"

That was all the inspiration that Joni needed: she stood and furiously returned to the mic. "You are very rude people," she said as part of a five-minute dressing down during which she expressed regret for having come to Stony Brook and said that she'd tell other performer friends not to do so. "You have to learn that you just don't go parading up and down the aisles while someone is singing. We have feelings, too, you know."

Science fiction writer Spider Robinson, then a student at Stony Brook, later told the *Globe and Mail*, "She maligned us and our relatives and ancestors until she ran out of breath, and stormed off stage. Leaving behind hundreds of baffled people . . . and a handful like me, cheering even louder than we had for her songs."

1978. Mitchell was a guest speaker at a class about the music business that David Geffen was teaching at Yale. A student in the class made the point that not *every* record label is obsessed with the profit motive—which made Geffen, who believed otherwise, furious. The two started arguing, and Geffen became increasingly vicious in his comments. Mitchell jumped into the fray, and asked the two to cool it. Referring to Geffen, she told the class, "Now you see how he negotiates those great recording contracts."

1991. At a dinner party in Los Angeles where Mitchell was seated with other musicians her age, a young fan came up to her and waxed romantic about hippies and 1960s idealism.

"Don't be romantic about it—we failed," Mitchell told the fan.

"Well, at least you tried."

"But we didn't try hard enough. If any progress is to be made, we must show you how we failed."

"Yeah, but at least you did something. Like, we did nothing."

"Look, the thing is, don't just ape our movement. Don't do hippie poses. Look at us. Admit to yourself that we only took it so far. Build from where we left off."

September 1999. As a favor to jazz drummer and composer Brian Blade for his having toured and recorded with her, Mitchell sings on a track of Blade's album *Perceptual*. The song, "Steadfast," has Mitchell repeatedly ask, "Can you hear the baby from the other room?"

In 2004, Mitchell visited the campus of McGill University, where she talked to a group of more than one hundred students. When she was asked what advice she had for someone wanting to get into the music business, Mitchell replied "Don't."

In 2007, Mitchell toured the Alberta College of Art, her former art college in Calgary, with David Yaffe. Yaffe told me that, during a Q&A that Mitchell conducted on campus, a female student asked, "Hi, Joni. I'm a singer-songwriter, do you have any advice for me?"

Mitchell replied, "Are you good?"

"Yeah, I'm good."

"OK, then you better get on it as soon as you can because they're gonna replace you with a fourteen-year-old."

Unfazed by Joni's cold blast of pragmatism, the young woman approached Yaffe after the Q&A and asked him if he could help her to get a little more face time with Joni.

Yaffe asked her, "Do you smoke?"

"Yeah."

"Bum an American Spirit from her."

The young woman did so, and she and Mitchell chatted while they each smoked a cigarette.

Later that day, as Mitchell and Yaffe were pulling away from the campus in a limo, the young woman called out, "Just you wait, Joni Mitchell! You'll see—I'm gonna be a big, big star!"

Yaffe shot Mitchell a "just another day at the office" look.

Mitchell said, "I wish I could hug them all."

Mitchell was sitting by herself at a crowded cafe in Santa Monica one day in 2001, eavesdropping on the two people seated next to her. She'd pieced together that the diners were a young musician and an A&R person from his record label (the artists and repertoire representatives sign and then help develop new acts). The young musician was tattooed and turned out in punk regalia—dog bracelets on wrist and neck, and spiky hair made stiff with hairspray. The musician alluded to the fact that his band, whose sound he didn't love, had broken up.

In a 180-degree reversal of all conversations ever held between musicians and their label, the A&R person was encouraging the musician to get inspired and then figure out his next musical incarnation; the musician kept bringing up audience expectations and the marketplace.

Joni could take it no more. After more than three decades in the business, she'd seen too many talented musicians fail out by trying to fit in. Without introducing herself, she turned to her two neighbors and called the musician out for not having the courage of his individuality. She suggested to him that he had disguised himself in his punk getup, and that he didn't like the music he was making. She said, "Do you want to be an artist or a star? I can answer that question by just looking at you—you'll do anything to fit in."

The kid responded, "Well, I don't want to be broke at forty-eight. It's good to have some business sense."

"Yeah, it's good to have some business sense *after*, but not at the point when you're making your art. Mr. A&R here is more of an artist than you are. Do you know how great it is to be told by your record company to be experimental? And you didn't even respond correctly to that. You go right back into your business head! Are you crazy?"

"Look, rock and roll is supposed to be dumb."

"Huh?" Joni asked. "Chuck Berry wasn't dumb, Bob Dylan's rock wasn't dumb. Hardly anybody else can reach such high standards. But at least try. Otherwise, when you wake up with little money in your pocket at forty-eight and you look at the dumb work, you'll have spent your whole life making shit while there's been spikes sticking out of you—all of which isn't you at all."

The musician said, "You hate me!"

"I don't hate you. I hate the music that's on the radio, because there's no muse to it—it's just ick!"

"Why are you judging me so harshly? Who are you to judge me?"

"That's what I hear from your generation all the time: 'Who are you to judge me?' The trouble is that nobody judged you, nobody told you how to judge your own work and judge yourself. You don't know how to think for yourself."

"You don't how I am. You don't know my work."

"I'm sitting next to your table, listening to how your head works. I don't even have to hear your musical work to know that if you're the fountainhead, then it's more of this. And you don't know who *I* am!"

In unison, the musician and the A&R man said, "Yes, we do."

"Oh."

2013. A Canadian journalist asks Mitchell what she's most proud of. Mitchell squirms a bit, says she tries not to indulge in pride too much, and then haltingly says, "But there are cases, on the street, where people come up . . . That it's meant a lot to them. For instance, two young girls who lost their mother in their early teens, who holed up in their bedroom with the music. It was cathartic. I kind of surrogate-mothered them."

In 2014, gossip writer Liz Smith wrote in her "New York Social Diary" column, "One admirer, who wishes [Lady Gaga] would just stand onstage and sing, is the great Joni Mitchell. The usually reclusive Joni reportedly phoned Gaga, and said, 'You have major talent as a singer and songwriter, don't let that voice get subdued by marketing tools, like music videos.' Even more surprising, Joni, known for her contemplative and heartfelt lyrics, suggested collaborating with Gaga on songwriting! No word on how Gaga took this advice, but even if she continues to vomit on-stage and otherwise divert us from her genuine talents, Lady G. should take Joni Mitchell up on her offer!"

38

1995. Joni was bustling around her neighborhood in Los Angeles, putting flyers in her neighbors' mailboxes.

Joni had initially turned down a request to write a mournful song for *Grace of My Heart,* Allison Anders's 1996 film, loosely based on Carole King, about a singer-songwriter who starts out by writing material for other acts. Joni wasn't feeling it. As she would explain later, "I'm not a hack. I have to feel what I write." (The profits spinning off her back catalog afford her a certain leeway; by 2021, according to *Billboard,* she was making about $735,000 annually just from publishing rights—i.e., from other people recording her songs.)

Saying no was not unusual for Joni. Throughout her career, no had been her friend. She'd turned down the first record deals offered her; she'd walked out on huge audiences who weren't listening intently. She'd turned down a $1.25 million offer for her publishing catalog in 1969 lest she feel like she was writing for money. She'd canceled a lot of dates in 1971 when she took the year off to woodshed after recording *Blue* and having her psychological crisis; she'd canceled more in 1976 after exhaustion from having the flu and breaking up with John Guerin. She'll axe the documentary *Joni Mitchell: Both Sides Now and Then* and tell her friend Carrie Fisher that she won't allow her to play "River" on a *Star Wars* TV special. She'll tell the choreographer whom she'll eventually work with on the ballet *The Fiddle and the Drum* that his first idea for a Joni ballet is "a little fluffy for the times"; she'll wiggle out of doing a subsequent ballet because she can't put together a list of her songs that encompasses everything she feels on the topic of love.

Many times Mitchell hasn't said no but has simply failed to respond at all (as happened to me with this book). "Joni Mitchell never returned my phone call," one of the producers of a 1986 concert in Vancouver that would draw the Prince and Princess of Wales told the *Toronto Star* in a lament not uncommon among us wannabe Joni-inveiglers. (The concert for Expo '86 ended up featuring Kenny Rogers, Bryan Adams, and Sheena Easton instead.) In 2013, actor Justin Long announced at the Tribeca Film Festival "Joni Mitchell, please return our calls!" because *A Case of You*, a romantic comedy that he and a collaborator had made with Brendan Fraser, Evan Rachel Wood, Sam Rockwell, and Peter Dinklage, hoped to use different versions of the song throughout the film. (Instead, the movie uses songs by Joan Baez and the Spin Doctors, among others.)

But with *Grace of My Heart*, something happened that made Mitchell change her mind. Her cat, Nietzsche, whom she adored—he's the yellow-eyed Abyssinian Joni is holding up on the cover of *Taming the Tiger*—couldn't control his bladder; maybe he'd taken an overly literal interpretation of his philosopher namesake's famous dictum "To do is to be." So one day Mitchell grabbed him by the scruff of his neck and told him, "If you're going to act like an animal, you're going to live like one!" She marched that bad boy Nietzsche outdoors. But, according to Mitchell, he was too "offended" to return.

Night after night, she called out anxiously for him. Nothing. She missed his weird ways of expressing affection. She had nicknamed him Man from Mars "because he's a little lavender lion who looks like an alien and walks on his hind legs as an expression of affection for me," she has said. Easily frightened, Nietzsche was devoted to Mitchell even if he wouldn't let her snuggle him. When Mitchell would stop playing guitar in the house, Nietzsche would start talking; when Mitchell started up again, he'd stop. "He'd give me these deep, long looks and chew on my hair while I rubbed his head. The absence of that ritual left a big hole."

Mitchell's sadness started to mirror the sadness of the character in *Grace of My Heart* whom she'd been asked to write for. After considering the thought that Nietzsche had drowned, Mitchell started working on a song called "Man from Mars" that ended up on the movie's soundtrack (and on *Taming the Tiger*). The song is a swoony lament for a lost love; the singer misses her unnamed love so much that she hears him in the wiring in her walls and in her water.

Mitchell also upped her search methods: "I only had a picture of him as a kitten," she told Elvis Costello when he interviewed her for *Vanity Fair* in 2004. "So I painted him, had it photographed, and on the third day took it to the printer, and got it back in laminate form on the fifth day, and hand-delivered it into everybody's mailbox in a three-mile radius. On the back it said, 'Have you seen my Nietzsche?' and gave the phone number to call."

The song took seventeen days to write, and on the final day, Nietzsche showed up in a neighbor's yard. "When I found him," Mitchell has said, "he just yelled at me, almost hyperventilating by telling me off. So I yelled back in his language, you know, 'Meow-meow-meow!' When I changed to coaxing tones, he stopped yelling and went belly up."

She brought him home. When she played him "Man from Mars," he stood on his hind legs and danced.

39

"God, maybe I should look for her," Joni would sometimes say to her husband Larry Klein. Joni couldn't always quiet the voices in her head. All this disquiet had tumbled out in her music over the years, of course—first with "Little Green," and then with "Let the Wind Carry Me" (Joni sings that she occasionally has the impulse to rear a child with someone, but that the impulse fades), "Woman of Heart and Mind" (Joni sings that being childless gives her more free time), "Man from Mars" (Joni's lament for her lost cat feels highly metaphorical), "The Magdalene Laundries" (Joni's tribute to the "fallen women" taken in by Irish institutions starts out in first person). Other than "Little Green," the most overt reference was in "Chinese Cafe" on 1982's *Wild Things Run Fast,* where Mitchell sings that the child she bore is a stranger to her.

Even though Mitchell had only told a few people about Kelly, the word was bound to get out at some point: there's very little that a famous person does or says that goes wholly unnoticed. As early as 1974, Shirley Eder, a columnist syndicated by Knight News Service, was floating the theory that Joni had a child; "May we hear from Miss Mitchell, please," Eder asked in her column. In September 1990, Mitchell gave an interview to Greater London Radio, to discuss an exhibition of her paintings that was about to open in London. Having heard the "Chinese Cafe" lyric ("I bore her / But I could not raise her"), the radio interviewer, Trevor Dann, figured the topic of the baby was in the public domain, so he asked Mitchell before the taping if it was OK to discuss it. Mitchell assented. Then, during the interview, while Mitchell was reminiscing about her parents, Dann asked, "Do you yourself miss having a close-knit family life of your own, or is that something—because you talk very fondly, and you always have done, about your childhood and about children and all that kind of thing, and yet your own family is you and your husband at the moment, isn't it?"

MITCHELL: Well, we have cats and also I have a lot of godchildren. I haven't had children by choice really. And there were children all the time growing up in my house and in Los Angeles. There were always children splashing in the pool. I have friends who would come and stay for long periods of time, bring their children. So, no, I didn't miss that. And I love children. I'm drawn to them, you know.

INTERVIEWER: You did have a child, didn't you, when you were very young?

MITCHELL: Yes.

INTERVIEWER: Do you know what happened to him or her?

MITCHELL: I do and I don't. Maybe I do. Maybe I know a little. Maybe I don't know anything. I'll tell you by that I think I've done my—people are too possessive about their children, too egocentric with their children anyway. I

> reproduced myself. I made a beautiful child, a girl. When—but at the time I was penniless. There was no way that I could take—she would have been—I was not the right person to raise this child. There was no indication that I would—I don't have a good education; I couldn't keep her. It was impossible under the circumstance. I had no money when she was born, none. Imagine. I mean none of the music would have come out. We would have just been—I would have been waitressing or something. It wouldn't have been—fate did not design this to occur.

In April 1995, after various tabloids had stirred the pot, Mitchell went public in the pages of *Vogue.* "I had a child," she told the magazine, "and I was broke, literally penniless." A year later, after one of Mitchell's art college classmates talked to the supermarket tabloid the *Globe,* the publication ran a brief story about Kelly. If the Greater London Radio broadcast and the *Vogue* piece had more or less slipped under the radar, the *Globe* article did not. Hundreds of wannabes and maybes and impostors got in touch with Mitchell's management; a waitress named Kelly at a restaurant in LA Mitchell frequented asked her mother if she'd been adopted. The foster mother who had cared for the real Kelly for seven months sent baby photos to Mitchell's managers; Weller writes in *Girls Like Us* that Mitchell looked at the photos and said, "'My daughter . . . my baby . . . my child' as if the sheer ability to mouth those words was intensely relieving." Mitchell thought the baby looked just like her maternal grandmother, Sadie, the one who'd kicked a door off its hinge.

Mitchell started looking for Kelly. Meanwhile, Myrtle told

the *Calgary Sun*, "We would have been supportive if we had only known." But she also told them, "It's Joni's fault this is coming out now; she's too open and frank about it. This is really embarrassing."

When Kelly was seven months old, she was adopted by David and Ida Gibb, schoolteachers who lived in the Toronto suburb Don Mills. "When [our son] David was three and a half," Mrs. Gibb told *Maclean's* magazine, "we were doing very well and we wanted to share it with someone. Taking a child into your home seemed like a good way of doing it." The Gibbs gave Kelly the new name Kilauren.

Kilauren led a fairly privileged life—private school, family vacations to warm, non-Canadian shores. At first, the Gibbs didn't tell Kilauren that she was adopted, because they wanted to protect her, and because they were afraid of losing her. But when Kilauren was fourteen, she started wondering why there were no pictures of her before the age of eight months. Her mother tried to explain it away by saying that a camera had not been handy at the time, or that Kilauren was a second child and that second children don't have as many pictures taken of them. These explanations did not sate Kilauren's curiosity. It didn't help that Kilauren's looks and personality were so different from the Gibbs'—she was much more headstrong and striking-looking than them.

That same year, 1979, Kilauren and her brother were walking on a beach in Jamaica during a school vacation when a talent scout from the Elite modeling agency spotted the young beauty. Kilauren would spend the next ten years as a professional model, working all around the world. Her face would grace the Evian spritzer bottle—a bottle that Joni, coincidentally, would sometimes clutch on airplanes to help with dehydration, totally unaware of the act of hydration-based pietá that she was engaged in.

While vacationing with her parents at a hotel in Miami Beach in December of 1991, Kilauren, twenty-six, told her parents that she was pregnant (with her boyfriend, Paul Kohler, a drummer), whereupon her parents told her that she'd been adopted. On hearing the news, Kilauren was confused and angry. She started searching for her birth mother in earnest.

Through a friend's connection, Kilauren got her name put at the top of the Children's Aid Foundation's Match Program list, through which adoptees at age eighteen could find out information about their birth parents without learning their parents' names. Kilauren received a registered letter from the foundation around 1996; it told her "Your mother was from a small town in Saskatchewan and left for the U.S. to pursue her career as a folksinger."

Eight years earlier, Duke Redbird, the Indigenous poet who had lived across the hall from Joni when she was pregnant in Toronto, had told fellow York University student Annie Mandlsohn, "Never tell this to anybody, but I lived in the same house as Joni Mitchell; she had a baby and nobody knows." Now, in 1996, Mandlsohn's boyfriend Tim Campbell introduced Mandlsohn to Kilauren. (The boyfriend had grown up in the same suburb as Kilauren and Kilauren's boyfriend.) When Kilauren showed Mandlsohn the Children's Aid letter stating that her mother was a folk singer who'd moved to the States, Mandlsohn said, "Kilauren! Your mother is Joni Mitchell!"

The name didn't mean much to Kilauren; she owned none of Joni's albums, though she had loved Joni's duet with Seal, "If I Could." (When Kilauren later hears "Little Green" for the first time, she'll tell Joni, "God, it's so cryptic, Joan. I never would have known it was for me," a statement that seems to echo *Rolling Stone*'s assessment of the song, which stated, "It passeth all understanding.") But Kilauren started Googling and, on JoniMitchell.com—a wonderfully encyclopedic website founded by longtime fan Wally Breese, who was looking for an "unselfish" project to commit himself to after he'd received a cancer diagnosis—found fourteen points of comparison between herself and Joni, including blond hair, blue eyes, and prodigious cheekbones. "The more I read, the more I realized how alike we were," Kilauren told the *Toronto Sun*. "She was a singer, I was into music. She was an artist. I painted. We both enjoyed the same things." Kilauren had started smoking at age eleven; had almost made Canada's Olympic swim team; and had become a professional model at age sixteen. "Like Joni, I was really headstrong," Kilauren will later tell the Toronto *Globe and Mail*. "My parents didn't like my doing modeling, but nothing could stand in my way."

After confirming with Duke Redbird that Joni had been pregnant during the winter—Kilauren was born in February—and then successfully filling out a questionnaire that Breese, the JoniMitchell.com founder, had devised to deal with the emails flooding his inbox, Kilauren was given the go-ahead to write to Joni's managers, who didn't write back for six weeks. Kilauren's parents, the Gibbs, found a photo of Kilauren taken the day she left her foster mother, and sent it to the managers, who matched it against the photos the foster mother had sent. Mitchell had one of the managers call Kilauren. "He came back and said it made his hair stand on end," Joni told the *Los Angeles Times*. "He said it's like you're talking to the same person." Joni was on vacation when the manager called her back with Kilauren's phone number. Joni called Kilauren and left a message on her machine: "It's Joni. I'm overwhelmed."

Kilauren has said that, in her first phone call with her birth mother, Joni "wanted to get it off her chest, how sorry she was that she gave me up. How broke she was at the time—she couldn't even get the money together to be in the musician's union. She couldn't tell her parents about the whole thing, having a baby—she was brought up in a Victorian household." Kilauren tried to allay Joni's feelings of guilt. "She asked me how my childhood was, and I was honestly able to tell her that it was fabulous," she said. "It was a great childhood, probably the best. I think now, that I could have been raised in California, and been a Bel Air brat. I'm really happy that I got my family to raise me, in down-to-earth style. I'll always be grateful for that."

When the news broke, Kilauren got interview requests from Oprah Winfrey, Barbara Walters, and Larry King. She disconnected her phone and abandoned her apartment. Strangely, she opted to let her then-boyfriend, an orthopedic parts salesman named Ted Barrington, speak for her. (Kilauren's friendship with Ted goes back to 1979; their parents were both members of the Donalda golf and tennis club.) When *Maclean's* magazine called, Barrington asked for $10,000 for an interview with Kilauren. *Maclean's*, being a legitimate publication, told him that they don't pay for interviews, whereupon Barrington told them, "It's all business to me. The money's for Kilauren. She's a student right now"—Kilauren was living on student loans while studying desktop publishing at George Brown College in Toronto—"and she should be able to profit from this, at least monetarily. . . . Joni's asset-rich, but not cash-rich." He added, "If you've got an offer, let us know. You have my pager number." Later, after Barrington spoke with Joni's Vancouver-based manager, whom Kilauren had by then put in charge of publicity, Barrington apologized to *Maclean's*: "I was out of line. All the good stuff is at the back end with book deals and all that. I'm just worried about Kilauren being exploited. I'm just worried about my girlfriend."

On Thursday, March 13, 1997, Kilauren and her five-year-old son, Marlin, flew to Los Angeles to meet Joni. It was dark by the time a limousine deposited Kilauren and Marlin at Joni's house in Bel Air; the duo walked up to the wrong door. "I heard a voice coming from above, looked up, and there she was like Juliet on her balcony," Kilauren has said. Joni had paintbrushes in her hand because she'd been working on a canvas.

The mother and daughter's initial contact felt both reassuring and fraught. Joni: "She looked at me and I looked at her, and we made the same sound at the same time: 'Mm-hmm.' We had the same speaking voice. She looks a lot like my mom." Kilauren: "When we met at the front door in the kitchen with hugs it felt like I had gone away on a trip for a couple months and I was coming home." Joni: "I've had pain and joy in my life, but nothing like this. It's an unparalleled emotional feeling."

During their nineteen-day "get acquainted" session, Joni and Kilauren found themselves talking for hours at a time. Sometimes they would simultaneously make the same remark. Amy Scholder, a writer and editor hired to work on a Joni autobiography that got shelved, had lunch with Joni and Kilauren and Marlin during this period; Scholder said, "It was uncanny how alike Joni and Kilauren were. When you think of the nature/nurture thing—they were meeting for the first time, and they were *so* similar."

But mostly the mood of the reunion seemed to be rhapsody. "Every once in a while I'd just blurt out, 'It's my kid!'" Mitchell has said. "We'd rush towards each other and hug and do some silly dance."

But if such outpourings of relief and communion and joy were perhaps to be expected, one outcome of the reunion was not: for the next ten years, Joni would write no new songs.

There's no accounting for inspiration or creativity. Their origins are mysterious. But certainly we have clues and intimations. The fact that Joni and Kilauren's reunion was followed by Joni's fallow decade would seem to give credence to the theory that Joni's deferred motherhood—and not other forces such as, say, her competitiveness, or her anger toward Myrtle—was the furnace of her artistry.

But of course, making art, like most actions in life, is the product of tens if not hundreds or thousands of tiny and sometimes unknowable factors, and thus we can't rule out any possible catalysts; the Great Wall of China, as we know, is partially held together with grains of sticky rice. Joni's pal Malka Marom once posited to Joni the theory that Joni's output was an effort to prove to Myrtle that she wasn't a quitter, whereupon Joni told her to desist with her stupid psychological theories. (Myrtle was very much alive during the fallow period, though—she died in 2007—so this reading doesn't quite scan.) When musician Ani DiFranco interviewed Mitchell for the *Los Angeles Times* in 1998, DiFranco wrote, "When I suggest to her that perhaps feminism is not just political slogans and short haircuts, that it can be something different for each person, she waxes poetic about the nobility of women staying in the home. She even cites the breakdown of the family and says children are not 'playing in the backyards anymore' because their 'mothers are not at home,' implicating feminism, and no other social or economic circumstances, as the cause of the problem. This seems ironic coming from a woman who, at a young age, made the difficult decision of adoption for her child, when confronted with the choice between motherhood and career." This last sentence caused the newspaper, days later, to run a response from the two managers who were handling Mitchell at the time: "Notwithstanding the emotional impact of this comment," the managers wrote, "it happens to be wrong. There are a number of infinitely more significant reasons for Joni to have made the difficult decision that she did."

And what does the woman herself say? "I quit everything in '97 when my daughter came back. Music was something I did to deal with the tremendous disturbance of losing her. It began when she disappeared and ended when she returned. I was probably deeply disturbed emotionally for those thirty-three years that I had no child to raise, though I put on a brave face," Mitchell told Camille Paglia when the social critic talked to her for *Interview* magazine in 2005. "Instead, I mothered the world and looked at the world in which my child was roaming from the point of view of a sociologist."

40

Joni remembers seeing Prince—whom she has called "the most amazing performer I have ever witnessed"—at one of her shows in the early seventies. "When he was fifteen, I think, I played Minneapolis," she has said, probably referring to her January 16, 1976, appearance at the University of Minnesota's Northrop Auditorium, when the wee dynamo of sensual funk and rock would have been two years older than her estimate. "I remembered him because he has those distinctive eyes—he's like a puffin, or an Egyptian wall painting. And he sat to the left of me in the front row with his head kind of cocked at me like a puffin bird. I played a lot of my stuff to him."

Ever the nonconformist, Prince claimed that his favorite Joni album was the one that had met with the greatest resistance from critics and Joni's fans at the time, 1975's *The Hissing of Summer Lawns*. Here Joni had turned away from confessional, first-person lyrics, training her gaze instead at marriage and suburbia in a series of ironical character portraits written in third person. (Prince's enthusiasm for the record has been equaled by no less a light than Elvis Costello, who has called *Hissing* "the masterpiece of that time.") Prince tried to get in touch with Joni via a letter written in his usual vegetable soup of U's and hearts and 2's and 4's; it is safe to assume that a letter from Prince, like a text from your twelve-year-old niece, resembles the Bayeux Tapestry. But, as Joni has put it, her employees threw the letter out because they assumed it hailed from "the lunatic fringe."

Regardless, Prince proceeded to pledge his troth. In his song "The Ballad of Dorothy Parker" from 1987's *Sign o' the Times,* he quotes a line from Mitchell's hit "Help Me" when Dorothy hears her favorite song on the radio. He also used Joni's tunes as the pre-concert music on his tours.

Once Prince and Mitchell became friends, he tried to tell her how to write and market a hit single, but she didn't want to listen. Nevertheless, when *New York* magazine asked Mitchell in 2005 which music, of all the music made by people who've cited her as an influence, she most admired, Mitchell said Prince's.

The Joni song that Prince is most readily identified with is "A Case of You," the song that the music director of the tastemaking New York City radio station WFUV once called "sort of our 'Stairway to Heaven.'" Prince called it "A Case of U" and covered it repeatedly, turning it, alternately, into a Jimi Hendrix–style guitar fantasia, a tender ballad, and a reason to flee the stage. (After running out on the audience at Atlanta's Fox Theatre in April 2016 days before his death, Prince returned to the stage to say, "Sometimes I forget how emotional these songs can be.")

After Prince and Mitchell had befriended each other, he sent her a song that he hoped she would cover, "You Are My Emotional Pump, You Make My Body Jump." But alas: "I called him up and I said, 'I can't sing this—I'd have to jump around in a black teddy,'"

Joni told *Mojo* magazine in 1994. "He's a strange little duck, but I like him." (Joni also balked in 1986 when she and Larry Klein went to a Prince show in Denver. When Prince asked Joni to join him on the chorus of his hit "Purple Rain," Joni said she didn't know the lyrics. Whereupon Prince helpfully explained that the song's chorus runs, "Purple rain, purple rain / Purple rain, purple rain.")

Though, at first blush, the impish His Royal Badness and the world-weary jazzcat troubadour would not seem to have much in common, both were creatively restless and prone to blurring genres on their mostly self-produced albums; each made music that was emotionally fraught and sexually frank; both flirted with androgyny and were associated with berets, cold weather, and falsettos. They both refused to play the promotional game (at one press conference, Prince responded to any question he didn't want to answer by playing the theme to *The Twilight Zone* on a keyboard; once asked by an MTV host how he felt, Prince responded, "I feel with my hands") and grew disenchanted with the music business around the same time: Prince wrote "SLAVE" on his cheek (he was pissed at how Warner Bros. had marketed one of his records, and thought the company was limiting his artistic freedom by stipulating how often he could release his work) with the same vigor that Joni once yelled "Slavery with tenure is not attractive!" at David Geffen.

But, in practical terms, the most important bond between Prince and Joni may have been their mutual love of parties. On the heels of the hugely successful film and soundtrack of 1984's *Purple Rain,* Prince held a listening party of his next record, *Around the World in a Day,* at the Warner Bros. offices in Burbank. How does such an event get arranged? By the seat of one's pants: Prince had one of his employees call Warner Bros. chairman and CEO Mo Ostin at noon on Thursday, February 21, 1985, to say that Prince would like to play the new record for key Warners executives that afternoon at 4:00. The Warners conference room was summarily decanted of its table and most of its chairs; the lighting was muted; flowers were spread on the floor. Then a small parade of Prince admirers—his stepbrother, Duane; collaborators Wendy and Lisa; Prince's father; Joni; and the tiny wonder himself—promenaded into the conference room, all holding flowers. (One Warners executive said at the time, "We're like, Haight-Ashbury.") Prince sat on the floor and was very quiet once the music started playing; when Joni, seated next to him, pointed out certain chords or progressions she liked and asked him where he got them from, he said, "From you." Lest he be forced to endure any uninspired reactions to this new music that was less commercial than *Purple Rain*, Prince, before the album ended, stood and left the room.

The following year saw a much more elaborate party thrown by Warners for *Under the Cherry Moon*, a film starring Prince. In this instance, the ten thousandth caller in a contest—a twenty-year-old hotel worker, who'd seen *Purple Rain* thirteen times—won a party for her tiny town of Sheridan (population: 10,369) in Wyoming. Prince arrived by private Learjet and flung his black silk sport jacket over a fence to a crowd of seven hundred fans waiting on the runway. A local at a coffee counter told a reporter that Sheridan was best known for fishing lures, adding, "We don't care about no boy who wears tight pants and struts around like a woman." The screening was held at the town's Centennial Theatre, where Prince, in makeup and a midriff-bearing shirt, played with the contest winner's hair and put his arm around her. Joni—whom Prince flew to the premiere along with Joni's friend Rosanna Arquette—slipped into the screening unnoticed; musician Ray Parker, Jr., conversely, received a burst of applause, but it was subsequently determined that the audience had thought he was Lionel Richie. At the premiere's after-party, Prince played a forty-five-minute-long set at the local Holiday Inn; many reported that they preferred the concert to the movie. "It went into the wee hours," Arquette told me. "There was an after-after-party. There's always an after-after-party."

In 2005, Prince threw an Oscars after-party at a mansion he was renting in the Hollywood Hills. An illuminated, purple Love Symbol—Prince's impossible-to-pronounce alias du jour—hung over the swimming pool, like an ankh at Gay Pride. At one point during the party, Oscars host Chris Rock, Penélope Cruz, Salma Hayek, Samuel L. Jackson, and Sean Combs were all standing in the kitchen, crowding the chocolate fountain. Meanwhile, Joni ran the pool table.

At four in the morning, Prince, in a gold, mandarin-collared outfit, was joined by some of the guests—Christina Aguilera, Sheila E., and Stevie Wonder, who had taken a disco nap on one of Prince's couches—for a jam session in the living room. When Prince simultaneously played keyboards and guitar during Wonder's "I Wish," various guests ran to other parts of the house to find their dates, so they, too, could witness the musical virtuosity on display.

When one guest left at 8:30 a.m., he found Joni chain-smoking on the patio. Mitchell smiled at him and offered, "Wasn't that incredible?"

That Mitchell can be described as both "hermit-like" and "highly social" is one of her more interesting paradoxes. On the latter score, she has been, over the years, an inveterate guest and a generous host. In 1992, she joined a passel of notables like Gregory Peck, David Bowie, and Shirley MacLaine at Elizabeth Taylor's sixtieth birthday party at Disneyland (Taylor rented out the entire park, and arrived in a carriage drawn by white horses). In 1993, Mitchell attended comedian Milton Berle's eighty-fifth birthday at the Beverly Hilton (where, amusingly, she looked out at a sea of cosmetically enhanced faces and performed her song "Face Lift"). Jimmy Webb told me that when he had members of the Los Angeles Philharmonic play a concert in the nude for a nude audience in Webb's backyard in Encino one day in 1970, "Joni and David Geffen came over and the first thing they did was take off their clothes."

She's been a regular to Clive Davis's annual pre-Grammys party—in 2013, she sat with Alice Cooper and Paul Stanley from KISS, and commented on Usher ("Now, he's the shit"), Scottish singer Emeli Sandé ("She's a real artist"), Miguel ("hot"), Sting ("He's the child James Taylor and I never had"). That night she danced during Gladys Knight's performance of "Midnight Train to Georgia," and was among the last to leave the ballroom.

And O, to have witnessed the burst of platinum incandescence that must have flared up at Ringo Starr's New Year's Eve shindig the year that Joni fell into conversation with that bombshell of yesteryear Mae West, who, dressed in a pink negligee, was escorted by two blond bodybuilders. (Like Georgia O'Keeffe, Mae West seems like a Granny Joni, but an NSFW one.)

"Had dinner with Joni Mitchell Saturday night," Jane Fonda wrote on her blog on October 11, 2011. "I can't remember when I've had a more intense, far-reaching, multifaceted conversation (right from the moment we sat down . . . no small talk with Joni)—from Christianity, Buddhism, the Gnostics, different forms of meditation, Ego as the original sin . . ." Then Fonda concluded her post, "Tonight I'm having a small gathering for Bonnie Raitt. Joni will be there and Robbie Robertson, [actor] Eddie Olmos, [philanthropist and film producer] Steve Bing, and [Microsoft co-founder] Paul Allen."

Given that show business is a microcosm fueled by schmooze, a world in which "I've heard good things about him" is code for "I have absolutely no idea who you're talking about because the demands of my own self-branding prohibit me from acknowledging other people," it would be easy to read too much into someone's appearance at a party. Show people sometimes go to parties because, yes, they want to catch up with friends, and, yes, they want to remove themselves from their feelings of isolation. But they also go for more expedient reasons—to meet people who can help their careers, to inhale fifteen complimentary mini quiches, and to have their photograph taken with Barry Manilow over near the crepe station for the *San Diego Union-Tribune*. Mitchell is, of course, hip to all this, as we know from *Court and Spark*'s "People's Parties," her deadly accurate depiction of how so many of us, in social situations, tend either to stand on the sidelines, or take center stage, "giving to get something."

Some of the gatherings set in motion by Joni, however, have had a more wholesome vibe to them. She has a small core group of five or so friends that she's known since childhood or since she was in her twenties. "There's a different sense of camaraderie in the prairies," one of these folks—childhood pal and onetime lover Tony Simon—told me. "Part of it stems from the weather—from the end of October to the end of March, it's no joke, the weather can be deadly. If you're on the highway and you see someone in a ditch, you fuckin' stop. They may die if you don't. It's a totally different way of thinking from other places, and that kind of camaraderie still governs what Joan is all about." The core group gets invited to Mitchell's birthdays and concerts; at the latter kind of event, Mitchell is understandably in high demand, so the group, according to Simon, doesn't "really give a rat's ass whether Joan hangs out with us or not, what with everyone bugging her and all. We can just get together and have fun ourselves. We're all friends."

One member of the group, longtime friend Sharolyn Dickson, a retired teacher and former homemaker who still lives in Saskatoon, told me she never feels awkwardness or imbalance as a result of Mitchell's fame because "she's genuinely interested in what's going on in our world"; during the Pandemic, one Zoom call between Mitchell and Dickson, heavy on childhood memories, ran more than three hours. A 2023 memoir written by Mitchell's five-decades-long friend Cary Raditz—the impecunious bohemian Joni met during her vacation on Crete in 1970—portrays a similarly salt-of-the-earth Mitchell who's willing to sleep in a cave or a youth hostel despite being able to afford a hotel.

Mitchell is generous about inviting people who aren't in the inner circle to gatherings, too—Beverley Straight, a former neighbor of Mitchell's on the Sunshine Coast whom Mitchell had once given a smudge stick after Straight broke up with a boyfriend, told me she loved being invited to one of Mitchell's birthdays: "It was a fascinating party because you'd walk around and think, 'Oh, there's the guy who owns the liquor store—and there's Diana Krall.'"

The most celebrated gathering hosted by Mitchell occurred one night in July 1968 when Graham Nash, still a member of the Hollies, albeit a disgruntled one, went to Joni's Laurel Canyon house, where she was hanging out and partying with David Crosby and Stephen Stills. Nash had met all three of them previously. After Nash had settled in, Crosby whacked Stills on the arm and said, "Hey, play Willy that song we were just doing." Stills grabbed a guitar, and he and Crosby launched into Stills's "You Don't Have to Cry," a love letter to his long-distance lover, Judy Collins (Stills has repeatedly insisted that this event took place at Mama Cass's house because he would have been too intimidated to sing in front of Joni). Crosby's smooth tenor brought grace to Stills's rougher, bluesier baritone.

"Fuck, that's a fabulous song!" Nash enthused when they'd finished. "Would you mind doing it again?"

Crosby and Stills plowed into the song again, after which Nash said, "OK, bear with me here. Do it *one* more time."

When Stills launched into the song's intro this third time, Nash, a quick study, walked over to Stills's left, and proceeded to sing a high harmony over the other two voices, thus launching the band that the world would come to know as Crosby, Stills & Nash. The trio's eponymous 1969 debut would inject sunniness into a musical landscape weighed down by power rock and heavy blues. ("I've seen Crosby, Stills & Nash," Jimi Hendrix would say. "They're groovy. Western sky music. All delicate and ding-ding-ding.") Indeed, so delightful was the vocal blend that, some sixty seconds or so into the song, the trio collapsed in laughter. Crosby enthused, "That's the best thing I ever heard!"

Nash asked Joni, "Did that sound as incredible to you as it did to me?"

"Yeah, it sounded pretty incredible."

In 2018, Joellen Lapidus, the woman who more than four decades earlier had made and sold Mitchell her first dulcimer (Mitchell took a dulcimer on her 1970 trip to Europe because it was easier to travel with than a guitar; she would write "All I Want," "A Case of You," "Carey," and "California" on it), got a phone call from a young English musician who told her "I'm a big fan of Joni Mitchell and I know she bought a dulcimer from you and I'd like to buy one."

"So I said to him, 'I'm in Culver City, why don't you come over,'" Lapidus told me. The musician and his collaborator, Tom, showed up at Lapidus's house—"Very sweet, nondescript guys," Lapidus said. "Not overly handsome, just nice guys. Very unpretentious." Lapidus showed the two musicians eight or nine dulcimers; then the three musicians each grabbed one of the instruments and had a jam session. The musician who'd initially contacted Lapidus bought four of her instruments, including one called a Crying Seahorse, for himself.

A few months later, a colleague of Lapidus's, who'd seen Lapidus's name mentioned in a *Rolling Stone* article, called Lapidus and asked, "How do you know Harry Styles?"

Lapidus said, "Harry *who*?"

"Harry Styles!"

Lapidus told me, "He had to explain to me who that was."

Lapidus got an even better sense of who Styles is when Lapidus's across-the-street neighbor, a teenaged girl, found out that the young pop star had had a little jam session astonishingly close to her home. The neighbor did "that teenage thing they do," Lapidus said. "She just screamed."

After her aneurysm in 2015, Mitchell's social life took on a new dimension by becoming a kind of barometer: it was Joni's visits with friends in their homes or at concert venues that helped us fans gauge how well she was recuperating. In August 2016, turned out in a wide-brimmed black hat and a beautiful, embroidered black shawl, Mitchell went with Herbie Hancock to hear her friend and collaborator Chick Corea play at Catalina Bar and Grill in Hollywood; though she was starting to walk again at the time, the dark recesses of the club made a wheelchair a more practical means of locomotion. In 2017, she went to Elton John's seventieth birthday party at Los Angeles's Hammer Museum. 2018 took her to see James Taylor at the Hollywood Bowl. "The pair shared a tender embrace backstage," the *Boston Globe* reported, "and despite reports of health problems in recent years, Mitchell looked terrific with her hair fixed in an exquisite fishtail braid." In the heartrending accompanying photo, James's muscular arms pull Mitchell into his chest while he, with his eyes closed, rests his chin on her head.

Gradually, she started to make other forays out into the world.

In 2018, an old friend of Joni's from the folk world—Eric Andersen, who, more than forty years earlier, had taught Joni how to open-tune her guitar—visited Joni at her house with his band.

Andersen and his colleagues played some music for Joni, who did not, or could not, sing along. Cut to the aforementioned dinner with Brandi Carlile after the Grammys, whereat Joni proposed the gatherings that would turn into the Joni Jams.

At the first Joni Jam, Carlile, bearing a giant orchid and a bottle of champagne, showed up with her wife, her two musical partners, and the Irish musician Hozier. Carlile didn't know what to expect, but, as she writes in her memoir, "Joni always has the mischief in her eyes." Mitchell was turned out in bright lipstick and a designer hat; she encouraged everyone to scarf down Mexican food that a friend had prepared, as well as Pinot Grigio. (Mitchell doesn't want people looking at their phones during Jams, so at her house's entrance for the New Year's Eve Jam in 2019, guests were greeted by a board that read "Leave your guns at the door"; they unloaded their phones and put them in individual Ziploc bags with their names on them. The no-pistols policy would become the norm at the Jams, though Joni allows for one group photo to be taken at the Jam's conclusion.)

Once inside Mitchell's house, the guests at the first Jam marveled at the coziness—Mitchell has hand-painted all the cabinets and wooden beams; behind a secret door that Joni has painted cats on, there's a hidden bathroom. Mitchell answered everyone's questions "like it was story time with a preschool class," according to Carlile. "She has the presence of a white cat. She could sort of take you or leave you."

Carlile played her song "Cannonball" and Hozier sang an Irish folk song . . . when in walked Chaka Khan and Herbie Hancock. Soon, Khan, aka the Queen of Funk, was grabbing Carlile's wineglass mid-conversation and pouring it into her own while saying,

"Bitch, you're not drinking this." Hancock had started playing some jazzy, diminished chords when a low, sultry voice started crooning the opening of "Summertime": Joni was singing for the first time since her aneurysm. Hancock burst into tears.

The Jams continued, mostly on a monthly basis. Harry Styles sang "River" at one Christmas-themed Jam. Mitchell played bongos and sang "Love Potion No. 9" at one. Meryl Streep showed up one night; Ellen DeGeneres came once in her pajamas. Elton John and Charlie Puth did a duet of John's "Don't Let the Sun Go Down on Me." When Marcus Mumford botched a lyric in his rendition of "My Funny Valentine," Khan leaned over to Joni and, in a stage whisper, said, "He really fucked that up. Do you want me to do it?" (Joni, clutching her frozen margarita, laughed and said, "No, no, no, it's fine. It was great.") When Joni told Celisse that she loved the R&B singer's version of "Help Me" and hoped she'd come to another Jam, Celisse joked that she'd be willing to sleep under Mitchell's pool table in the interim, whereupon Mitchell told her, "Sarah Vaughan slept right under that pool table many times." One night Elton told Joni, "I just want to say this is such a gift to see you doing so well. And to be here, and to tell you how much we love you. . . . We just love you," prior to serenading her with a lustrous, world-weary "Moon River."

Joni was clearly thrilled by all the musical camaraderie. She seemed mellowed. "I was at the second Joni Jam in Bel Air at Joan's place," Mitchell's longtime friend Tony Simon told me when I interviewed him in his backyard in North Vancouver. "Everyone was drunk. They'd say, Sing something, or sing a verse, and Joan didn't really want to because she didn't sound great. Afterwards,

Brandi said, 'You know, you should get a vocal coach. I can line you up with mine if you want,' and I thought"—here he inhaled quickly as if anticipating fireworks—"if you'd said that to Joan a few years ago: watch out. But this time she said, 'Yeah, that's a good idea.'"

Mitchell didn't start playing instruments again until the night that actress Kathy Bates showed up for one of the Jams in 2021. Prior to this night, whenever Carlile had mentioned guitar playing to Mitchell, Mitchell had said, "I don't do that. I don't play guitar." But Bates showed up with a prized electric guitar that she proceeded to place on Mitchell's lap. "My breath got caught in my chest," Carlile has written about the moment. "I just didn't know what would happen. And Joni just goes, 'This is a beautiful guitar. Does anyone have a cord or an amp?'"

Carlile reached down to take the guitar from Mitchell and tune it. But Mitchell swatted Carlile's hand away, saying, "Hey, don't, I'm going to put this in one of my tunings."

Mitchell proceeded to put the guitar into the tuning known as an open D. Once she'd done so, Mitchell was about to put the guitar down when her assistant and friend Marcy said, "Wait! Does anyone know anything in this key?" Taylor Goldsmith, of the band Dawes, realized that his favorite of Joni's late-career songs was written in the key. "I started singing it, looking her dead in the eye, and I was terrified," Goldsmith would later recount. "I'm like, 'I don't know if this is appropriate.'" But Mitchell took the bait, and started playing and singing along on the song whose title, given the circumstances, could not have been more appropriate: "Come In from the Cold."

41

2022. On a flight from Vancouver to Calgary, I told my seatmate—a smiley Canadian woman in her early thirties—that I was writing a book about Joni Mitchell. The woman looked slightly confused and said, "I know my mom loves her, but . . . is she the one who does 'You're So Vain'?" No, I said, that's Carly Simon. "Oh! Oh! Wait, I know who she is," the woman said. "'Paving Paradise'!" Close enough.

While, as previously mentioned, people occasionally confuse Mitchell with Judy Collins, and while I myself have alluded to her similarities with Georgia O'Keeffe, Mae West, Neil Young, Prince, and Shelly from *Northern Exposure*, there is one luminary who is an even more apt point of comparison: beloved singer-songwriter Carole King. King has denied the alikeness: "We do the same thing but we do it in *such* different ways," said the most successful American female songwriter of the latter half of the century in a gracious video testimonial she made when Mitchell won the Gershwin Prize in 2023. "She goes to the place of total creativity" whereas "I was trained to write on assignment. I *have* been struck by the muse, I have worked at the direction of the muse. But that's Joni's native habitat."

Nevertheless, consider: both have blue eyes, came from humble beginnings, gave birth early (Carole: eighteen, Joni: twenty-one), changed their names, initially wrote songs that were hits for singers other than themselves, were skittish about performing live, lived in Laurel Canyon, performed with James Taylor and a lot of the same musicians, are white but buoy their music with traditionally Black music (Carole: R&B, Joni: jazz), recorded their biggest individual records at the same time and at the same studio with the same piano, included on their breakout albums—albums that trafficked heavily in romance and the use of the first person—third-person songs about outlaws who let their freak flags fly (Carole: killer Smackwater Jack, Joni: the prostitute in "Raised on Robbery"), freaked out at fame, retreated into the wilds (Carole: Idaho, Joni: B.C.), put their cats on their album covers, played Carnegie Hall, received a lot of the same honors, have implanted our brains with artisanal word pronunciations (Carole: the sky comes "tum-BOOL-ing" down, Joni: children are let out of "skoo-ells"), are associated with entities that are either hanging above our heads (Carole: "Up on the Roof," Joni: clouds) or are furry and adorable (Carole: the theme song to *The Care Bears Movie*, Joni: various boyfriends), appeared in ads for The Gap, performed with their daughter, became increasingly vocal about environmental issues, and continued recording, despite having announced their retirement, after turning seventy-five.

But perhaps most auspiciously, King wrote the song "Jazzman," and Mitchell [lower your voice two octaves here] . . . *is a jazzlady.*

42

May 7, 1996. Stockholm, Sweden. Joni has just been awarded the Polar Music Prize, an annual award referred to by Swedes as "the Nobel Prize of music," usually given simultaneously to one classical musician and one popular musician for their contribution to the field. Joni was the first woman ever to win the prize; her co-recipient was Pierre Boulez, one of the dominant forces of post-war classical music, whose accomplishments range from leading the New York Philharmonic to conducting Wagner's Ring Cycle at Bayreuth to collaborating with rock weirdo Frank Zappa.

At the press conference for the prize, an interviewer asked Mitchell, who was seated next to Boulez, if she had any kind of relationship with the maestro. "No, we are sitting beside one another, that's our relationship!" Mitchell said.

"But surely you'd *heard* of Maestro Boulez when the prize was announced," the interviewer followed up. At which point Mitchell, who has never gone in for computers or cellphones, apologized for "living in isolation" and said no.

Joni Joni Joni, those of us who lead lives guided by manners and deference to elders want to scream when we witness such a lapse of decorum, have ya heard about this crazy new thing called the Google? (Similarly, in 1998 when celebrated musician and maverick Ani DiFranco interviewed Mitchell for the *Los Angeles Times*, we learned that Mitchell had neither listened to any of DiFranco's music before the interview nor learned how to pronounce DiFranco's name.)

The unflappability in the face of social norms, the relentless candor, the utter dedication to her craft at the expense of certain interpersonal niceties: for many of us, Joni represents what it means to be an artist, if not an Artist. Her career is full of examples of Joni prioritizing art over commerce. Her management begged her not to make the full departure into jazz that they knew *Mingus* would be, but she did it anyway (and, even more iconoclastically, made it a jazz record with no solos on it). There are many examples of Joni opting not to play her hits at concerts, focusing instead on new material that she feels strongly about (in 1998 the Toronto *Globe and Mail* carped about the "sheer perversity" of just such a set). She didn't put fan favorites "The Circle Game" or "Both Sides Now" or "Urge for Going" on her first album. In 2023 when *Rolling Stone* reviewed her third volume of archival material, the magazine gave the story the headline "Joni Mitchell Did Whatever the Hell She Wanted. A New Box of Unheard Music Proves It."

Her dedication to her craft is a large part of the equation here. She has said that she wrote some two hundred verses to her song "Taming the Tiger," keeping only four. Jimmy Webb, whose songwriting credits include classics like "By the Time I Get to Phoenix," "MacArthur Park," and "Wichita Lineman," told me that, while sitting with Joni in his living room in London once, he got a glance of

Court and Spark's lyrics-in-the-making. "She would write out different versions of a single verse four or five times," he said. "Look, let's be honest about songwriters," Webb continued, "if they get a couple of verses and a chorus strung together, they'll usually run off to a recording studio and cut it." But not Joni: "Every strike of the chisel is premeditated."

Roger McGuinn told me that, during Rolling Thunder, "Joni came back to the dressing room one night and said, 'Why do I get so scared out there, McGuinn?' I said, 'Well, you're doing brand-new material and the audience doesn't recognize it.' And she said, 'But I have to!'" (On YouTube there's an excerpt from Scorsese's *Rolling Thunder* documentary, with more than 3 million views, wherein we see McGuinn and Mitchell and Bob Dylan playing "Coyote" at singer-songwriter Gordon Lightfoot's house. McGuinn introduces the song by admiringly saying "Joni wrote this song about this tour, and *on* this tour, and *for* this tour.")

Mitchell's commitment to art extends to defending art that is not of her own making, too. In 1980, James Taylor, JD Souther, and Waddy Wachtel wrote a song, "Her Town Too," inspired by the divorce between Taylor's manager Peter Asher, formerly of the pop duo Peter and Gordon, and his wife, Betsy. But Betsy Asher thought the song—despite the fact that its only specific detail was that the wife would get the house and the garden in the settlement while the husband would get the boys in the band—was an insult and that everyone would know it was about her and Peter. So Taylor and Wachtel were summoned to the Ashers' house to meet with Betsy, who'd invited her friend Joni for moral support. Asher pleaded her case, whereupon an exasperated Wachtel turned to

Joni and said, "Joni, why don't you tell her everything's fiction no matter whose fuckin' name is in it, or no matter who wrote what or who inspired what! It's all a bunch of bullshit, and it's all fiction!" Whereupon Joni said, "Well, he's right. He's basically right, Betsy. Nothing's really literal around here, you know, it's just art." (Released in March 1981, the song "Her Town Too"—a duet between Taylor and Souther—stayed in the Top 40 for ten weeks. Most listeners assumed it was about Taylor's marital troubles with Carly Simon.)

While the net yield of Mitchell's commitment to artistic ideals or bullheadedness was several albums that her listeners didn't necessarily want to listen to, Joni has never given us the impression that she makes decisions based on wanting to get more airplay or sating her fan base or appeasing her label. You can dislike or be unmoved by her music or her tart comments or even her persona, but it would be almost impossible to accurately call her inauthentic; when Mitchell was given a Lifetime Achievement Award by the National Academy of Songwriters in 1996, she said, "I actually feel humbled, which, considering how arrogant I am, is very unusual."

Her coolness in the face of honors and awards can very occasionally seem like bad manners, but more often it further underlines her commitment to her artistic ideals. She didn't go to Cleveland to collect her trophy from the Rock & Roll Hall of Fame in 1997: she was miffed that it took four years for her to be admitted once she became eligible, and it was going to cost her $20,000 to take her family to see her unpaid performance. But a year after the ceremony, Graham Nash presented Joni with the remnants of her trophy, which had been smashed by an airline's baggage check:

in the middle of Joni's Painting with Words and Music concert, Nash handed over the broken trophy, which he'd put in a green plastic bag.

"I'm sorry I didn't wrap this a little more genteelly," he said.

Joni looked at the offering and said, "It's perfect in a garbage bag."

What's particularly sweet and unexpected about Mitchell's artistic idealism is that the world has rewarded her for it—which we see best, ironically, when we compare her music with her painting. Although Mitchell often describes herself as a painter derailed by circumstances, the bulk of her artwork—or, at least, the artwork that she has shared with the world—tends to be, with the exception of her 1980s abstracts, both traditional and figurative. "I don't paint for galleries, I don't paint for museums. I paint to go with my couch," she once told a Los Angeles radio interviewer; in 2013 she'll tell the CBC, "Paintings are square things to hang on the wall to decorate your house." In 1999 she confessed to KCSN-FM that she has even painted over other people's artwork given to her, to make it jibe with her decor.

Her music, by contrast, is the product of a much less quotidian impulse, and is less like a poofy chair warmed by the afternoon sun than it is a boat ride with unforgettable scenery but no life preservers. Yet of the two mediums, it's Mitchell's music for which she is lionized—a rare instance of the world exalting the progressive and the unusual rather than the comfortable and the familiar.

Score a win for Art.

43

One day in 1998, Joni and Kilauren and Kilauren's son, Marlin, accompanied by Joni's friend Paul Starr, a makeup artist, went to the Hollywood Athletic Club so Mitchell could play pool. To amuse young Marlin while Grandma banked some shots, Starr told the five-year-old, "Pretend like you're excited." Marlin duly took on a look of pop-eyed joy. "Now pretend like Joni's going away," Starr said, whereupon Marlin paused before arranging his face.

"That was hard," Marlin responded. "I couldn't imagine why Joni would be going away."

If only Joni and Kilauren's relationship were so sweet. Though the mother and daughter's reunion was full of familial grace notes, their subsequent interactions were something less than a cakewalk. The initial meeting's burst of marathon talking sessions and silly dancing gradually subsided. An initial period of practicality post-reunion saw Kilauren deciding to keep living in Toronto, Joni calling Kilauren's parents to assure them that she wasn't trying to take their daughter away, and Joni and Kilauren having dinner with Kilauren's birth father, Brad McMath. When biographer David Yaffe met Kilauren and saw that she had had "Little Green" tattooed on her arm, Kilauren told him, "Don't tell my mother"; when Yaffe later told Mitchell about it, Mitchell—who probably numbers among the mothers in the world *least* likely to take exception to a tattoo—responded, "She doesn't know me."

Joni, spending increasing amounts of time with her grandchildren—Kilauren gave birth to a daughter, Daisy, in June 1999—found herself glued once more to her television, which she enjoyed (though she worried a little about it: "I thought, 'Uh-oh, is this the rest of my life? Smoking in front of Ted Turner?'"). Her friends noticed a new lightness to her demeanor; Herbie Hancock said that his collaborator looked "so overjoyed, she was like a little child. Joni's face had changed." Mitchell's friend drummer Brian Blade told me, "Man, it was such a deep time! Any restoration in life—you're thankful to see it, to witness it."

Joni and Kilauren liked swimming in Joni's pool; they watched two movies about people tracking down their birth parents—*Secrets and Lies* and *Flirting with Disaster*. "My relationship with my daughter is coming along beautifully," Mitchell told the BBC in 1999, "and my relationship with my mother is improving probably because of it, so maybe that hole was at the root of it."

Soon, however, the stress marks revealed themselves. "There were easier reunions for other people," Mitchell will say. "This was not easy. She had a lot of things to work out. You know, she had a lot of issues, and a lot of blame, and couldn't understand my circumstance, and didn't want to in the beginning." A confidante of Joni's told *Girls Like Us* author Sheila Weller that Kilauren, like her birth mother, is "brutal to argue with."

Kilauren's relationship with Ted Barrington, who has ADD and is prone to depression, did not make her life easier. The birth of their daughter led to a nasty custody dispute. Barrington, in a questionnaire he filled out as part of a court-ordered investigation, alleged that, after Daisy's birth, "Frequent emotional outbursts and her alienating manner were now the norm" for Gibb. When Gibb and her two children headed to Joni's for Christmas that year, Barrington was not invited.

During that visit, on January 3, 2000, Joni and Kilauren's troubles came to a head. While they were busily getting ready to go to a party at Michael Douglas and Catherine Zeta-Jones's house, Kilauren had plunked Marlin down in front of the TV to watch the movie *The Green Mile*, which includes an agonizing torture scene in which we see a man in an electric chair burn to a smoky death. Joni thought this wasn't appropriate fare for her young grandson; Kilauren vehemently disagreed.

"Don't talk back to me—I'm your mother!" Joni said.

"What do *you* know about being a mother? You gave me away!" Kilauren—whose name, when typed into a computer or phone, autocorrects to the Hawaiian volcano Kīlauea—shot back.

At which point Mitchell slapped her daughter's face.

Kilauren called the cops, but, on their arrival, didn't press charges, though she wanted the alleged assault reported. She took Marlin to a friend of Joni's to spend the night.

In his court-ordered questionnaire, Barrington alleged, "The months following the Christmas trip, as I had suspected, Kilauren took no responsibility for this horrendous incident and she was increasingly hostile towards her biological mother, the children and me." He further alleged that she began to drink heavily. Gibb, who will apply for sole custody in September 2000, will, according to the *National Post,* claim that Barrington is a mentally unstable and alcoholic porn addict who abused his own daughter, and who wants custody to be "connected financially" to Mitchell. (The Children's Aid Society of Toronto concluded that "there is no evidence to suggest any immediate child protection concerns." Barrington, who has copped to depression and ADD but denied all other claims, won limited supervised access to Daisy.)

The set of tensions swirling around Joni and Kilauren are hard for us outsiders to fully fathom. It would be more surprising if Joni and Kilauren's relationship *weren't* at least a little rocky. Biographer Sheila Weller thinks that the two women's differing levels of engagement with life played a big part here, too; she told me, "Kilauren was frustrating to Joni because Joni is such a doer and Kilauren is not."

Joni has not been afraid in the past to extend her competitiveness to situations involving her family. In her essay "Fear of a Female Genius," music critic Lindsay Zoladz writes, "Joni Mitchell retaining Chuck's last name for decades after their divorce has always struck me as a defiant, deliciously cruel act of revenge." When Mitchell once asked if her teenaged granddaughter, Daisy, would play something for her on the ukulele, Daisy said she couldn't because she was only in her second year of playing. "Second year?" Mitchell said later when recounting the incident. "I had it mastered in six months."

Mitchell has always had high standards and has not been afraid to express them: when she and her friend Daniel Levitin, the neuroscientist and musician, were in the habit of getting together to play their own songs to each other, Mitchell told Levitin at one point, "You've gotta quit at some point because I've got a higher standard and your songs are never gonna be up to my standard. But at some point they're gonna be good enough for other people to hear." In a truth teller's backyard lie the corpses of her allies.

Regarding Mitchell's relationship with Gibb, Joni's longtime friend Tony Simon told me, "I said to Joan, 'You question your own mother and father, who were totally devoted to you, and now you talk about what a loaded situation it is to meet up with your own kid. You have to look at that not in terms of who *she* is but who *you* are: you're a fucking perfectionist! How many people find out in their twenties or thirties that their mother is world famous? I wouldn't wish that on anybody.'"

In the wake of her reunion with her birth mother, Gibb had endured a two-month-long separation from her adoptive parents, and a strained relationship with her brother, David. Meanwhile, Gibb's friends assumed that Gibb would be picking up bar tabs now that she was a celebrity's daughter (when in fact Gibb was doing odd jobs like refinishing boats and interior decorating). At one point Gibb found herself in an emergency ward, where she was diagnosed as being heavily stressed. When Mitchell had her aneurysm in 2015, Gibb was not listed as her next of kin; in 2023, when Mitchell made her triumphant appearance at The Gorge, Gibb was not in attendance.

Had Gibb never fully reconciled herself to Mitchell's having put her up for adoption? When Gibb was asked this by the Toronto *Globe and Mail* in April 1998, she equivocated and shifted the spotlight onto her birth mother: "That's an issue, a tough issue. It's hard to tread there. I think she really has a guilty feeling about that." In the same article, we learned that Gibb and Mitchell were talking three or four times a week, but that Gibb didn't feel comfortable calling Mitchell "Mom" yet. Gibb also confessed, "I feel like I don't get enough time with Joni. She's very busy."

People with no experience of adoption often make the assumption that once adoptees are reunited with birth parents, the ache and pain will eventually subside—that both parties will "get over it," and settle into some kind of equanimity. But the testimony of adoptees tells a different story: the implicit pain of the experience is usually *not* something you conquer, but, rather, something you live with for the rest of your life. As Toni Morrison once said, "Sometimes you don't survive whole, you just survive in part. But the grandeur of life is that attempt."

Maybe it's this grandeur that has helped smooth some of the rougher edges of Joni and Kilauren's relationship. By 2002, Mitchell was telling *W* magazine, "Now we're hummin'. We're more like sisters. Our relationship is beautiful—since I didn't raise her, we don't have the scar tissue that's frequently built up between mother and daughter."

In 2006, Mitchell started writing music again, after her almost decade-long pause. She'd grown disenchanted with the music industry (again), and had reunited with her daughter, and . . . the music . . . just . . . stopped . . . coming. Then one day while she was sitting with a neighbor out on her deck at her house on the Sunshine Coast, as they drank coffee and rhapsodized to each other about how heavenly their view of the water and land was, the neighbor said to Mitchell, "If I get to Heaven and it's not like this, I'm coming right back down here."

That night, Mitchell sat down at her piano, flooded with gratitude for getting to live in such a beautiful place, and wrote "One Week Last Summer," which she originally titled "Gratitude." A pastoral instrumental, the song opens Joni's most recent studio album, *Shine,* which is dedicated to her grandchildren, Marlin and Daisy. "One Week Last Summer," which would win the 2008 Grammy Award for Best Pop Instrumental Performance, is possibly the weirdest entry in Mitchell's oeuvre by virtue of its not being recognizably a Joni Mitchell song. An incantatory and repetitive piano phrase lushly backed by alto saxophone and a wash of synthesized instruments, the tune would probably be the perfect accompaniment to the part of a nature documentary where a merganser chick that we've been trailing finally takes flight—the part where Morgan Freeman's voice-over tells us "Up, up he goes—off to a faraway land for heavy molting." Over the years, studies of various artists' late-in-life works have pinpointed a few common traits among these artists' last creative gasps: a distillation or simplification of the artist's lifelong forces into something called the "senile sublime," and a tendency toward timelessness if not an outright denial of death. It would not be peculiar to cite these themes at work in the spectral "One Week Last Summer."

If the other songs on *Shine* took a solemn and doomed view of the environment and the state of the world, the mood of their creator was now anything but. The workhorse was once again working. Mitchell seemed elated. Moreover, soon the Alberta Ballet would call and get her started on what would be one of her favorite-ever projects she'd work on: a ballet set to her songs, which would be called *The Fiddle and the Drum. The Fiddle and the Drum* sees dancers thrashing and jeté-ing to heavy hitters like "Woodstock" and "Ethiopia" as well as a bouncy zydeco version of "Big Yellow Taxi."

The natural order of things was shifting on the family front, too. Myrtle passed away in 2007 at age ninety-five; in her *Saskatoon Star-Phoenix* obit, she was praised for her modesty—she wasn't one to brag about having a famous daughter—and for her laugh, which, like Joni's, was 50 percent giggle. She and Bill cross-country skied well into their eighties; aided by Myrtle's dietary fastidiousness, they were both on no medications until their health faltered in their nineties. Bill passed away in 2012 at age one hundred. He made good on his lifelong vow to golf on his hundredth birthday (he was advised merely to putt).

One hopes that, as Joni grieved her mother's demise, the fact that Joni was now an inspiration to practitioners of a *second* medium (dance) provided succor. For any Joni die-hards who'd turned to the internet for Joni updates, her relations with her daughter appeared to be easing up a bit. Kilauren sang backup when Joni performed "Woodstock" at the close of the Luminato Festival's Joni tribute in 2013; by the end of the song, as you can see on YouTube, mother and daughter are holding hands and exchanging knowing glances. A year later, when Mitchell was asked about Kilauren and her grandchildren by *Maclean's*, she told the magazine, "We've become this funny little dysfunctional family that I'm so glad exists."

The following year saw the publication of a memoir called *Shameless: The Fight for Adoption Disclosure and the Search for My Son,* written by Marilyn Churley. Living in bohemian circumstances in Ottawa in the 1960s, eighteen-year-old Churley got pregnant and had to put the child up for adoption; but some twenty years later, as the Ontario government's New Democratic Party minister responsible for all birth, death, and adoption records, Churley reunited with her son and waged a battle to help reform adoption laws. "*Shameless* is a fantastic book," one blurb on the book's cover read. "Marilyn's story reflects a similar journey that both myself and my birth mother, Joni Mitchell, experienced and the joy we felt when we reunited. Secrecy was so entrenched that it took years just to get a piece of paper that didn't even have her name on it. Because of the changes in adoption disclosure laws, people can now get the information they need to search. Thanks Marilyn!"

The blurb is signed "Kilauren Gibb (Little Green)."

44

Posts from Kilauren Gibb's Facebook page:

- (A color photo of a winding country road going nowhere. On the side of the road is a traffic sign which is simply the letter "K.")
- (Gibb updated her profile pic with the nude portrait of Joni from the *For the Roses* gatefold.)
- (A painting of a tube of paint. The tube of paint is labeled "BONES." Emerging from the tube of Bones is a human skeleton that is pressing its left hand and knee against the tube in a struggle to break free.)
- (A photo of Kilauren standing onstage, wearing snakeskin pants and a vintage tee. She is standing, peering at us through the center of a headless tambourine.)
- (Gibb updated her profile picture with the famous black-and-white still from the 1962 film *What Ever Happened to Baby Jane?* in which Joan Crawford's wheelchair-bound character's

dead bird is being served to her by her sister—played by Bette Davis—on a platter.)

- (A photo of Gibb labeled "Birthday candle wax mishap?" The photo has her staring into the camera's lens, with several beads of wax or milk on her face. Gibb's expression is one of irritation or alarm.)

- (A photo of a field in winter on an overcast day. We see tree stumps that are covered with snow.)

- (Gibb updated her profile picture with a photo of Kurt Cobain wearing a T-shirt bearing the name of Daniel Johnston's album *Hi, How Are You: The Unfinished Album.*

- (A black-and-white photo of Gibb, who is lying on the ground barefoot, her head resting against a tall tombstone.)

- (Gibb updated her profile picture with a photo of trees on a rock promontory. The trees have been severely bent by the wind.)

- (A photo of Gibb playing an acoustic guitar.)

- (Gibb has created a Facebook "Life Event" which reads "QUIT SMOKING.")

- (A photo. We see the spine of an old-looking hardcover book, *The Little Green Book.* Directly over the book is someone's arm on which a tattoo in fancy script reads "*LITTLE GREEN*.")

- (A photo of Gibb with her daughter, Daisy.)

- (A blurry photo in which we see half of Gibb's face in the foreground. Behind her we see a sign on a dressing room door that reads, "Luminato Festival. JONI DRESSING ROOM.")
- (A post in which Gibb quotes Andy Warhol's dictum that in the future we'll all be famous for fifteen minutes.)
- (Gibb writes, "Last week to check out my art show 'LOST IN THE MUSIC' at the Cameron House.")
- (A blurry photo of a youngish woman's hand on a Yamaha piano keyboard. The hand is holding a lit, black cigarette.)
- (A YouTube video of Joni playing "Little Green.")
- (A painting that is signed "Kilauren." We see bare trees in winter; the middle of the picture is dominated by a snow-covered, downed tree trunk that forms a big upside-down U.)
- (A Christmas video with no sound. We see Gibb staring at two nutcrackers—one of whose jaws she is making gnash, gnash—that are standing on a counter next to a bottle of spirits. Gibb smiles as she takes a big slug from the bottle, makes the "Shh" gesture, and then lifts one of the nutcrackers very close to her face and makes it gnash her cheek.)
- (A YouTube video titled "Joni Mitchell finding her daughter.")
- (Gibb writes, "The greatest mystery in life is who you really are.")

45

Joni was doing a show at the Avon Theatre in Stratford, Ontario, in July 1969. As she plopped herself down on the stool in front of the theater's piano, she confessed, "I'm a little nervous playing for people. I just started to play the piano." The audience breathed a collective sigh of relief: nothing soothes quite like modesty.

Two minutes later, she fumbled on the keyboard, causing her to give a look of faint horror. "Oh dear, I'm so sorry. I'm going to start that all over again," she offered. Whereupon the audience, according to the *Toronto Star* reporter in the room, "seemed to unbend with a spontaneous sympathetic laugh." When Joni started up again and flubbed it again, she said, "Same place, isn't it? Definitely a mental block," whereupon the audience only loved her more.

"By the time she got through the spot successfully with a we're-all-in-this-together wink the third time," the reviewer reported, "they were eating out of her hand. Suddenly the show had become a very personal thing. And it stayed that way, like a fine fantastical trip she was taking each person on."

There are scores of artists who are influential and revered yet whose work doesn't necessarily spark with later generations, whereas Joni's younger fans—Taylor Swift, Harry Styles et al.—bespeak an ongoing fascination. What's going on here? What has caused Mitchell to lodge so securely in her fans' consciousness?

Mitchell's disarming candor, as evidenced by her Avon Theatre performance above, is one of the ways she has taken root in our cerebellums. But there are others.

One of the biggest clichés in music writing is the phrase "rewards repeated listening," which is applied to songs that are complex enough that after tens or even hundreds of plays, they still yield freshness. Mitchell's songs have this quality in spades. Consider, for instance, "Songs to Aging Children Come," on *Clouds*: it has been called by one music critic "perhaps the most remarkably sophisticated chord sequence in all of pop music." Also, the song's lyrics, in addition to offering a terrific rhyme of "silver" with "will their," are like a restaurant proprietor in a foreign country: hugely welcoming but slightly incomprehensible. If, at first blush, you're intrigued, then you'll want to stick around to figure out what the hell's going on.

The surprise element of humor plays a part here, too. Consider the great, aforementioned "Rainy Night House" on *Ladies of the Canyon*, a moody, if not downright eerie, song probably inspired by a trip Mitchell made with Leonard Cohen, about going to a lover's mother's house on a rainy evening. (When David Yaffe read the song's lyrics to Leonard Cohen once, Cohen said, "Oh, yeah, that's my autobiography.") The mother has vacated the house for Florida, leaving her son behind with her husband's gun; the son stays up all night and stares at the song's singer as she sleeps on the mother's small bed.

The song ticks off a lot of boxes on the depressing dirge front—its tempo is slow-verging-on-lugubrious; it is written in D minor; it includes the word "thee"; it ends with choral keening. In short, "Rainy Night House" is, outside of a women's clinic in Kandahar, possibly the *last* place in the world where you would expect to find something comic. But:

You called me beautiful
You called your mother—she was very tanned.

This throwaway "joke" works on several fronts. There's the felicity of "called"/"called," of course. We can also enjoy the surface sarcasm of "very tanned," complete with its veiled disapproval of the shallowness of spending time lolling in the sun. (The song was written before sunbathing was demonized as a cause of cancer, so we can't read SPF boosterism into the lyrics.) But better yet is the implicit assertion that mom is *so* tanned that you can hear it over the phone.

Another possible engine of Mitchell's staying power relates to the word "protective," a word that pops up from time to time in the history of the woman Leonard Cohen sometimes called "little Joni." "I seem to bring out [men's] protectiveness," Mitchell told the *Sunday Times* of London in 1983. "I could go to the wildest places and the toughest person would look out for me." She has mentioned both the toughs in the divey Saskatoon bars of her childhood and the drug-soaked musicians of Laurel Canyon as having been "protective" of her. James Taylor has mentioned Mitchell's longtime engineer Henry Lewy as being "fiercely protective" of her music.

After Joni and Kilauren had found each other and then reunited with the birth father, Brad MacMath, MacMath's wife said that MacMath felt very "protective" toward Joni. "My attitude about Joni from day one was wanting to protect her," Beverley Straight, Mitchell's former neighbor on the Sunshine Coast, told me. "She's on a mile of waterfront. If anyone got near her property, I would let her caretaker know." Mitchell's longtime friend Tony Simon told me that when he heard about the abuse Mitchell was suffering from one boyfriend, Simon told her to invite him and the boyfriend over—"he won't be leaving there on his own." Indeed, even some fans, particularly once they know Mitchell's history with polio, an unwanted pregnancy, and an aneurysm, feel like they want to keep Mitchell from encountering more of life's harsh realities.

If, as is commonly stated, our memory tends to cling to phenomena that are either novel or emotional, then a feeling of protectiveness would certainly constitute an emotion-based reason why people fixate on Mitchell. For some of us sensitive types, Mitchell has emerged as a kind of lightning rod or scapegoat for emotion: we've attached so much suffering and disquiet or joy and gratitude onto her songs over the years that we need only look at a photograph of a post-aneurysm Mitchell to get the waterworks up and humming. Novelist Zadie Smith feels this pain: "This is the effect that listening to Joni Mitchell has on me these days: uncontrollable tears," she wrote in the *New Yorker* in 2012. "An emotional overcoming, disconcertingly distant from happiness, more like joy—if joy is the recognition of an almost intolerable beauty." Smith continued, "I can't listen to Joni Mitchell in a room with other people, or on an iPod, walking the streets. Too risky. I can never guarantee that I'm going to be able to get through the song without being made transparent—to anybody and everything, to the whole world. A mortifying sense of porousness." Which sounds weirdly similar to how Mitchell has described her own emotional state when she was writing *Blue*.

Or consider the scene in Martin Scorsese's 1985 black comedy *After Hours* in which waitress Julie (Teri Garr), seeing that computer data entry worker Paul (Griffin Dunne) is having such a hellish night that he is sobbing, says, "Hang on," and then replaces the bouncy Monkees tune playing on her stereo with a Joni song. Then Garr asks, "That better? 'Chelsea Morning.' Go on. Talk to me."

That some of us have allowed Mitchell and her music to be a representation or synecdoche for sorrow would seem to beg the question, Is Joni our Jesus? Because, what, after all, is religious faith if not a glamorous misunderstanding of the most exalted kind? Not being a spiritual sort, I'm loath to extend this simile much further—however, I will point you to the August 31, 1979, issue of a New Jersey newspaper called the *Salem Sunbeam*, which contended that when Mitchell performed at Philadelphia's Academy of Music in 1974, 1975, and 1976, "the concerts always happened to take place in March and were always preceded by at least a week of the most blustery, frigid weather. But when she came to town each year uncannily the weather changed. It became warmer by maybe 20 degrees. The sun came out, birds sang, the whole bit. As soon as she left Philly after her series of concerts the weather returned to late winter bluster."

The *Sunbeam* has the information wrong—Mitchell was at the Academy of Music in January of 1974, but not at all in '75 or '76.

Yet this would seem only to make my point more strongly. For this one writer at a New Jersey newspaper, Joni isn't simply Jesus. She's Jesus *and* Mother Nature.

My own long-lasting fascination with Mitchell, I've come to decide, revolves around all of the paradoxes and dualities that she represents, besides the aforementioned facts that she doesn't like poetry, and is simultaneously both reclusive and highly social. In the same way that Mitchell's artisanal guitar chords cause us to listen more attentively in an effort to resolve them, her contradictions find me pulling out my proverbial magnifying glass. She's a musician who considers herself a painter. She's a feminist icon who regularly bad-mouths feminism. She says too much in interviews, but she rarely gives interviews. She once said, "The problem is probably that I'm the least pretentious [contemporary singer] and that's what's most pretentious about me." She wrote her timeless paean to innocence, "Woodstock," while holed up in David Geffen's suite at the Pierre Hotel; she told us to go back to the garden, but she herself mostly lives adjacent to the Bel Air Country Club's golf course. She's an avatar of ecological lament who doesn't drive an electric car, is neither a vegan nor an avowed vegetarian, and who has confessed to being a litterer. She's thought of as a soprano but she's really an alto; she's an untrained singer who, when overdubbing, could match her own vibrato note for note, time after time. She's a rebel who couldn't fully escape the puritanical juggernaut of her own mother. She's credulous enough to take her yoga instructor's suggestion to see a psychic dietitian, but ironical enough to later call it "California nonsense." She is quite pushy—her own term—about playing her new music to friends and colleagues, but she turns down a lot of publicity and performance requests. She's a polio victim who loves to dance. She's a musical visionary who doesn't read music. She's hilarious but sometimes has no sense of humor. She's tough but soft. She's patrician but raucous. She's immodest but Canadian.

It's not in my interest to try to resolve these contradictions, and it may not be possible to do so. I just want to spill them out on a tabletop and watch them sparkle in the light.

46

2010. Fallbrook, California. A local newspaper is interviewing a married couple, both musicians, who are about to put on one of the many Joni tribute concerts that get staged yearly around the world. It's easy to put on these kinds of shows, the wife says, given how many Joni fans there are around the world and how supportive of one another these fans are—"It's like belonging to AA or something."

For many creative people, there is no greater feeling of satisfaction than seeing your work, years after its completion and dissemination, reverberating in the culture. On this score, Mitchell sits pretty. There's a cookbook based on Joni songs, and a collection of crime stories each based on a Joni song. NASA's *Stardust*, the first spacecraft to bring samples from a comet to earth, was named partly after the "Woodstock" lyric; Tom Cruise's line "You complete me" in *Jerry Maguire* is a lift from "Court and Spark." The world has seen a Big Yellow Taxi cab company, a National Lampoon song parody called "You Put Me Through Hell," a Tina Fey song parody called "Paints and Brushes," "Coyote"-themed bras and briefs, a tribute band called Foni Mitchell, and a noisecore band called Moni Jitchell that the music website *The Quietus* says will "fully submerge you into a disturbed world of feral math rock riffs and doom-inducing screamo."

Mitchell's work has long been associated with the *other* kind of screamo, too—her music, particularly the songs on *Blue*, is used by psychiatrists and counselors as a form of therapy. Her tear-inducing song about unmarried Irish mothers sent to asylums, "The Magdalene Laundries," for instance, has helped counsel survivors of abuse from religious institutions in Ireland.

During the years that performance artist John Kelly appeared as Joni at Wigstock, the annual outdoor drag festival held in New York City between 1984 and 2005, Kelly's rewrite of the lyrics to "Woodstock"—originally rewritten as "I dreamed I saw the drag queens spraying hair spray in the sky / And they make all the yuppies die across our nation," but then re-rewritten to "And I dreamed I saw the drag queens and they were all dressed up like maids / And they found a cure for AIDS across every nation"—became a kind of rite or yearly commiseration for attendees who would sing along while holding lighters or candles.

A 2007 study published in the *Washington and Lee Law Review* found that Mitchell was the ninth most popular musician to be quoted in judicial opinions (Dylan and the Beatles came in at #1 and #2); "Mitchell is not a lawyer," one legal scholar wrote in 2018, "but in her chorus [of "The Circle Game"], she captures pretty well the essence of our precedent-based system of *stare decisis*."

Mitchell has been an especial source of inspiration for writers over the years. *Eats Shoots & Leaves* author Lynne Truss has written a radio play in which a Joni-like librarian sings a parody of

"A Case of You" ("Oh I could read a stack of you, David / . . . And my eyesight would never be vexed!"). A journalist has wondered whether long straight hair on professional women over forty who are "desperately trying to rechannel Joni Mitchell in her heyday" is "playing havoc with their careers"; Mitchell's ad-libbed comment "Nobody ever said to van Gogh, 'Paint another *Starry Night*, man'" has been used by an ESPN sportswriter to discuss why fans yell at foul shooters at basketball games.

Mitchell has popped up fairly frequently in novels. In Wally Lamb's 1992 *She's Come Undone*, a character who's trying to make the point that "a bunch of equals [share] the same small planet" claims she was "two people back from Joni Mitchell in the portable toilet line" at Woodstock. In *About a Boy*, Nick Hornby's 1998 novel—and its subsequent film adaptation starring Hugh Grant, Toni Collette, and Nicholas Hoult—a twelve-year-old, Marcus, who has been raised by his depressed, anti-materialistic mother has been taught to like Mitchell's music.

Some allusions to Mitchell in fiction are so subtle as to not even mention her by name. Stephen King adorns a scene in 1978's *The Stand*—when a character who is giggling happens to step on a rock and bite her tongue, and immediately stops giggling—with the aside "you turn me off, I'm a radio."

Mitchell's oeuvre has also inspired a healthy amount of nonfiction. A philosophy professor has written that "Woodstock" is a defense of Rousseau's view of human nature against Hobbes's. Writer Clifford Chase has written about whether or not Mitchell can be considered camp (Chase examines how, in *Ladies of the Canyon*'s "Conversation," Joni brings her lover apples and cheeses, plural, and not simply apples and cheese), and has owned up to mistakenly thinking that when Joni sings in *Night Ride Home*'s "Passion Play" that Magdalena, the object of much kindness from men, is "trembling" as well as "gleaming," Joni is singing about her own genitals (a friend of Chase's asks Chase, "You mean, Joni goes to the drugstore and says, 'Give me some Magdalena cream'?").

Meghan Daum's essay "The Joni Mitchell Problem" posits that Mitchell is not a confessionalist: Daum takes pains to separate the difference between artistically "letting it all hang out" and "putting yourself out there," the latter—which she thinks is Mitchell's way—being a generous rather than a needy act. "The artist who puts herself out there is not foisting a confession on her audience as much as letting it in on a secret, which she then turns into a story. That's Joni's entire modus operandi." (Daum also espouses the opinion, shared by former *New Yorker* music critic Ellen Willis and possibly by Mitchell herself, that *For the Roses,* not *Blue,* is the echt Joni album. Though melodically thornier than *Blue, For the Roses* has all the introspection of its predecessor as well as more overtures to jazz; it was made before cigarettes and vocal nodes had inhibited Mitchell's ability to sing long lines.)

One subgroup of the Joni industries is formed by those writers who are friends with Mitchell—like journalist turned filmmaker Cameron Crowe (*Say Anything, Jerry Maguire*), or Malka Marom of *Joni Mitchell: In Her Own Words* fame—and who thus parlay their friendship into decades of journalistic access. Joni's friend Daniel Levitin, the neuroscientist and author of *This Is Your Brain on Music,* has written about Mitchell in, yes, five of his books, two of them chronicling the custom-designed drawers that Mitchell had built in the kitchen of her house in British Columbia: there's one drawer for Scotch tape, one for masking tape, one for mailing and packing products, one for string and rope, one for batteries, and one for spare lightbulbs. Science!

Screenwriters love Mitchell, too. They have often employed the inter-gender tangle—biographer Michelle Mercer has called this "the litmus test" when it occurs between two lovers, and Mitchell herself has called it "the Joni Mitchell device." As Mitchell has pointed out, "Like *You've Got Mail,* where he [the Tom Hanks character] hates me and loves boats, and she [the Meg Ryan character] hates boats but loves me."

The most affecting of these tangles is probably in Lisa Cholodenko's 2010 film, *The Kids Are All Right,* wherein tough-minded obstetrician Nic (Annette Bening) grows dubious of Paul (Mark Ruffalo), the laid-back, hipster-y sperm donor of Nic and her wife Jules's (Julianne Moore) two children (Mia Wasikowska as Joni and Josh Hutcherson as Laser). So Nic asks that Paul invite her and Jules and the two kids over for dinner so that Nic can try to bond with him in the same way that the other three members of her family seem to be so ardently doing. And bond they do: when Nic finds *Blue* in Paul's record collection, she says to the group, "You don't meet too many straight guys who love Joni Mitchell." ("You like Joni?" Paul asks. Nic responds jestingly, "No, not really. We just named our daughter after her." Nic tells him that *Blue* is her favorite of Joni's records, whereupon Paul calls her "my brother from another mother.") Soon, Nic and Paul—to Nic's wife and children's growing squeamishness—are singing an a cappella "All I Want" together at the dinner table, at the conclusion of which Nic looks fondly at Paul and announces, "I like this guy!" Bonding completed. But then: seconds later, on excusing herself to use the bathroom, Nic finds some of Jules's hair in Paul's hairbrush and in Paul's bathroom drain and figures out that Jules and Paul are having an affair. Bonding derailed.

Cholodenko, who directed *The Kids Are All Right* and cowrote it with Stuart Blumberg, told me that after she and Blumberg realized they were both Mitchell fans, they resolved to try to use some of her music in the film somehow. Originally their idea was to play "All I Want" at the very end of the film, as the moms and Laser are driving away from the college where they've dropped Joni off, but "as the script and the story evolved and became clearer," Cholodenko told me, "we thought, 'Why don't we put it here, in the dinner scene, and have this be what bonds Annette Bening's character with Mark Ruffalo's character?'"

This was not Cholodenko's first allusion to Mitchell in a film: her previous movie, 2002's *Laurel Canyon,* starring Frances McDormand as a bohemian but uncompromising record producer forced to co-house with her son and his uptight girlfriend (Christian Bale and Kate Beckinsale), was inspired by Cholodenko's having listened a lot to *Ladies of the Canyon.* Asked what it is about Mitchell or her music that inspires her, Cholodenko—who had just finished cowriting the film adaptation of the Carole King musical *Beautiful,* which she is slated to direct—said, "She had her own kind of artistry that was inimitable. She's doing her own thing, to her own tunings."

Given the frustration that Joni has expressed over the years about her fans or critics abandoning her, you'd think that all of these reverberations in the culture of her work would provide balm—that maybe these tiny signposts might help erase the pain of having a mother who, after you've put out fifteen albums and played Carnegie Hall and been on the cover of *Time*, still brings up those piano lessons that you quit in childhood ("All that money we spent and you quit!" an eightysomething Myrtle told her. Joni responded, "Look, I think you got some bang for your buck").

But when Joni was given an honorary doctorate by Berklee College of Music in 2022, her comments suggested that she still felt Myrtled. "My mother in particular would be really proud of this because she wanted me to go to college," Mitchell said. "I went to art school and I quit after a year. She thinks of me as a quitter. So to see this achievement would be very impressive to her. I wish I could share it with her."

47

In October 2004, Mitchell was given an honorary degree by the music faculty of McGill University in Montreal. In a celebratory daylong symposium held to discuss Mitchell's music, audience members got a chance to see, among many other things, a tape of performance artist John Kelly performing "Woodstock" as Joni, and to hear one scholar describe Joni's work as "a sonic document of feminism."

But for many people, the highlight of the symposium was when music critic Ann Powers broke down while talking about "Little Green," the song about Kilauren on *Blue*, while Joni and Kilauren were in the audience listening to Powers's talk. "It's impossible in light of the revelation seven years ago that Mitchell had entrusted a daughter to adoption when she was twenty-one years old . . . ," a casually dressed Powers said while sitting at a long conference table onstage; in the audience, Mitchell turned to Kilauren with a look of sympathy. Kilauren, who sat with her legs crossed, played ruminatively with the necklace she was wearing, as if steeling herself.

". . . to hear the song 'Little Green,'" Powers continued, quietly waxing with emotion, "as anything but a relic of that arduous moment, an outline of the story, uh, Mitchell must have told herself, um, in order to survive the moment, the story of her child's happy ending."

Then, as Powers started reciting a line from the song, she adlibbed laughingly, "I'm gonna cry!" She touched her face with her hands and added, "I'm an adoptive mother so this is really emotional for me!" She laughed, touched her face again, and then put her clasped hands in front of her mouth.

Powers continued, "She sings . . . ," but, as her voice started to crack with emotion, she looked at Mitchell in the audience and said, "I know you're sitting there."

As Powers buried her face in her hands and sighed heavily, Mitchell, who had a microphone in front of her, said, "Awww," and then put down the water bottle she'd been holding; she looked as if she were going to stand and go comfort Powers. Instead, she remained seated but urged Powers, "Go on, go on."

Taking a breath, Powers, holding back tears, recommenced.

After Powers's speech, Mitchell spoke into the mic that had been stationed in front of her; she thanked Powers for "the beauty of her emotionality" and confessed, "I'm kind of speechless."

"I can put that on my résumé," Powers responded. "'I made Joni Mitchell speechless!'"

Interestingly, sixteen years later, when Powers, who'd gone on to become NPR Music's critic and correspondent, recounted the incident on air to her colleague Bob Boilen, the host of *All Songs Considered*, she misremembered, or slightly altered, Mitchell's response.

POWERS: I had recently become an adoptive mom to my daughter, and Joni was there. At the time, she had recently reunited with her daughter, and they were in the front row, and I started crying when I got to the part in my paper about this song. And I heard this little voice, Bob, from the front row: "You can do it. You can do it."

BOB BOILEN: Oh my God.

ANN POWERS: It was Joni.

BOB BOILEN: Oh my God.

ANN POWERS: I know. I know. I know.

BOB BOILEN: Life.

ANN POWERS: At the time I was mortified, but now I realize that was a gift.

BOB BOILEN: That is beautiful.

ANN POWERS: And now sometimes I just try to hear that voice again in my dark moments. "You can do it." That's what Joni says to all of us.

I don't bring up this alteration—from "Go on, go on" to "You can do it, you can do it"—in an attempt to zing the reliable and wonderfully talented Powers; we all constantly alter anecdotes that we tell, sometimes consciously, sometimes not, particularly when we are more than a few years away from the incident and/or nervously staring down the headlights of a large audience. (When I wrote Powers in 2023 about the alteration, she was putting the finishing touches on *Traveling*, her book about Mitchell. She wrote me, "I honestly haven't watched that YouTube clip ever, so you are revealing something to me. I guess I needed to hear 'You Can Do

It.' In a way you've served as an important fact checker." In *Traveling*, Powers writes, "At the small reception after the conference, where Joni stood looking for conversation partners while nibbling on carrots and dip, I avoided her. I surrendered my chance to make her acquaintance because I felt barren in that moment, worthless.") Rather, I lump Powers's act of sweetening with other glamorous misunderstandings like Stevie Nicks's comment about her collaborators all living in a mythic house together like Joni and CSN, or with the breathless University of New Mexico student who wrote about Mitchell in the school's newspaper in 1974, saying that "when she dies, music—as we know it—will vanish from our lives."

Apparently, Joni Mitchell is a story that we tell ourselves. And sometimes this story shifts.

The larger point here, of course, is that Mitchell's and her daughter's story has provided succor to others. In 2000, Mitchell told a radio interviewer from the CBC, "It was a healing for a lot of women. It made it—it enabled women to be able to say, 'I had a child.' You know. There were millions of women holding on to this terrible, painful secret. I mean my mother received all kinds of calls. The neighbor woman leaned over the fence and said, 'I had a child out of wedlock.' A teacher called her. 'Can you imagine?' she said. 'A teacher called me. Why is she telling me all this?' Because, you know, my mother is, like, a private person. And I got letters. Women sent me flowers. It was really kind of a beautiful and cathartic experience."

Novelist Lorrie Moore mentioned "Little Green," the song about Kilauren, in her 1994 novel *Who Will Run the Frog Hospital?*. Moore's protagonist writes that "at a cocktail party, I would watch an entire roomful of women, one by one and in bunches, begin to sing this song when it came on over the sound system. They quit conversations, touched people's arms, turned toward the corner stereo and sang in a show of memory and surprise. All the women knew the words, every last one of them, and it shocked the men."

In 2023, almost sixty years after Mitchell gave her baby up for adoption, people were still talking about it. First we learned from the published emails of Steve Jobs, the founder of Apple who died in 2011, that the song "Little Green" had reminded Jobs of his own adoption: "I cry every time I hear it."

Then, a few weeks later, writer Claire Dederer published the book *Monsters,* in which she considers how to reconcile our appreciation of the work of "problematic" artists like Roman Polanski and Miles Davis with the moral outrage that some of their actions in private life provoke. With female artists, Dederer contends, the ultimate taboo is the abandonment of their own children; here she considers Mitchell and writer Doris Lessing, who, when she moved to London from Rhodesia in 1949, took her youngest child with her, but left her older two kids with her husband. ("For a long time I felt I had done a very brave thing," Lessing would say later. "There is nothing more boring for an intelligent woman than to spend endless amounts of time with small children. I felt I wasn't the best person to bring them up.")

Despite her book's scary title, Dederer comes out pro-Joni: "I needed the model of her, the blazing comet trail of her life as an artist," she writes in *Monsters.* "I read her story, and was galvanized." Though she contends, as Chuck Mitchell seems always to have done, that Mitchell's putting her baby up for adoption was a willful act done to protect her career, Dederer finds sustenance in this act of rebellion, as well as in Mitchell's uncompromising and principled approach to her career over time: "She did what a great artist does: vigorously, aggressively protected her ability to make something vulnerable and tender . . . Joni Mitchell was an asshole on behalf of her own vulnerability."

To cast judgment on someone else's decision to put their baby up for adoption is fairly presumptuous—particularly when, as seems to be the case with Dederer, that judgment is based purely on having read Weller's *Girls Like Us* and Yaffe's *Reckless Daughter.* Casting such a judgment begs the question, Who's the real asshole here? (Maybe me, for fanning the flames.) But the fact that some people feel free to cast judgment on a highly personal aspect of Mitchell's life circles back to Mitchell's larger contribution to music. We're allowed to talk about Mitchell's music, of course, because she has put it out into the world—and given that all of the music is partly inspired by the loss of her daughter and that a tiny part of this music is *about* her daughter, it would seem to follow that we're thus allowed to talk about her daughter, too.

Such is the curse of the memoirist. When Joni decided, in making *Blue,* to start showing us her real and emotionally battered self, she opened the floodgates of our curiosity and expectation. That she was one of the first singer-songwriters to expose herself thusly only stacked the deck. "Outside of Woody Guthrie and the blues," the authors of *Faking It: The Quest for Authenticity in Popular Music* write, "there just wasn't much autobiographical song, even by the early 1960's," and autobiography in the blues was the exception rather than the rule. But the singer-songwriter movement of the 1960s and '70s changed all that by turning musicians' gaze navel-ward, a tendency that hasn't gone away ever since; in 2004 alone, we're reminded in *Faking It,* Ashlee Simpson, Usher, and Alicia Keys had #1 albums titled, respectively, *Autobiography, Confessions,* and *The Diary of Alicia Keys.*

While Dylan and Bowie developed characters or personas that helped put distance between them and their fans, Mitchell did not; she was almost always, with the possible exception of songs like "Twisted" or "Free Man in Paris," herself on every track of her albums. This took its toll. Writing an album's worth of introspective songs, like writing a memoir, presumably forces you to sit down and spend many hours summoning feelings and memories, trying to accurately capture these feelings and memories, and then deciding which of these capturings you're willing to share with the world. Given how exhausting this kind of psychic inventorying must be, maybe it makes sense that such a writer would be thin-skinned in the face of her work's reception.

Mitchell's freak-out over her fame in 1970—not to mention her irritation with critics or with people who have tried to categorize her or put her in boxes—speaks to a larger psychological point, too. In 1971, psychologists Edward Jones and Richard Nisbett conducted an experiment in which they asked subjects to rate a series of individuals—their fathers, their friends, Walter Cronkite, and themselves—in terms of traits like aggression and generosity. If the subjects wished, they could choose "depends on situation" as a rating. To a large degree, the subjects in the experiment chose "depends on situation" only for themselves, while positing more definite character traits for the other three categories of people.

While we tend to think of other people as having fixed personalities and traits, we view ourselves as inherently flexible—and not something as limited as a "folk singer" or a "confessionalist" or a "bad mother." These kinds of labels sequester; they impinge on one's sense of self, maybe even on one's freedom. And lord knows Joni Mitchell is all about her freedom—it's there in the songs, from "Cactus Tree" to "All I Want" to "River" to "Free Man in Paris" to "Hejira" to "Taming the Tiger."

Joni's friend Malka Marom asked Joni in 1974 to define freedom. "Freedom to me is the luxury of being able to follow the path of the heart," Joni said. "I think that's the only way that you maintain the magic in your life, that you keep your child alive."

48

1979. Mitchell is being interviewed by her friend Cameron Crowe in her house in Bel Air. When the conversation turns to the differences between men and women, Mitchell says, "I believe that I am male and I am female."

Though Joni has always distanced herself from feminism, which she finds "too apartheid," she is rightly perceived by many as a feminist icon. "We are living in a rock white male world and because of this," Bjork said in 2007, "Joni is being ignored while someone like Bob Dylan for instance has become a saint."

To have excelled in a male-dominated industry is no small thing. The societal conservatism leading in to the sixties certainly hadn't helped women who were trying to make a name for themselves: in 1958, when sixteen-year-old Maria Muldaur ("Midnight at the Oasis") proudly brought home her first recording contract, her mother ripped it to shreds, certain that her daughter was being led into human trafficking. Though female singer-songwriters could build a reputation and name for themselves, they struggled on the fronts of creative control and financial remuneration. The smash success of Carole King's *Tapestry* in 1971 was the exception that proved the rule. In the early sixties, chart-topping girl groups like the Ronettes and the Crystals were the pawns of mogul Phil Spector, who wrote their songs, produced the records, and raked in all the profits. Later, hugely talented female singers who broke off from their bands, like Janis Joplin and Grace Slick, went the way of Laura Nyro: lost in the shuffle, sometimes fueled by drugs.

All this said, it can seem like an act of music critic elitism when people point at Mitchell's career and crow, "There weren't many women at the time," as if crowd-pleasers like Helen Reddy and Anne Murray and Olivia Newton-John don't count. I was only ten years old when Helen Reddy's song and album "I Am Woman" came out in 1972; initially my friends and I giggled at the song's breathless swagger, but soon I found myself singing its lines about being strong (strong!) and invincible (in-VIN-cible!) when I needed to psych myself up for a daunting task, always stopping at the crescendo of "I am wuh-monnnn" lest I clobber bystanders with my proverbial pocketbook. Or what about Roberta Flack's 1973 gem "Killing Me Softly with His Song"? It would take me years to realize that Flack, in singing about a male singer who had exposed all her vulnerabilities when he sang about her, was exacting delicious revenge on him by returning the favor. But somehow, between Reddy's and Flack's songs—both inescapable to radio listeners by the mid-seventies—even a self-involved, preteen male got the distinct impression that women had been mistreated and were now storming the castle.

Sometimes feminists' appreciation of Joni is less about her ability to prosper professionally than it is about her celebration of a woman's sexual agency. In this light, it's easy to see why someone like Madonna would say that *Court and Spark* was "my coming-of-age record." In a post-Madonna, post–Alanis Morissette, post–Taylor Swift world, we take it for granted that song lyrics will raise a glass to a woman's prerogative to sleep with whomever she wants to, whenever she wants to. But in the 1960s and '70s, when the Pill was wreaking havoc with traditional, patriarchal mores, this worldview was much less common. The 1962 publication of Helen Gurley Brown's *Sex and the Single Girl* had helped foster the idea that sex outside of marriage was not dirty; soon, in a refreshing twist on various girl groups' subservient bleatings about puppy love and the leader of the pack, Dionne Warwick would be beseeching the world "Don't Make Me Over," and Lesley Gore would be announcing "You Don't Own Me"—two cris de coeur that set the world up for Aretha Franklin's devastating 1967 mic drop, "Respect." But all three of these songs, unlike the later "I Am Woman" and "Killing Me Softly," were written entirely by men.

Joni's lyrics shaded in more nuance and details here by celebrating cohabitation without marriage ("My Old Man"), love that encourages your partner's autonomy ("All I Want"), the loneliness of being without a lover ("Song for Sharon"), an acceptance of having a lover without any expectations of commitment ("Cactus Tree," "Coyote"), the heartbreak of an unwanted pregnancy ("Little Green"), the intermittent urge to procreate ("Let the Wind Carry Me")—all while beseeching, in "California," "Will you take me as I am / Strung out on another man."

Not only did Joni espouse a new freedom in her songs, but she was its exemplar as well: "It was well known in London in the early

1970s that every time she came to town, it was on the arm of a new male singing star. David Crosby, Graham Nash, James Taylor, Jackson Browne," author Angela Bowie, David's ex, has said. "In the past, it was *de rigeur* that male rock stars would have a series of girls on their arms. Never before had a female rock star had multiple affairs so publicly, like there was nothing even remotely questionable about such behavior. It was like Joni was saying, 'If no one thinks twice about the guys behaving like this, then why shouldn't I behave the same way?'"

For women of Mitchell's generation who were fed the fiction that having a family and a career was an either/or equation, Mitchell's commitment to her art makes her a powerful symbol of the lives these women might have led, or dreamed about living, or once led but had to sacrifice. One place where we see this acutely is on TV shows that reference Mitchell—on *This Is Us,* we learn that Rebecca Pearson (Mandy Moore) was once an aspiring musician who loved Joni's music, an enthusiasm that prompts Pearson to look for Joni's house in Laurel Canyon; on *The Wonder Years,* when young Kevin Arnold (Fred Savage) doesn't heed his mother's warnings about tackle football and Kevin gets hurt, the mother (Alley Mills) lets him lick his wounds alone, and then we cut to home movies of Mom playing with toddler Kevin while "The Circle Game" plays; on *Six Feet Under* Claire (Lauren Ambrose) witnesses an alternate version of the mother she often argues with when she hears her mother (Frances Conroy) singing along to "Woodstock."

Let's hope that the world's attitudes about whether or not women raise families or have careers or do both or do neither are, like the world's attitudes about gender identification and sexual orientation, gradually growing wider. That Mitchell has seen herself, since 1979, at least, as both male and female seems wonderfully progressive. What's more, even that most unlikely person, her quasi-nemesis Bob Dylan, agrees with her. "She's not really a woman," he once said. "Joni's kind of like a man."

49

Los Angeles. 1976. A Halloween party at the home of Betsy and Peter Asher, the couple from the previous "Her Town Too" anecdote. Peter Asher is the producer and manager who signed James Taylor for his debut at Apple, the Beatles' label, before becoming his manager (as well as Linda Ronstadt's, and, briefly, Joni's).

JD Souther, the singer-songwriter who would write many of the Eagles' biggest hits ("Best of My Love," "Heartache Tonight," "New Kid in Town")—and who'd had, or was having, a fling with Joni—walked into the gathering, whereupon the Ashers introduced him to a thin Black dude named Art. Art, who didn't say much, was dressed in a suit jacket, vest, and fedora, all in a robin's egg blue; his face was appointed with big sunglasses and a mustache. Souther took him to be a pimp. The Ashers, Souther, Art, and the guitarist Danny Kortchmar stood and chatted for about ten minutes, after which the mostly silent Art casually removed his hat. Then Art removed his wig. And then Souther realized that Art—full name Art Nouveau—was Joni in blackface.

It is a marker of the reverence and admiration that Joni has elicited from the world as a musician that so few people have taken her to task for having done blackface. Joni long maintained that she identified with Black men so acutely that the first line of her unfinished memoir, should she ever write one, would be "I was the only Black man at the party." ("Yes, that was going to be the first line," Amy Scholder, the ghostwriter who worked on Mitchell's aborted autobiography in a pre–Black Lives Matter 1997, told me, rolling her eyeballs slightly. "Sigh.")

Joni's embrace of blackface started when a dentist who was capping her teeth told her, "Oh, you've got the worst bite I've ever seen. You have teeth like a Negro male." This casually racist comment was still percolating in Joni's head when, a short while thereafter, she found herself walking down Hollywood Boulevard while in search of a costume for the Ashers' Halloween party, and beheld a Black gentleman bopping down the boulevard. Taking in Joni's pink stilettos and her summery jersey dress, the man said to Joni, "Mmm, mmm, mmm, looking good, sister, looking good." Joni smiled at him and followed him down the sidewalk, trying, in her heels, to imitate his bop. The man smiled at Joni's efforts, but kept on walking.

Joni decided to go to the party dressed up as the man. She went to a wig shop and bought an Afro, and then gradually accumulated other elements of her costume, including Egyptian-brown Max Factor pancake. "I was amazed when I put on the costume and saw the transformation," Joni told *Musikexpress* years later. "For several days it was like Black Like Me. I was able to feel what it was like, I received prejudice in restaurants. It was a very strange and interesting experience."

But Joni's effort to pass off her tone-deaf act as a feat of Nellie Bly–type undercover journalism, if that's what the *Musikexpress* comment was, feels deluded. More likely, Art Nouveau, like Joni's disinclination to open a concert with a familiar hit, or like her impulse to sing a breakup song to someone at a party two times in a row, is another example of how someone who feels things too intensely is, ironically, someone who can't always read a room. (And, similarly, who is in the habit of injecting conversations with references to, say, "Leslie," without having previously mentioned or identified who this Leslie is.) This occasional inability to read a room was prominent when Joni played for a mostly Black audience at a prison as part of Rolling Thunder. She was met with catcalls and jeers shortly into her set and lost her composure. "We came here to give you love," Joni lectured the inmates. "If you can't handle it, that's your problem." Joan Baez has said, "I was just praying she'd get off the stage." Another musician on the tour, Rob Stoner, later commented, "Talk about wrong moves—that warmed-over sixties shit was the worst thing she could have said to them. . . . I mean, you could see guys giving each other looks that said, 'Throw that bitch out here and we'll teach her a thing or two about *clouds*!'"

While Joni would probably like us to view her embrace of blackface as an extension of her sympathy for Native Americans and other disenfranchised people—she has made the point that someone at the Ashers' party asked Art if he was sure he was at the right party—it's tempting to instead lump Art Nouveau in with Joni's painting of a naked Don Alias: he's a provocation. After the Ashers' party, Joni decided to bring the costume to the photo shoot for the cover of *Don Juan's Reckless Daughter*, which was being shot by a photographer whom she found to be bossy and irritating. "I brought it in a bag," Joni has said. "I could do the makeup in about four minutes, and then I step out of the curtain. I just stood there till they noticed me. I walked really showily, going, *Heh heh heh.* It was a great revenge. That was all to get his ass. To freak him out. I had to keep him on the defensive."

Had Joni consigned Art Nouveau to the recesses of her closet after his first two forays, or had she apologized for trotting him out in the first place, we wouldn't have to be having this conversation. But she trotted him out again—he not only takes up half the cover of *Don Juan's Reckless Daughter* (the album's title comes out of his mouth in a speech bubble), but Joni wrote a ten-minute segment about him (and then played him) for the 1982 anthology movie *Love.* Then in 1988 she played a Black soldier in the video for "The Beat of Black Wings." As late as 2015, when she was interviewed by *New York* magazine, she was still under her delusion: "When I see a black man sitting," she said, "I have a tendency to nod like I'm a brother."

Joni scored a lot of cool points, to be sure, when Charles Mingus, who was Black and an irascible and outspoken critic of racism who'd written an inflammatory composition called "Fables of Faubus," not only praised Joni for having the nerve to appear as Art Nouveau on the cover of *Don Juan's Reckless Daughter,* but then chose Joni shortly before his death to record his last music, even allowing her to put words to his classic instrumental "Goodbye Pork Pie Hat." (Mingus was running out of money and probably wanted Joni's popularity, as Joni has put it, to give him a bigger funeral. But still.) Other defenders of Joni's embrace of blackface point to the various Black musicians Joni has hired and collaborated with over the years, including singer Chaka Khan, who is a former member of the Black Panther Party. Art Nouveau is not a Stepin Fetchit character crudely drawn on Joni's face with burnt cork, these defenders say, but, rather, an incarnation. Should we chide Elvis Presley and Mick Jagger for appropriating Blackness in their performance style? Should we cancel Patti Smith and Lenny Kaye for writing "Rock N Roll [N Word]" or John Lennon and Yoko Ono for "Woman is the [N Word] of the World"?

In 2023, when I asked Mitchell's collaborator Brian Blade, the fifty-two-year-old Black drummer who played on *Taming the Tiger* and *Shine* and various gigs, whether he cared that Mitchell had done blackface, he exploded with a burst of unhinged laughter and said, "Oh, you mean Art Nouveau? I don't have a problem with it at all—and God bless anyone who does, you know? If she says something like, 'I'm the only black man at the party,' I just laugh because she's been pushed to the fringe herself, she's been left out. We all can't know the true struggles of every other person."

A month later, when I interviewed Jeremy Dutcher, a thirty-two-year-old, two-spirit, operatic tenor who is a Wolastoqiyik (Maliseet) member of the Tobique First Nation and who sang one of his own compositions at Joni's seventy-fifth birthday celebration at the Music Center in Los Angeles, he brought up Art Nouveau without my prompting. Dutcher told me that, at the Music Center, after he'd performed his song in his native Wolastoq language (he sang "a chief song—it's for someone you really admire, who has done good work for the people"), he literally got down on bended knee to express his gratitude to Mitchell for the honesty in her songs, but that "I didn't take that chance to bring up, 'Hey you really shouldn't have done blackface on your album cover.'"

"Does it bother you that she did it?" I asked.

"I'm certainly not gonna give her a stamp of approval on that one. But this is not my fight to have—I'm not Black. I know as an Indigenous person that whenever someone, say, dons our regalia when it hasn't been offered to them, it gets super nuanced and complicated. It's not something I would do in my practice, let's say that."

For some listeners, Mitchell's nods to Black culture have a trace of Magic Negro solipsism to them; as Janet Maslin wrote in her review of *Don Juan's Reckless Daughter*, "there seems to be the notion that Blacks and Third World people have more rhythm, more fun and a secret, mischievous viewpoint that the author, dressed as a Black man in one of the photos on the front jacket, presumes to share."

The rare criticism of Art Nouveau—Maslin has been joined by author Francine Prose in her *New York Times Book Review* of Yaffe's *Reckless Daughter*; the queer, alt-country group Kym Register + Meltdown Rodeo; and the singing group Sweet Honey in the Rock, who performed "The Circle Game" at the 2000 tribute to Mitchell at the Hammerstein Ballroom—has not been substantial enough for Mitchell to apologize or desist (though, when *Don Juan's Reckless Daughter* was remastered in 2024, the album cover's redesign did not include Nouveau).

At a 2014 screening of *The Fiddle and the Drum*, the ballet set to Mitchell's music, a young Black man in the audience stood up during the Q&A and said, "I grew up a Black kid in the sixties in an all-white neighborhood and all white schools. Your music was a big part of me getting through that." To which Mitchell responded,

"I grew up a woman in a man's world, it's kinda the same thing." Whether such a response is a presumptuous act of false equivalency, or a neutral or even admirable act of candor and empathy, depends on your worldview. Discuss.

For some Mitchell fans, the only good thing to have come out of the Art Nouveau narrative is "How Black Is Joni Mitchell," a tender and hilarious poem that the beloved music critic Greg Tate, who was Black and wrote for the *Village Voice*, composed about Mitchell for an honorary ceremony at McGill University in 2004. The poem praises Joni for being, among other things, "So Black that we need to consider her the gnostic Mary Magdalene of Afro-bohemia's post-soul culture," and "So Black that even as a rock star she gets read as an outsider artist."

It's easy to file Art Nouveau into a slightly battered file labeled "The Past"—after all, it's been almost fifty years since the world first beheld the cover of *Don Juan's Reckless Daughter*. But I thought about him in the summer of 2022, when Joni made her surprise appearance at the Newport Folk Festival.

Sitting on her gilded, Louis XIV–style throne on the Newport stage, wielding her cane like a tribal staff, exuding buckets of regality and warmth—*Pitchfork* would liken her voice to "a piece of high-pile cotton velvet warmed in the daylight"—Mitchell in her beret and sunglasses could have easily passed for a beloved blues singer. She's never looked so Black.

50

1998. Sitting outside at a restaurant in the Brentwood neighborhood of Los Angeles, Mitchell told a reporter from *Mojo* that, though she has always loved songs and stories, she has never much liked poetry. "Poetry was kind of like shelling sunflower seeds with your fingers—it just was too much work for too little return, a lot of times," Mitchell said. "I like things more plainspeak."

The greatest surprise in re Joni Mitchell—besides the fact that she has often worked with her exes long after they've broken up—is that she, one of the all-time-great lyricists, a wordsmith who comes up with lines like "Newsreels rattle the Nazi dread," does not like verse. Yes, she has set both Rudyard Kipling's "If—" and William Butler Yeats's "The Second Coming" to music ("I disagreed with a couple of [Yeats's] ideas," she said in 1997. "I put in some qualifications, and I rewrote a part that I thought he hadn't really finished"). But in the main, her response to verse is a resounding meh. When asked in the past about this disinterest, she has trotted out the Nietzsche quote about poets, "They muddy the water, to make it seem deep."

But Mitchell's oversight is even more intriguing given that the things she says in conversation—particularly when she talks about music—often sound like poetry. As His Bobness once said, "To be a poet does not necessarily mean that you have to write words on paper."

Every line of the following poem is something Joni has said about her or other people's music, either in interviews or to collaborators during recording sessions.

I want us to be all woven together like colored threads into
a tapestry.
Like inside my head there's a whole boardinghouse full of
people
Like a pack of wolves stomping around—nervously
Like Marlon Brando
Like a jazz donkey
Like a bra
Like Picasso's portrait of Gertrude Stein: he put his own
eyes in it
She said, "It doesn't look like me," and he said, "It will."

The keyboards should break like a wave.
That intimidates some people:
"It's getting too Bergman, Joan."

It's a very tricky business to laminate a band onto my
chunk-a chunk-a.
I wanted the bass to be less supportive and more of a show-
off.

You can play any note you want on top. Why can't you play any note you want on bottom?
I wanted them to stop putting dark polka dots all over the bottom
I craved patterns on the bottom
But the bass and drums buddied up and polka-dotted along the bottom, ignoring what my voice was doing.
Deaf ears.
Nothing.
Constant coitus interruptus.
You have to understand that in jazz circles at the time, the girl singer was called "the chirp."

51

If, apart from the joy Joni has experienced spending time with her grandchildren, the Joni/Kilauren narrative hasn't yielded the kind of fairy-tale ending that some Joni fans might crave, a parallel story has. In 2019, researchers at Mount Rainier in Washington State made the rare sighting of a wolverine; wolverines became locally extinct in the state in the 1920s partly because of unregulated trapping, shooting, and poisoning. Because this particular wolverine was found in the Paradise section of Mount Rainier, the researchers named her Joni (think "Big Yellow Taxi"). In 2020, when Joni gave birth to two male kits—she sometimes visits with a male of her species whom researchers call Van—Joni and her kits became the first wolverine family in the park in more than one hundred years. In 2021, Joni gave birth to a male and a female kit.

By July 2023, Joni had mothered nine children in total. It's uncommon for wolverines to rear kits three years in a row, so Joni's doing it for four was a cause for celebration. Wolverines are born in the spring; their birth reflects the fact that their mother was able to find enough food the previous winter. So a wolverine who reproduces four years in a row is a wolverine who shows the world that her habitat is thriving.

"Joni is a mama again, and this time it's TRIPLETS!" the Cascade Carnivore Project wrote in a Facebook post in 2023. "Joni, a wolverine mama living in and around Mount Rainier National Park, has birthed kits for the fourth year in a row, and this year it's triplets!" The alternative Seattle weekly *The Stranger* weighed in, "You are an inspiration to us all, Joni. You are life as what it always strives to be: a force of nature."

To a world increasingly subject to the grueling dynamic of Man v. Nature, Joni the wolverine's fecundity was a cause for hope. Species may go extinct, the world's temperature may keep rising, Mother Nature's reign may increasingly be unseated by human appetites.

But somewhere, high on a mountaintop in the Northwest, a wolverine is replicating.

52

Imagine going to a concert being held on the lip of the Grand Canyon at sunset; then add to this fantasy the idea that the performer you're listening to—who hasn't given a ticketed, live performance in more than two decades—has recently made a startling medical breakthrough.

That's how I'd describe the spectacular concert that Joni and Brandi Carlile and others gave in June 2023 at Washington State's outdoor amphitheater The Gorge.

The Gorge is located on a bluff overlooking the majestic Columbia River about three hours east of Seattle; it takes only one glance at the sky there to be reminded of the Joni lyric

These are the clouds of Michelangelo
Muscular with gods and sungold.

While I waited in a long line to be admitted to the concert, the crowd buzzed with theories as to which musical luminaries might be joining Joni and Brandi Carlile onstage. "James Taylor is in Las Vegas now, so . . . ," a woman who'd traveled from Santa Cruz told me. Another person correctly guessed that Wendy & Lisa, the duo who had once backed up Prince and who had performed the evening before at The Gorge, would be in attendance; she added that it would be "really cool" if Prince joined them from the afterlife via hologram.

The concert was styled as a Joni Jam, complete with a semicircle of couches and comfy chairs and a coffee table bearing framed photographs of pets. Joni, who'd only recently mastered standing up on her own, ambled on stage without assistance but with a lot of deliberation, though her assistant Marcy and her physical therapist Sauchuen lurked on either side of her; Joni sat center stage for the entirety of the concert, while other performers (Carlile, Annie Lennox, Sarah McLachlan, Celisse, Marcus Mumford et al.) shifted chairs, orbiting around her. Joni's voice sounded even better than it had the previous year at Newport, and the fact that she opened with a hit ("Big Yellow Taxi") and then served up a lot of fan favorites ("Raised on Robbery," "A Case of You," "The Circle Game") betokened a performer who, at last, was thinking about what an audience wants rather than what she wants to play. She found lots of interesting new melodic variations to her songs. She thrilled to the crowd's enthusiasm. She drank Pinot Grigio out of a brown Yeti.

When Joni and Brandi sang "Shine," a late-career Joni song, many of us in the audience held our illuminated cellphones up in the air, swaying them in time to the music; Joni looked out at the wash of twinkly lights and told us, "You look like a fallen constellation." Then Joni asked Brandi, "Where did they get all the lights from?"

"Those are cellphones."

"Those are cellphones?" asked Joni, who doesn't use one except to take photos with. "Oh, wow."

This was one of a handful of allusions to aging during the show; at one point Joni would yell "Viva la old age!" and she'd end the show with a cover of the standard "Young at Heart."

I don't know why group singing felt so potent to me, but during more than one of the sing-alongs ("Big Yellow Taxi," "Why Do Fools Fall in Love," "Love Potion No. 9"), I was suffused with the kind of deep-seated relief and completion that I'd normally only get from staring at a campfire or a Zamboni. Some primal urge within me was being sated, but this time without the distraction of woodsmoke or hockey parents. For one of the very few times in my life, crying in public didn't feel like bleeding in public.

Even a sing-along of the one Joni song that I thought I never needed to hear again, "The Circle Game," got the better of me.

But my most emotional moment came during "A Case of You." I completely and entirely lost it when Joni got to the line about how, even after drinking an entire case of "you," she would still be on her feet.

Because she wasn't.

Six days later, I headed off to Saskatoon to meet Joni's friend since third grade, Sharolyn Dickson. Prior to having Sharolyn drive me around Saskatoon to show me all of her and Joni's childhood haunts, she and I had met for lunch at the restaurant located on the former site of the Louis Riel, the club where Joni had her first professional singing engagement. The restaurant is called Calories, which is kind of like calling a brand of cigarettes Cancer.

Though the extent of my relationship with the wonderfully polite and self-deprecating Sharolyn was, at this point, a thirty-minute phone interview and twelve emails, I felt so immediately at ease with her that I told her about sobbing when Joni sang "A Case of You." I sensed that Sharolyn's response to this confession was slightly conflicted: as a friend of Joni's, she'd invested a lot of hope in Joni's rehabilitation, and the fact that Joni hadn't been able to be on her feet during the show was slightly off-message for Sharolyn. She didn't say anything, but it was there. She started telling me about how Joni's physical therapist was having Joni swim and play Ping-Pong with a couch behind her in case she falls. Then: "Her living room has a mezzanine floor up above. So he rigged up some kind of cords, bungee cords, that hang from above and hook onto her. They put music on, and she dances."

Even if I hadn't spent the previous year researching Joni, this image would have haunted me. But, given my time in the stacks, all I could think about was the time Myrtle walked young Joni around town on a leash—and how, when they passed a Woolworths and Joni started dancing to music coming from the store, Myrtle tugged on the leash. Or how producer Paul Rothchild once taped Joni's restless feet to a recording studio's floor. The next time I heard "Free Man in Paris," the line about feeling "unfettered and alive" would definitely hit differently.

About ninety minutes later, Sharolyn had driven me all around the neighborhood, showing me the Joni sites—Joni's childhood home on Hanover Avenue, the pool where Sharolyn

mind, and so it flows freely through time on that level. And I don't really have any optimism for the future, for us getting out of this mess, but while there are still pockets of greenery and birds flitting by, you know, I just try to make the best of what is left. For a long time, in my twenties especially, I would look at nature in its voluptuousness and feel sad, you know, like, 'It's going! It's disappearing!'"

She added, "Now I can look at the smallest piece and enjoy it for what it is."

AUTHOR'S NOTE

HUSBAND (*With a look of confusion or mild distaste*): What is this we're listening to?
WIFE: Joni Mitchell.
HUSBAND: I can't believe you still listen to Joni Mitchell.
WIFE: I love her. And true love lasts a lifetime. Joni Mitchell is the woman who taught your cold English wife how to feel.
HUSBAND: Did she? Oh, that's good. I must write to her sometime and say thanks.

It's entirely possible that the above dialogue, held by characters portrayed by Alan Rickman and Emma Thompson in Richard Curtis's 2003 movie *Love Actually*, has been conducted in thousands of households across the globe. The scene distills the prevailing common wisdom, or should we say cliché, about our favorite singer-songwriter: that Joni Mitchell, the bard of heartbreak and longing, taught the world how to feel. That, through her oversharing and self-deprecation, Mitchell, particularly on 1971's *Blue*, made it okay for us to admit that we're sometimes selfish and sad, that love relationships sometimes make us feel "strung out," and that, when our partner hurts us, our inclination is to hurt him, too.

While this interpretation has the bold outlines of truth, it can also feel generalized and glib—as if, had Mitchell not made her early work, a sector of the population would have resorted to poking each other in the eye with sharp sticks. Mitchell, to be sure, is wildly successful at defining how people's wheels spin in the sand when they're caught between ambition and long-lasting love—and also how, once we find love, it sometimes floods us with ambivalence. But isn't this a victory of naming rather than a victory of inspiration, let alone creation?

In my own experience, the more accurate reading of Mitchell's legacy would be: Joni Mitchell taught me what to expect from an amorous relationship. My father died on a Saturday in the spring of 1978, when I was sixteen and enrolled in a boarding school in northwestern Connecticut. Having heard from friends the previous summer that *Blue* was sad and beautiful, I had bought the album prior to moving away from home; now, in my mourning, I put the record on my turntable, lifted my record player's tone arm so that the music would play on repeat, and then holed up in my dorm room to grieve. The next morning, when I realized slightly embarrassedly that the record had played through the night, I flipped it over and started playing Side B.

My *Blue* weekend would serve as a template for how I would respond to emotional pain for the rest of my life: I like to listen to music that is even sadder than I am, because it provides a sense of scale. But as *Blue*'s lyrics started to colonize my brain over the years—I had already started playing guitar in high school, and would soon buy a dulcimer to learn "A Case of You"—they did something even more telltale. The lyrics created expectations about what romance might look like. For a closeted homosexual whose relationship with the topic was entirely notional, this was huge; no wonder my efforts to stop hearing the lyric "We don't need no piece of paper / From the city hall" were like trying to wash Crisco off my hands. Thrillingly, *Blue* made romance sound like a whirlwind—you'd simultaneously love and hate your partner, and you'd advertise this fact in song; he'd do a goat dance and then he'd steal your camera; you'd end up with beach tar on your feet; he'd tell you pretty lies, only pretty lies; and once you'd broken up with him, you'd spend a certain amount of time in the bar. "A Case of You" put it all too succinctly: I should be prepared, among all things, to bleed.

As much as Mitchell's lyrics were a seedbed for contemplating what a relationship might look like, they were also a way to warn myself of how difficult it would be to find and start that relationship ("I am on a lonely road and I am traveling"). We're told that early man drew pictures on cave walls of the beasts that he hoped to slaughter—but how do we know that he didn't also draw these pictures to metaphorically defang these beasts? It wasn't as if, while I continued to listen to Mitchell through college in the early eighties, I needed a reason to practice celibacy—the difficulty of finding a suitable dude pre-internet, not to mention during the rise of AIDS, was taking care of that all too well. But a bit of dampening pragmatism was probably a healthy thing for someone who was overidentifying with song lyrics and who'd once, in the privacy of his bedroom, stealthily kissed the album cover of James Taylor's *Sweet Baby James*. If I was *prepared* to bleed, then maybe I wouldn't bleed *out*? Then, I figured, if I could keep my wits about me, maybe I'd finally understand what Joni means when she sings "I love you when I forget about me." Because, to a young person trying to forge his identity, such a sentiment was all but meaningless.

I look back on all this emotional trauma from the vantage point of my twenty-year-long relationship with my boyfriend, Greg. (On our second date, after music sophisticate Greg had expressed admiration for several musicians I was entirely unfamiliar with, I had searchingly asked "And how do you feel about Joni Mitchell?" and was met with a reassuring "Everybody loves Joni.") I'd like to think that, had Miss Mitchell never graced the planet, I would have found some other songster or writer under whose aegis I could have engaged in the formative process of overthinking romance. But the fact is, I didn't.

A lot of fandom is, at its base, essentially narcissistic, revealing more about the fan than his lodestar. But what if the object of your veneration is herself a symbol of self-reflection and solipsism? Then the experience of fandom is only heightened. The early Joni records should come with a warning sticker: "Listening to Joni Mitchell can lead to talking about yourself in the third person." Furthermore, what if, forty-five years after your father's death, while you are in the last throes of writing a book about Mitchell, your ninety-five-year-old mother dies, causing you to burrow once more under the comforting enclosure of Mitchell's sonic security blanket? And what if this burrowing, just as it did four and a half decades earlier, helps you to slowly transition from the egoistic storm that is grief to the brittle but more sociable flatline that is post-grief? Then you can only conclude, counterintuitively, "Joni Mitchell has once again helped me to forget about me."

Which brings me to why I wrote this book. Given the totemic role of *Blue*'s naked emotionalism in so many of our lives, and given the fact that young Mitchell—blond, beatific, extraordinarily sensitive—was so easily "typed" both by the media and fans, she has often been perceived as an emotionally fragile hippie goddess, the kind of person who might see a pigeon and earnestly conclude, "Oh, wow. A dove."

But she is so much more.

SOURCES

This book was loosely inspired by Craig Brown's 2017 book, *99 Glimpses of Princess Margaret.* Some of its content comes from the periodicals mentioned in the text, as well as from the following.

1.

AUTHOR INTERVIEWS: Joellen Lapidus. ARTICLES: Rick Pope, "Joni Shows Mystique," *Daily Illini,* January 22, 1974. Alex Frank, "Joni Mitchell on Love, Her New Box Set, and Music Today," *Vogue,* December 2014. Ron Rosenbaum, "The Best Joni Mitchell Song Ever," *Slate,* December 14, 2007. Brittany Spanos, "Unpacking the Clues and Conspiracy Theories Swirling Around Harry Styles' New Album," *Rolling Stone,* March 31, 2022. "Joni Mitchell: 15 Great Artists Influenced by the 'Blue' Singer," *Rolling Stone,* June 22, 2016. Ken Tucker, "Impresarios Will Find It Tough to Top Megabucks 'Live Aid' Rock," *Chicago Tribune,* June 30, 1985. OTHER: CBC-AM interview of Elliot Roberts, February 3, 1974. Mitchell's onstage patter from her appearance at the Troubadour in November 1972.

2.

VIDEOS: The video "Joni Mitchell—Lifetime Acheivement [*sic*] Award" on YouTube, March 21, 2014. The Library of Congress's video "A Conversation with Joni Mitchell" posted on YouTube March 15, 2023. "Reckless Daughter: A Portrait of Joni Mitchell," an August 22, 2019, video of a David Yaffe lecture that Case Western University put on YouTube. OTHER: Ann Crews Melton's essay "Lady of the Canyon, the Prairie, and the Sky" in the *Playbill* for Lincoln Center's American Songbook series, February 20, 2014.

3.

AUTHOR INTERVIEWS: Charlie Clark, Sharolyn Dickson, Vicki Gabereau, Joellen Lapidus, Roger McGuinn, Tony Simon, Jimmy Webb, Sheila Weller, David Yaffe. ARTICLES: Anne Bayin, "Joni & Me," *Elm Street*, November 2000. Lee Hedgepeth, "How an Alabama Winn-Dixie Changed Joni Mitchell," CBS42.com, August 10, 2022. Joe Jackson, "The Second Coming of Joni Mitchell," *Hot Press*, March 30, 2000. Steven Rosen, "Joni in Person," *Sounds*, December 9, 1972. Ingrid Sischy, "A Major Cool Cat," *Interview*, May 2000. Giles Smith, "Joni Mitchell," *Independent* (UK), October 29, 1994. Timothy White, "Joni Mitchell—A Portrait of the Artist," *Billboard*, December 9, 1995. Dave Wilson, "An Interview with Joni Mitchell," *Broadside*, February 14, 1968. David Wild, "Morrissey Interviews Joni Mitchell: Melancholy Meets the Infinite Sadness," *Rolling Stone*, March 6, 1997. Hilde Staalesen Lilleøren, "She Was Told She Was Samí," *Bergens Tidende*, July 22, 2009. BOOKS: Sheila Weller, *Girls Like Us: Carole King, Joni Mitchell, Carly Simon—and the Journey of a Generation*. Karen O'Brien, *Joni Mitchell: Shadows and Light*. Malka Marom, *Joni Mitchell: In Her Own Words*. OTHER: Mitchell's liner notes to *Archives—Volume Two: The Reprise Years (1968–1971)*. Mitchell's appearance on *Tavis Smiley*, PBS, November 9, 2007.

4.

See citations within chapter.

5.

ARTICLES: Vic Garbarini, "Joni Mitchell Is a Nervy Broad," *Musician*, January 1983. Leonard Feather, "Joni Mitchell Makes Mingus Sing," *Downbeat*, September 6, 1979. OTHER: Mitchell's November 15, 2007, appearance on PBS's *Charlie Rose*.

6.

AUTHOR INTERVIEWS: Sharolyn Dickson, Tony Simon. ARTICLES: Deirdre Kelly, "I Sing My Sorrow and I Paint My Joy," Toronto *Globe and*

Mail, June 8, 2000. Michael Small, "She's Looked at Life from Up and Down, So Now Joni Mitchell Has New Ways to Write About 'Both Sides Now,'" *People*, December 16, 1985. BOOKS: Katherine Monk, *Joni: The Creative Odyssey of Joni Mitchell*. Larry "Ratso" Sloman, *On the Road with Bob Dylan*.

7.

AUTHOR INTERVIEWS: Roger McGuinn, Chris O'Dell, Larry "Ratso" Sloman, David Yaffe. ARTICLES: Peter Watts, "Inside Bob Dylan's Rolling Thunder Revue: 'A floating ship of crazies!,'" *Uncut*, May 11, 2021. Cameron Crowe, "The *Rolling Stone* Interview: Joni Mitchell," *Rolling Stone*, July 26, 1979. Brantley Bardin, "Joni Mitchell," *Details*, July 1996. Gordy Bowman, "The Rolling Thunder Revue," *Ann Arbor Sun*, December 17, 1975. BOOKS: Robert Shelton, *No Direction Home: The Life and Music of Bob Dylan*. Joan Baez, *And a Voice to Sing With*. Sam Shepard, *The Rolling Thunder Logbook*. Sloman, *On the Road with Bob Dylan*. Joe Hagan, *Sticky Fingers: The Life and Times of Jann Wenner and Rolling Stone Magazine*. Weller, *Girls Like Us*. Robert Greenfield, *True West: Sam Shepard's Life, Work and Times*. Chris O'Dell, *Miss O'Dell: Hard Days and Long Nights with the Beatles, the Stones, Bob Dylan and Eric Clapton*. David Yaffe, *Reckless Daughter: A Portrait of Joni Mitchell*. OTHER: "Ronee Blakley discusses Dylan and Baez on Rolling Thunder Tour," a 1978 interview with Patrick Carr, on YouTube.

8.

AUTHOR INTERVIEWS: Rosanna Arquette, Tony Simon, Beverley Straight. ARTICLES: Sean O'Hagan, "Idol Talk," *New Musical Express*, June 4, 1988. Neil Strauss, "The Hissing of a Living Legend," *New York Times*, October 4, 1998. BOOKS: Michelle Mercer, *Will You Take Me as I Am: Joni Mitchell's* Blue *Period*.

9.

ARTICLES: John Mackie, "On war, peace, memories and dance," CanWest News Service, January 15, 2010. BOOKS: Marom, *Joni Mitchell: In Her Own*

Words. OTHER: "Teacher Handbook," New Jersey Department of Transportation (www.state.nj.us/transportation/works/njchoices/pdf/education.pdf).

10.

AUTHOR INTERVIEWS: Brian Blade, Nathan Joseph, David Yaffe. AUTHOR CORRESPONDENCE: Liz O'Brien. ARTICLES: Steve Pond, "Wild Things Run Fast: Eighty miles of bad road for two teaspoons of paint and other adventures in the sensitive lane," *Rolling Stone*, November 25, 1982. Crowe, *Rolling Stone*. Jenny Gabruch, "Mitchell Art Has Prairie Roots," *Saskatoon Star Phoenix*, July 1, 2000. Stewart Brand, "The Education of Joni Mitchell," *Co-Evolution Quarterly*, June 1976. Guy D. Garcia, "The State of Her Art: Joni Mitchell," *Interview*, August 1983. Leonard Feather, "Joni Mitchell Makes Mingus Sing," *Downbeat*, September 6, 1979. Barbara Schultz, "Classic Tracks: Los Angeles Edition," *Mix*, October 1, 2014. Daniel Levitin, "Joni Mitchell: I Know What I Want and I'm Not Afraid to Stand Up for It," *New Statesman*, December 9, 2020. John Mackie, interview with Mitchell, *Vancouver Sun*, January 15, 2010. O'Hagan, *New Musical Express*. BOOKS: Yaffe, *Reckless Daughter*. Monk, *Joni*. Herbie Hancock, with Lisa Dickey, *Possibilities*. Michelle Mercer, *Footprints: The Life and Work of Wayne Shorter*. OTHER: Wikipedia entry for O'Keeffe's *Black Iris* painting. Mitchell's liner notes to *Love Has Many Faces: A Quartet, A Ballet, Waiting to Be Danced*, Rhino, 2014. From a February 9, 2008, interview with Herbie Hancock on Australia's ABC RadioNational. Michael Buday's interview of Mitchell in the short film *Life of a Recording*, Grammy Museum, 2008.

11.

AUTHOR CORRESPONDENCE: Beth McDonald. ARTICLES: Bill Flanagan, "Lady of the Canyon," *Vanity Fair*, June 1997. Dyana Williams, "Chaka Khan," *Hits*, February 2023. Hilton Als, "Birthday Suite," *New Yorker*, December 11, 1995. Abby Wilson, "Q&A: Kazuo Ishiguro on Joni Mitchell, 'War and Peace' and the future of storytelling," *Washington Square News*, October 4, 2022. "Kazuo Ishiguro: By the Book," *New York Times Book Review*, March 5, 2015. Elisabeth Bumiller, "Bush's iPod

Is a Little Bit Country, Rock'n'Roll," *New York Times*, April 12, 2005. Cameron Crowe, "The Durable Led Zeppelin," *Rolling Stone*, March 13, 1975. Ellie Muir, "Courtney Love says she's only ever known two 'true musical geniuses,'" *Yahoo! News*, December 28, 2022. Stephen Holden, "Rolling Her Classical Voice Around Pop Songs," *New York Times*, May 21, 2005. BOOKS: Rob Jovanovic, *Kate Bush: The Biography*. OTHER: "Jamie Lee Curtis on *Halloween Ends* and her love for Joni Mitchell," a video put on YouTube by Greatest Hits Radio on October 10, 2022. Interview of Mitchell by Steve Warden on Toronto's Q107-FM in September 1994. k.d. lang's introduction at the Canadian Governor-General's Award in December 1996. An April 10, 2002, entry on the "Ask Carly" part of CarlySimon.com. Mitchell's interview on CTV's *Canada AM*, April 22, 2005.

12.

AUTHOR INTERVIEWS: Sharolyn Dickson, Matt Diehl, Tony Simon. AUTHOR CORRESPONDENCE: Estrella Berosini, Jeffrey O'Brien. ARTICLES: Wayne Studer, "Mitchell Returns to a Packed House; Audience Appreciated Two-Hour Set," *Flat Hat*, February 13, 1976. Tom Waseleski, "Mitchell Is Pgh's Valentine," *Pitt News*, February 18, 1976. David Wild, "Q&A: Joni Mitchell," *Rolling Stone*, October 31, 2002. Doris G. Worsham, "Joni Mitchell flawless in concert at Berkeley," *Oakland Tribune*, March 15, 1972. Flanagan, *Vanity Fair*. Steve Newton, "Voodoo Shoots for Versatility," Straight.com, April 15, 2004. Guy Trebay, "Of Joni Mitchell and David Hockney Holding Hands," *New York Times*, February 28, 2019. Divina Infusino, "A Chalk Talk with Joni Mitchell," *San Diego Union-Tribune*, April 3, 1988. BOOKS: Weller, *Girls Like Us*. OTHER: Getty Images, "Joni Mitchell in London (photo by Michael Putland/Getty Images). Also: "Joni Mitchell-Wembley 1983" put on YouTube on December 10, 2019, by uphollandlatic. The PBS video "Joni Mitchell Accepts the Gershwin Prize," from April 5, 2023, on YouTube.

13.

AUTHOR INTERVIEWS: Estrella Berosini, Nathan Joseph, Roger McGuinn, Amy Scholder, David Yaffe. ARTICLES: Lisa Robinson, "An Oral History of Laurel Canyon, the 60s and 70s Music Mecca," *Vanity Fair*, March 2015. Crowe, *Rolling Stone*. Bryan Appleyard, "The Lonely Painter," *Sunday Times* (of London), November 23, 2014. Ivan Kreilkamp, "Joni Mitchell's Ferocious Gift," *Public Books*, August 31, 2020. David Remnick, "Leonard Cohen Makes It Darker," *New Yorker*, October 10, 2016. "Joni Mitchell's Deepest Cuts," the April 4, 2022, entry on David Yaffe's Substack, *Trouble Man*. Bill DeMain, "*Bella Donna*: How Stevie Nicks escaped chaos and proved a point," Loudersound.com, June 7, 2021. Geoff Edgers, "What pushed Graham Nash, the quiet one, to record his solo masterpiece," *Washington Post*, September 17, 2019. Cameron Crowe, "Joni Mitchell opens up to Cameron Crowe about singing again, lost loves and 50 years of *Blue*," *Los Angeles Times*, June 20, 2021. Jon Bream, "Review: Thoughts of Joni Mitchell and David Crosby spark Graham Nash concert in Minneapolis," *Star Tribune*, May 2, 2023. A. L. McClain, "Two Single Acts Survive a Marriage," *Detroit News*, February 6, 1966. Susan Gordon Lydon, "In Her House, Love," *New York Times*, April 20, 1969. BOOKS: David Browne, *Crosby, Stills, Nash and Young: The Definitive Saga of Rock's Greatest Supergroup*. Michael Walker, *Laurel Canyon: The Inside Story of Rock-and-Roll's Legendary Neighborhood*. Graham Nash, "Wild Tales: A Rock & Roll Life." Marc Myers, *Anatomy of a Song: The Oral History of 45 Iconic Hits That Changed Rock, R&B and Pop*. David Crosby and Carl Gottlieb, *Long Time Gone: The Autobiography of David Crosby*. Jimmy McDonough, *Shakey: Neil Young's Biography*. Rita Coolidge, with Michael Walker, *Delta Lady: A Memoir*. OTHER: Mitchell's interview on *The Nicole Sandler Show*, September 1998. VH1's "Crosby, Stills, Nash & Young" episode of *Legends* that aired March 13, 2000. Graham Nash's interview with Terry Gross on *Fresh Air*, October 15, 2013. *Hallelujah: Leonard Cohen, a Journey, a Song*, a documentary by Dan Geller and Dayna Goldfine, Sony Pictures Classics, 2022.

14.

AUTHOR INTERVIEWS: Sharolyn Dickson, Tony Simon, David Yaffe. ARTICLES: *Life* magazine's interview of Robert Plant in October 1987. David DeVoss, "Rock 'n' Roll's Leading Lady," *Time*, December 16, 1974. Kristine McKenna, "The Dream Girl Wakes Up," *New Musical Express*, December 4, 1982. Jaelyn Molyneux, "Joni Riffs on Joni," *Calgary Her-*

ald, February 2, 2007. Michael Anthony, "Views and reviews," *Minneapolis Star Tribune,* July 30, 1974. Gene Stout, "Bob Dylan Sparkles in Triple-Treat Performance at the Gorge," *Seattle Post-Intelligencer,* May 18, 1998. Stephen Holden, "The Ambivalent Hall of Fame," *New York Times,* December 1, 1996. BOOKS: Joe Smith, *Off the Record: An Oral History of Popular Music.* Hugh Barker and Yuval Taylor, *Faking It: The Quest for Authenticity in Popular Music.* St. Augustine, *Confessions.* OTHER: Peter Gzowski's interview of Mitchell on CBC Radio's *Sunday Morning* on July 11, 1983. D. A. Pennebaker's documentary *Don't Look Back,* Leacock-Pennebaker, 1967. Mitchell's December 29, 1980, interview with radio host Jim Ladd on *Innerview.*

15.

ARTICLES: Barney Hoskyns, "Our Lady of the Sorrows," *Mojo,* December 1994. Bardin, *Details.* Vic Garbarini, "60 Minutes with Joni Mitchell," *Guitar World,* September 1996. Graeme Thomson, *Uncut* magazine's *Ultimate Music Guide,* May 19, 2017.

16.

AUTHOR INTERVIEWS: David Yaffe. ARTICLES: Thom Duffy, "7 Sublime Moments from Brandi Carlile's Performance of Joni Mitchell's 'Blue' at Carnegie Hall," *Billboard,* November 7, 2021. BOOKS: Brandi Carlile, *Broken Horse: A Memoir.* OTHER: Joni's November 9, 2007, appearance on PBS's *Tavis Smiley.*

17.

BOOKS: Marom, *Joni Mitchell.* Tom King, *The Operator: David Geffen Builds, Buys, and Sells the New Hollywood.*

18.

ARTICLES: "I Am My Words," an unsigned article about Bob Dylan in the November 4, 1963, issue of *Newsweek.* Adam Gopnik, "Harvest Time,"

The New Yorker, April 11, 2011. BOOKS: Nash, *Wild Tales*. Weller, *Girls Like Us*. OTHER: Mitchell's liner notes to *Archives, Volume 2*, Rhino Records, 2021.

19.

AUTHOR INTERVIEWS: Sharolyn Dickson, Tony Simon, Sheila Weller, David Yaffe. AUTHOR CORRESPONDENCE: Marion Garden and Chuck Mitchell. ARTICLES: Katherine Orloff, "Joni Mitchell, Artist, Is Simply That," *Los Angeles Times*, January 14, 1973. Joseph Lelyveld, "Little Joan Baezes Sing U.S. Protest Songs in Japan," *New York Times*, January 17, 1967. Bill Higgins, "Both Sides At Last," *Los Angeles Times*, April 8, 1997. "Witness of Life," an unsigned article in the *Irish Times*, February 26, 1999. Arthur Zeldin, "Joni and Chuck Mitchell: Both are rising folk stars," *Toronto Daily Star*, November 10, 1966. Lindsay Zoladz, "Joni Mitchell: Fear of a Female Genius," *Ringer*, October 16, 2017. BOOKS: Nicholas Jennings, *Before the Gold Rush: Flashbacks to the Dawn of the Canadian Sound*. Sloman, *On the Road with Bob Dylan*. OTHER: *Both Sides Now*, a BBC2 show, hosted by Mary Black, that aired February 20, 1999. Barry Berg's interview of Chuck and Joni Mitchell on Temple University's radio station, November 17, 1966. A speech that Mitchell gave to San Francisco's Commonwealth Club on April 22, 2005. *Joni Mitchell Archives—Vol.1: The Early Years (1963–1967)*, Rhino Records, 2020. The documentary *Joni Mitchell: Woman of Heart and Mind*, directed by Susan Lacy, PBS, 2003.

20.

AUTHOR INTERVIEWS: Vicki Gabereau, John Kelly. ARTICLES: White, *Billboard*. Flanagan, *Vanity Fair*. BOOKS: Marom, *Joni Mitchell: In Her Own Words*. OTHER: The website of Fort Macleod's public library: https://fortmacleodlibrary.ca/about-us/library-history.

21.

AUTHOR INTERVIEWS: David Yaffe. ARTICLES: Brian D. Johnson, "Joni's Secret: Mother and Child Reunion," *Maclean's*, April 21, 1997.

BOOKS: Weller, *Girls Like Us*. OTHER: *Diary of a Decade Interview*, hosted by Trevor Dann, on Greater London Radio, September 6, 1990.

22.

AUTHOR INTERVIEWS: Sharolyn Dickson, Roger McGuinn, Vince Mendoza, Tony Simon. ARTICLES: Carl Swanson, "Joni Mitchell, Unyielding," *New York*, February 9, 2015. Cameron Crowe, "Joni Mitchell: 'I'm a fool for love. I make the same mistake over and over,'" *Guardian*, October 27, 2020. Brad Wheeler, "When Joni Mitchell talks, the songwriting neuroscientist Daniel Levitin listens," Toronto *Globe and Mail*, February 24, 2022. Josh Eells, "22 Things You Learn Hanging Out with Taylor Swift," *Rolling Stone Australia*, September 11, 2014. William Doyle, "Free, Open Spaces: Brian Eno's Favourite Records," *Quietus*, April 13, 2016. Tim Murphy, "Joni Mitchell Gets Angry, Hugs It Out," Vulture.com, September 26, 2007. Bayin, *Elm Street*. BOOKS: Peter Erskine, *No Beethoven: An Autobiography and Chronicle of Weather Report*. Yaffe, *Reckless Daughter*. Monk, *Joni*. Daniel J. Levitin, *The World in Six Songs*. Lloyd Whitesell, *The Music of Joni Mitchell*. James Bennighof, *The Words and Music of Joni Mitchell*. Eric Olsen, Paul Verna, and Carlo Wolff, *The Encyclopedia of Record Producers*. OTHER: Lacy, *Joni Mitchell*. Mitchell's liner notes to *Love Has Many Faces: A Quartet, A Ballet, Waiting to Be Danced*, Rhino, 2014. *A Special Conversation for Radio*, with David Jensen and Mitchell, Capital Radio (London), April 1988. *Words and Music—Joni Mitchell and Morrissey*, Reprise Records, October 18, 1996.

23.

AUTHOR INTERVIEWS: Jancee Dunn. ARTICLES: Jancee Dunn, "Question and Answer: Joni Mitchell," *Rolling Stone*, December 15, 1994.

24.

AUTHOR INTERVIEWS: Rosanna Arquette, David Yaffe. AUTHOR CORRESPONDENCE: Estrella Berosini. ARTICLES: Jenny Stevens, "'I was a bad influence on the Beatles': James Taylor on Lennon, love and recovery," *The Guardian*, February 17, 2020. Jane Stevenson, "Musical spectrum lauds Joni Mitchell," *Toronto Sun*, January 29, 2007. Timothy Crouse, "James Taylor: The First Family of the New Rock," *Rolling Stone*, February 18, 1971. "A Conversation with Buffy Sainte-Marie," posted on jonimitchell.com on March 6, 2013. Will Blythe, "A December Night," *Oxford American*, November 20, 2018. Mary Lou Sullivan, "Kinky Friedman on the Night Bob Dylan, Jack Nicholson Crashed His Wild House Party," *Rolling Stone*, November 16, 2017. Dave Simpson, "Joni Mitchell's 'Blue': my favourite song—by James Taylor, Carole King, Graham Nash, David Crosby and more," *Guardian*, June 22, 2021. Bill Flanagan, "Joni Mitchell Builds Shelter from the Rainstorm," *Musician*, May 1988. BOOKS: David Browne, *Fire and Rain: The Beatles, Simon & Garfunkel, James Taylor, CSNY and the Lost Story of 1970*. Mercer, *Will You Take Me as I Am*. Weller, *Girls Like Us*. Ian Halperin, *Fire and Rain: The James Taylor Story*. Yaffe, *Reckless Daughter*. Lester Bangs, *Psychotic Reactions and Carburetor Dung*. Elijah Wald, *How the Beatles Destroyed Rock 'n' Roll: An Alternative History of American Popular Music*. Carly Simon, *Boys in the Trees: A Memoir*. Carole King, *A Natural Woman: A Memoir*. OTHER: James Taylor, *Break Shot: My First 21 Years*, Audible Originals, 2020. Ladd, *Innerview*. Mitchell's liner notes to *Love Has Many Faces: A Quartet, A Ballet, Waiting to Be Danced*, Rhino, 2014. Sam Stone, "Treasure Somewhere: Patrick Milligan Talks 'Joni Mitchell Archives, Vol. 2,'" JoniMitchell.com, February 18, 2022.

25.

AUTHOR INTERVIEWS: John Kelly, Vince Mendoza, David Yaffe. ARTICLES: Mary S. Aikins, "Heart of a Prairie Girl," *Reader's Digest*, July 2005. "Joni Mitchell: Free love? It's a ruse for guys," *Uncut*, November 2013. Adrian Ewins, "Joni Mitchell: Seeing Art in the World," *Western People*, May 22, 1980. Marci McDonald, "Joni Mitchell Emerges from Her Retreat," *Toronto Star*, February 9, 1974. BOOKS: Peter Doggett, *There's a Riot Going On: Revolutionaries, Rock Stars, and the Rise and Fall of the 60's*. Marom, *Joni Mitchell: In Her Own Words*. OTHER: Liane Hansen, "Music Icon Joni Mitchell Discusses Her Music," NPR's *Weekend Edition*, May 28, 1995. "Ed Sciaky Interviews Joni Mitchell," *The Broadside Program*, WRTI-FM,

March 17, 1967. *The Joni Mitchell Interview*, with Jian Ghomeshi, CBC Music, June 4, 2013. Ladd, *Innerview. David Bowie—The Flo and Eddie Interview, Plaza Hotel, NYC, 90 Minutes Live (1977)*, CBC TV, November 25, 1977.

26.

AUTHOR INTERVIEWS: Tony Simon, David Yaffe. ARTICLES: Tom Doyle, "The Jazz Singer," *Mojo*, July 2023. David A. Kaplan, "David Geffen Unplugged," *Fortune*, July 25, 2013. Les Irvin, "Pass the Salt, Please," JoniMitchell.com, September 26, 1997. John Seabrook, "The Many Lives of David Geffen," *The New Yorker*, February 23 and March 2, 1998. Barb Geraud, "What's Going Down?" *Pitt News*, October 4, 1972. Barney Hoskyns, "Sex, Drugs, and the Billion-Dollar Rise of David Geffen," *Independent*, November 18, 2005. Dave Hobill, "Review: Joni Mitchell, a Real Person," *Tech News* (Worcester Polytechnic Institute), December 16, 1969. Bernard Weinraub, "David Geffen, Still Hungry," *New York Times*, May 2, 1993. Candace Bushnell, "Candace Bushnell on Joni Mitchell's 'Free Man in Paris,'" *Wall Street Journal*, July 21, 2015. James Reginato, "The Diva's Last Stand," *W*, December 2002. BOOKS: Robbie Robertson, *Testimony*. King, *The Operator*. Jimmy Webb, *The Cake and the Rain*. Nash, *Wild Tales*. Yaffe, *Reckless Daughter*. Weller, *Girls Like Us*. Larry F. Norman, *The Public Mirror: Molière and the Social Commerce of Depiction*. Lisa and John Sornberger, *Gathered Light: The Poetry of Joni Mitchell's Songs*. OTHER: The Leon Levy Center for Biography's video of David Yaffe's October 3, 2018, lecture at the Center. The documentary *Inventing David Geffen*, directed by Susan Lacy. *American Masters*, PBS, 2012. Mitchell's December 8, 1995, appearance on *CBS This Morning*.

27.

ARTICLES: Crowe, *Rolling Stone*. Michael Watts, "The public life of a private property," *Sunday Times* (London), April 17, 1983. Ben Fong-Torres, "Joni Rocks Again," *Chatelaine*, June 1988. David Wild, "A Conversation with Joni Mitchell," *Rolling Stone*, May 30, 1991. Barney Hoskyns, "Our Lady of the Sorrows," *Mojo*, December 1994. William Ruhlmann, "From Blue to Indigo," *Goldmine*, February 17, 1995. Flanagan, *Vanity Fair*.

Adam Sandler, "Van Morrison; Joni Mitchell; Bob Dylan," *Variety*, May 26, 1998. Amanda Ghost, "Come In from the Cold: The Return of Joni Mitchell," JoniMitchell.com, March 20, 2007. Bob Clark, "Mitchell on the Warpath," *Calgary Herald*, February 10, 2007.

28.

AUTHOR INTERVIEWS: Brian Blade, Kazu Matsui, Vince Mendoza, Jimmy Webb. ARTICLES: Giovanni Russonello, "Ambrose Akinmusire Learned to Let Go (with Help from Joni Mitchell)," *New York Times*, September 10, 2023. David Yaffe, "Didn't It Feel Good?," David Yaffe's Substack from August 20, 2023. Steven Daly, "Rock and Roll," *Rolling Stone*, October 29, 1998. Wesley Strick, "Joni Mitchell Meets Don Juan's Reckless Daughter," *Circus*, March 2, 1978. Steve Pond, "Mitchell 'storms' back," *Rolling Stone*, March 10, 1988. Johnny Black, "The Greatest Songs Ever! 'Free Man in Paris,'" *Blender*, September 2004. Angela Alexis, "Native Son: After a Career as Hollywood's Noble Indian Hero, Iron Eyes Cody Is Found to Have an Unexpected Heritage," *New Orleans Times-Picayune*, May 26, 1996. Jennifer Van Evra, "Joni Mitchell: 20 things you didn't know about one of Canada's greatest musicians," *CBC Music*, November 7, 2013. BOOKS: Marom, *Joni Mitchell: In Her Own Words*. Mercer, *Will You Take Me as I Am*. Weller, *Girls Like Us*. OTHER: Mitchell's liner notes to *Complete Geffen Recordings*, Geffen Records, 2003. Mitchell's liner notes to *Love Has Many Faces: A Quartet, A Ballet, Waiting to Be Danced*, Rhino, 2014. An interview Malka Marom gave on a panel at the University of Connecticut's Joni symposium, April 2020. Lloyd Whitesell's interview on WICN 90.5's *Inquiry* on April 10, 2009.

29.

ARTICLES: White, *Billboard*. Steve Ponsonby, "Sweet Joni," *Shadows and Light* zine, July 1996. Madison Bloom, "Neil Young Pens Tribute to Late Manager Elliot Roberts," *Pitchfork*, June 22, 2019. Deirdre Kelly, "The Matador: Landmark Decision," Toronto *Globe and Mail*, September 29, 2007. Crowe, *Los Angeles Times*. Liel Leibovitz, "Leonard Cohen releases his 12th studio album," *Tablet*, January 31, 2012. Flanagan, *Vanity Fair*.

Stephen Thomas Erlewine, "Joni Mitchell: 50 Essential Songs," *Rolling Stone Australia*, June 25, 2021. Kaya Burgess, "Musicians seen as Cold War weapons," *The Times* (London), October 4, 2013. BOOKS: Weller, *Girls Like Us*. Yaffe, *Reckless Daughter*. Marom, *Joni Mitchell: In Her Own Words*. OTHER: Mitchell's liner notes to *Mingus*, Asylum, 1979. The video "NAMM TEC Awards 2000 (Joni Mitchell Receives the Les Paul Innovation Award)" posted on YouTube February 25, 2020.

30.

AUTHOR INTERVIEWS: Roger McGuinn, Tony Simon, Sheila Weller, David Yaffe. ARTICLES: Howard Cohen, "Mitchell Romantic, Brilliant," *Miami Herald*, May 19, 2000. Jim Wirth, "Both Sides Now," *New Musical Express*, March 10, 2000. Dan Jones, "Joni Mitchell Sizzles at Garden State Arts Center," *Bernardsville News*, July 21, 1983. "Joni Mitchell: The Words Come Spilling Out," *Ann Arbor Argus*, March 13, 1969. Dave Wilson, "An Interview with Joni Mitchell," *Broadside*, February 14, 1968. Remnick, *The New Yorker*. Crowe, *Rolling Stone*. Joe Tiller, "'Court and Spark': Joni Mitchell's Commercial and Creative Breakthrough," *Dig!*, January 17, 2022. Alice Echols, "Thirty Years with a Portable Lover," *L.A. Weekly*, November 25, 1994. Eric Lott, "Tar Baby and the Great White Wonder: Joni Mitchell's Pimp Game," in Ruth Charnock's *Joni Mitchell: New Critical Readings*. Wild, *Rolling Stone*. Bill Flanagan, "Secret Places," *Musician*, May 1988. Small, *People*. Steve Baltin, "Who I Am: Larry Klein on Joni Mitchell, Beatles, Jazz and More," *Forbes*, September 13, 2023. Corey Blake, "Larry Klein talks Joni Mitchell," *Troubadour Tribune*, March 20, 2012. Mary Campbell, "New-fashioned girl," Associated Press, November 18, 1994. Tom Valeo, "Old school singers ring in new venue," *Chicago Daily Herald*, September 20, 1998. David Cavanagh, "Turbulent Indigo: Can Joni Mitchell really be the Siren of Sorrow? And why is she so disillusioned with the world and the music business this time?," *Uncut*, December 2020. Dave DiMartino, "The Unfiltered Joni Mitchell," *Mojo*, August 1998. Allison Rapp, "The Joni Mitchell Request That Shocked Andy Summers," UltimateClassicRock.com, August 9, 2023. Steven Dougherty, "Both Sides Now," *People*, March 20, 2000. BOOKS: Mercer, *Will You Take Me as I Am*. Monk, *Joni Mitchell*. Marom, *Joni Mitchell: In*

Her Own Words. Weller, *Girls Like Us.* Miles Davis, *Miles.* Cary Raditz, *Carey: Genesis of the Song.* Sornberger, *Gathered Light.* OTHER: David Yaffe's interview on "The 1A Record Club celebrates the songwriting of Joni Mitchell," WAMU, March 30, 2023. Mitchell's interview in the liner notes from *Artist's Choice: Music That Matters to Her. Joni Mitchell,* Starbucks, 2005. Mitchell's liner notes to *Love Has Many Faces: A Quartet, A Ballet, Waiting to Be Danced,* Rhino, 2014. Mitchell's interview on BBC2 TV's *Old Grey Whistle Test,* November 26, 1985. Liza Richardson, "Joni in conversation with Liza Richardson," KCRW's *Morning Becomes Eclectic,* February 13, 2015. A reproduction of Mitchell's painting of Don Alias on the Tumblr account *bobdylan-n-jonimitchell.*

31.

ARTICLES: Phil Sutcliffe, "Joni Mitchell," *Q,* May 1988. Alex61, "Joni's Vocal Range," *The Range Place,* September 1, 2016. Swanson, *New York.* Garth Cartwright, "Elliot Roberts: Music Manager who shepherded Neil Young and Joni Mitchell to fame," *Independent,* July 8, 2019. Alanna Nash, "Joni Mitchell," *Stereo Review,* March 1986. James F. McCarty, "Man Admits Guilt in Beating Death Plea Consoles Jazz Great's Kin," *Miami Herald,* November 8, 1988. Adam Sweeting, "David Crosby obituary," *Guardian,* January 20, 2023. Jim Farber, "David Crosby, Folk-Rock Voice of the 1960s Whose Influence Spanned Decades, Dies at 81," *New York Times,* January 19, 2023. Jo Livingstone, "Both Sides of Joni Mitchell," *New Republic,* October 19, 2017. "Snow, High Winds and Heavy Surf Batter the West," *New York Times,* January 19, 1988. White, *Billboard.* Wild, *Rolling Stone,* 1991. Hugh McIntyre, "Legendary Label Geffen Records Relaunches After Disappearing," *Forbes,* March 23, 2017. BOOKS: Joni Mitchell, *Joni Mitchell: The Complete Poems and Lyrics.*

32.

AUTHOR INTERVIEWS: Amy Scholder. AUTHOR CORRESPONDENCE: Joshua Brand, Christopher Guly. ARTICLES: Christopher Guly, "Music world courts and sparks Joni Mitchell," Toronto *Globe and Mail,* December 16, 1996. OTHER: *Northern Exposure,* CBS, 1990–1995.

33.

AUTHOR INTERVIEWS: Matt Diehl, John Kelly, Amy Scholder. ARTICLES: James Reginato, "The Diva's Last Stand," *W*, December 2002. Wild, *Rolling Stone*, 2002. Victoria Ahearn, "Joni Mitchell writing 'vignettes' for autobiography; 'squelched' film on her life," *Saskatoon StarPhoenix*, June 16, 2013. Matt Diehl, "It's a Joni Mitchell concert, sans Joni," *Los Angeles Times*, April 22, 2010. Robert Hilburn, "The Mojo Interview: Joni Mitchell," *Mojo*, February 2008. Doug Fischer, "Joni Mitchell's Fighting Words," *Ottawa Citizen*, October 7, 2006. Kristine McKenna, "Chalking It Up to Experience," *Los Angeles Times*, March 27, 1988. Jeremy Warren, "Items on way back to Joni," *Saskatoon StarPhoenix*, August 17, 2013. Nic Harcourt, "Joni on Point," *Los Angeles Times*, June 7, 2009. Garcia, *Interview*. Sacha Reins, "Joni Mitchell, Maitresse Flammes," *Paris Match*, December 22, 2014. Swanson, *New York*. BOOKS: Shelton, *No Direction Home*. Yaffe, *Reckless Daughter*. Mercer, *Will You Take Me as I Am*. N. K. Jemisin, *The City We Became*. OTHER: Marc Rowland's interview of Dylan, as quoted in John Bauldie's sleeve notes for *The Bootleg Series Volumes 1–3 (Rare and Unreleased) 1961–1991*, Columbia Records, 1991. Ghomeshi, CBC Music. Ladd, *Innerview*. Richardson, *Morning Becomes Eclectic*. Brandi Carlile's interview on *CBS This Morning*, July 29, 2022.

35.

ARTICLES: Bill Higgins, "Both Sides At Last," *Los Angeles Times*, April 8, 1997.

36.

AUTHOR INTERVIEWS: Sharolyn Dickson, Nathan Joseph, Tony Simon. ARTICLES: Jonathan Bernstein, "'She Schooled Us All': Inside Joni Mitchell's Stunning Return to Newport Folk Festival," *Rolling Stone*, July 28, 2022. Diehl, *Los Angeles Times*. Sheila Weller, "Why We Can't Get Enough of Joni Mitchell and Brandi Carlile," *Next Tribe*, August 3, 2022. Aleandra Steigrad, "Joni Mitchell alive and 'well' after People magazine mistakenly posts obituary," *New York Post*, October 7, 2022. David Yaffe, "Joni Mitchell Rises Again,"

Tidal, August 7, 2023. Brandi Carlile, "Brandi Carlile: How I got Joni Mitchell back on stage," *The Times* (London), July 28, 2022. BOOKS: Marom, *Joni Mitchell: In Her Own Words*. Yaffe, *Reckless Daughter*. OTHER: Renee Montagne, "The Music Midnight Makes: In Conversation with Joni Mitchell," NPR's *Weekend Edition Saturday*, December 9, 2014. Mitchell's 1996 interview on CBC TV, "Joni Mitchell a 'bad' girl?" Lindsay Zoladz's interview on "The Joni Mitchell Renaissance," the June 17, 2023, episode of *Podcast!*, a *New York Times* podcast hosted by Jon Caramanica.

37.

AUTHOR INTERVIEWS: Estrella Berosini, David Yaffe. ARTICLES: Estrella Berosini, "A Child Came Out to Wander," Part 1, JoniMitchell.com, April 1, 2008. Harold Rubinstein, "The Privilege of a Concert," *SUNY Statesman*, October 25, 1968. Jim Frenkel, "Don't Ask for Music If You Can't Take It!," *SUNY Statesman*, October 22, 1968. Spider Robinson, "Ballad of the Rude Canadian," Toronto *Globe and Mail*, February 22, 2001. Claire Potter, "Live! In class at Yale! David Geffen!," *Yale Daily News*, December 6, 1978. Wild, *Rolling Stone*. Timothy White, "Words from a Woman of Heart and Mind," *Billboard*, September 8, 2001. Ghomeshi, CBC Music. Liz Smith, "Friday potpourri—Cher, Gaga, Joni Mitchell, Gwyneth and Chris," *New York Social Diary*, March 28, 2014. OTHER: Sciaky, *The Broadside Program*. Lloyd Whitesell's interview on WICN 90.5's *Inquiry* on April 10, 2009.

38.

AUTHOR CORRESPONDENCE: John Mackie. ARTICLES: Edna Gunderson, "The Cat's 'Meow-meow-meow!,'" *USA Today*, September 29, 1998. Colin Stutz, "Here's What It Costs Neil Young and Joni Mitchell to Leave Spotify," *Billboard*, January 30, 2022. White, *Billboard*. Hubert Saal, "The Girls—Letting Go," *Newsweek*, July 14, 1969. John Mackie, "On War, peace, memories and dance," CanWest News Service, January 15, 2010. Greg Quill, "Adams headlines Expo gala," *Toronto Star*, April 22, 1986. Roger Friedman, "Justin Long and Friends Paging Joni Mitchell for Song Rights on Charming New Rom-Com," *Showbiz 411*, April 23, 2013. Elvis Costello, "Joni's Last Waltz?," *Vanity Fair*, November 2004. BOOKS:

Sheila Weller, *Carrie Fisher: A Life on the Edge*. OTHER: Mitchell's interview by Rene Engel on KCSN-FM, December 21, 1999.

39.

AUTHOR INTERVIEWS: Amy Scholder, Tony Simon, David Yaffe. AUTHOR CORRESPONDENCE: Trevor Dann. ARTICLES: Dougherty, *People*. Shirley Eder, "Where Is Joni Mitchell's Baby?," *Philadelphia Inquirer*, December 21, 1974. Charles Gandee, "Triumph of the Will," *Vogue*, April 1995. "Heartsick Joni Mitchell Hunts Baby She Gave Up," *The Globe*, April 16, 1996. Laila Fulton, "Alberta Native Gave Up Daughter," *Calgary Sun*, December 1996. Brian D. Johnson, "Joni's Secret: Mother and Child Reunion," *Maclean's*, April 21, 1997. Timothy Crouse, "Blue," *Rolling Stone*, August 5, 1971. Nicholas Van Rijn, "How Joni Mitchell's daughter found mom and became whole," *Toronto Sun*, April 8, 1997. Michael Posner, "Little Green a Little Blue," Toronto *Globe and Mail*, April 11, 1998. Higgins, *Los Angeles Times*. Gunderson, *USA Today*. Tom Arnold, "The reunion, from both sides now," *National Post*, March 3, 2001. Ani DiFranco, "Court and Spark," *Los Angeles Times*, September 20, 1998. Sam Feldman and Steve Maclam, "Joni-Ani Postscript," *Los Angeles Times*, January 17, 1999. Camille Paglia, "The Trailblazer Interview," *Interview*, August 2005. BOOKS: Weller, *Girls Like Us*. Yaffe, *Reckless Daughter*. OTHER: Mitchell's interview with Trevor Dann on Greater London Radio on September 6, 1990. Malka Marom's interview at the University of Connecticut's Joni symposium, April 2020.

40.

AUTHOR INTERVIEWS: Rosanna Arquette, Sharolyn Dickson, Joellen Lapidus, Tony Simon, Beverley Straight, Jimmy Webb. ARTICLES: Neal Karlen, "Prince Talks: The Silence Is Broken," *Rolling Stone*, September 12, 1985. Costello, *Vanity Fair*. Ethan Brown, "Influences: Joni Mitchell," *New York*, April 29, 2005. Melinda Newman, "Joni Mitchell offers Hits and Misses," *Billboard*, August 24, 1996. Michael Wood, "The best Joni Mitchell cover? How Prince blended purple and 'Blue' on 'A Case of You,'" *Los Angeles Times*, June 22, 2021. Hoskyns, *Mojo*. Alexis Petridis,

"Prince: Transcendence. That's what you want. When that happens—Oh, boy," *Guardian*, November 12, 2015. David T. Friendly, "Prince for a Day in Wyoming," *Los Angeles Times*, July 3, 1986. "In 1986, one lucky Wyoming woman got to meet Prince," *Billings Gazette*, February 17, 2017. James Patrick Herman, "A Remembrance of Prince as the Ultimate A-List Party-Thrower (Bring on the Superstar Guests)," *Billboard*, May 2, 2016. Lynn Elber, "Actress Celebrates 60th Birthday with Disneyland Bash," Associated Press, February 28, 1992. Bill Wyman, "Car wrecks, drug binges and a naked Joni Mitchell: Jimmy Webb's wild ride," *Sydney Morning Herald*, October 13, 2023. Roger Friedman, "Whitney Houston Remembered at Clive Davis's All Star Pre Grammy Bash," *Showbiz 411*, February 10, 2013. Edward Kieran, "David Crosby," *Spin*, October 1985. Del Cowie, "Joni Mitchell makes rare public appearance at Chick Corea concert," CBC Music, August 23, 2016. Mark Shanahan, "Joni Mitchell makes rare public appearance at James Taylor show in Los Angeles," *Boston Globe*, June 4, 2018. Cameron Crowe, "The inside story of Joni Mitchell's return to the stage," *The Times* (London), July 20, 2023. Eric Todisco, "Brandi Carlile on Jam Sessions at Joni Mitchell's House with Dolly Parton, Chaka Khan, and Harry Styles," *People*, April 2, 2021. Bernstein, *Rolling Stone*. Kevin Stairiker, "Taylor Goldsmith of Dawes reflects on Long's Park concerts, Joni Mitchell in advance of Harrisburg show this weekend," *Lancaster Online*, March 9, 2023. Karen Herman, "The Interviews: Martha Quinn," Emmys.com, October 28, 2019. BOOKS: Raditz, *Carey*. Nash, *Wild Tales*. Carlile, *Broken Horses*. Duane Tudahl, *Prince and the "Parade" and "Sign O' the Times" Era Studio Sessions, 1985 and 1986*. Ronin Ro, *Prince: Inside the Music and the Masks*. Ira Nadel, *Various Positions: A Life of Leonard Cohen*. OTHER: Mitchell's video message for Prince's induction to the UK Music Hall of Fame, November 14, 2006. Mitchell's interview on *The Tonight Show with Jay Leno*, February 3, 1995. Rosanna Arquette's interview on *The Joni Mitchell Podcast* hosted by Zachary Scot Johnson, Episode 27. Mitchell's interview on KCSA-FM, October 25, 1994.

41.

BOOKS: King, *A Natural Woman*.

42.

AUTHOR INTERVIEWS: Roger McGuinn, Tony Simon, Jimmy Webb. ARTICLES: DiFranco, *Los Angeles Times*. Nick Hasted, "Mingus," *Uncut*, December 2020. Chris Dafoe, "Unpredictable Icons Can Still Rock When They Want To," Toronto *Globe and Mail*, May 16, 1998. Les Irvin, "Pass the Salt, Please," JoniMitchell.com, September 26, 1997. BOOKS: David Jacks, *Peter Asher: A Life in Music*. OTHER: Mitchell's interview at the Polar Music Prize press conference, May 7, 1996. The video "Joni Mitchell—Coyote (Live at Gordon Lightfoot's Home with Bob Dylan & Roger McGuinn, 1975)," on YouTube. Mitchell's December 21, 1999, radio interview with Rene Ingle on KCSN-FM. Ghomeshi, CBC Music.

43.

AUTHOR INTERVIEWS: Brian Blade, Amy Scholder, Tony Simon, Sheila Weller, David Yaffe. ARTICLES: Neil Strauss, "Joni with an 'I,'" *New York Times*, October 18, 1998. Posner, Toronto *Globe and Mail*. Natasha Stoynoff, "Catching Up with Joni Mitchell," *People*, November 5, 2007. Swanson, *New York*. Arnold, *National Post*. Larissa MacFarquhar, "Living in Adoption's Emotional Aftermath," *The New Yorker*, April 3, 2023. Reginato, *W*. Jeremy Warrren, "Myrtle Anderson, mother of Joni Mitchell, dies at 95," *Saskatoon StarPhoenix*, March 21, 2007. "Father of music legend Joni Mitchell dies," *Saskatoon StarPhoenix*, January 23, 2012. Elio Iannacci, "The Interview: Joni Mitchell," *Maclean's*, November 22, 2014. BOOKS: Weller, *Girls Like Us*. OTHER: Mitchell's interview on *The Nicole Sandler Show*, April 3, 2015. Mitchell's interview on BBC2 with Mary Black, February 20, 1999. An interview Daniel Levitin gave on a panel at the University of Connecticut's Joni symposium, April 2020. Mitchell's appearance on *Charlie Rose*, 2007.

45.

AUTHOR INTERVIEWS: Tony Simon, Beverley Straight, David Yaffe. ARTICLES: Marci McDonald, "Joni Mitchell has daringly come of age," *Toronto Star*, July 11, 1969. Michael Watts, "Joni Mitchell: the public life of a private property," *Sunday Times* (London), April 17, 1983. Posner, Toronto *Globe and Mail.* Zadie Smith, "Some Notes on Attunement," *The New Yorker,* December 9, 2012. Iain Blair, "Lucky Girl," *Los Angeles Herald,* March 9, 1986. BOOKS: Barney Hoskyns, *Hotel California.* Yaffe, *Reckless Daughter.* OTHER: David Cleary's album description of *Clouds* on Pandora. James Taylor's interview with PBS on the red carpet of the Gershwin Prize, 2023.

46.

AUTHOR INTERVIEWS: Lisa Cholodenko, John Kelly. ARTICLES: Annie Dru, "Robin Adler and Dave Blackburn Breathe Spirit and Soul in the Music of Joni Mitchell," *San Diego Troubadour,* February 10, 2010. Steve Connor, "NASA takes off in search of stardust," *The Independent* (UK), February 3, 1999. Laviea Thomas, "Moni Jitchell," *Quietus,* May 25, 2023. Sandhya Bathija, "Oh, the Legal Cites, They Are A-changin,'" *National Law Journal,* November 8, 2006. Vivia Chen, "Too Old for that Joni Mitchell Look?" *Careerist,* July 25, 2012. Kevin Arnovitz, "Why do we scream at foul shooters?," ESPN.com, February 14, 2012. Clifford Chase, "Trouble Child," JoniMitchell.com, June 17, 1996. BOOKS: James F. Harris, *Philosophy at 33 1/3 RPM: Themes of Classic Rock Music.* Meghan Daum, *Unspeakable.* Marom, *Joni Mitchell: In Her Own Words.* OTHER: Cameron Crowe's speech at the Hammer Museum's Gala in the Garden honoring Mitchell, November 2014. Anita Tedder, "Pleasant Distractions or Life Savers," a paper delivered by Tedder at Court & Spark, an international symposium on Joni Mitchell, held at the University of Lincoln, on July 3, 2015. Richardson, KCRW.

47.

AUTHOR CORRESPONDENCE: Ann Powers. ARTICLES: Jeffrey Hudson, "Joni Mitchell Is Music," *New Mexico Daily Lobo,* March 15, 1974. Christina Passariello, "Steve Jobs has a new 'memoir,' more than 11 years after his death," *Washington Post,* April 1, 2023. Henry Alford, "This Is the Story of My Life. And This Is the Story of My Life," *New York Times,* January 10, 2019. Malka Marom, "Face to Face," *Maclean's,* June 1, 1974.

OTHER: "Joni Mitchell Symposium: Ann Powers," October 27, 2004, video posted on YouTube. CBC TV's "Dr. Joni Mitchell" video, January 7, 2005. "Hear Joni Mitchell's Previously Unreleased Early Recordings," NPR's *All Songs Considered*, November 5, 2020. Mitchell's February 11, 2000, interview with Brian Stewart on CBC.

48.

AUTHOR INTERVIEWS: Amy Scholder, Sheila Weller. AUTHOR CORRESPONDENCE: Estrella Berosini. ARTICLES: Crowe, *Rolling Stone*, 1979. Gary Graff, "Joni Mitchell looks at the darker side," *Detroit Free Press*, October 23, 1994. Björk's post on the A Tribute to Joni Mitchell website, April 2007. DeVoss, *Time*. Wild, *Rolling Stone*, 1992. BOOKS: Mark Bego, *Joni Mitchell*. Greil Marcus, *Folk Music: A Bob Dylan Biography in Seven Songs.*

49.

AUTHOR INTERVIEWS: Brian Blade, Jeremy Dutcher, Amy Scholder, David Yaffe. ARTICLES: Swanson, *New York*. Syvie Simmons, "An Interview with Joni Mitchell," *Musikexpress*, 1988. Les Ledbetter, "Knockin' on Heaven's Door," *Rolling Stone*, January 15, 1976. Janet Maslin, "Joni Mitchell's Reckless and Shapeless 'Daughter,'" *Rolling Stone*, March 9, 1978. Grayson Haver Currin, "Joni Mitchell at Newport," *Pitchfork*, July 29, 2023. BOOKS: Weller, *Girls Like Us*. Yaffe, *Reckless Daughter*. Marom, *Joni Mitchell: In Her Own Words*. Spitz, *Dylan: A Biography*. OTHER: Kris Griffiths, "When Joni Mitchell wore blackface for Halloween," BBC, October 28, 2016. The Hammer Museum's video "Hammer Presents: Joni Mitchell Q and A and Birthday Celebration, November 6, 2014" and the video "Joni Mitchell Symposium: Greg Tate," shot at McGill University in 2004, both on YouTube.

50.

ARTICLES: Dave DiMartino, "The Unfiltered Joni Mitchell," *Mojo*, August 1998. Morrissey, *Rolling Stone*. Robert Shelton, "How does it feel to be on your own?," *Melody Maker*, July 29, 1978. Iannacci, *Maclean's*. Mitchell's interview with CBC's *CBC Magazine*, February 11, 2000. Barbara Gail Rowes, "Joni Mitchell's Search for Satisfaction," *Circus Raves*, June 1974. Winston Cook-Wilson, "On Joni Mitchell's Enduring *Hissing of Summer Lawns*, 40 Years Later," *Pitchfork*, November 30, 2015. Ben Brooks, "Joni Mitchell's Independent Art," *Music Connection*, November 25, 1982. Daniel Levitin, "A Conversation with Joni Mitchell," *Grammy*, March 1977. BOOKS: Marom, *Joni Mitchell: In Her Own Words*. OTHER: Mitchell's liner notes to *Love Has Many Faces: A Quartet, A Ballet, Waiting to Be Danced*, Rhino, 2014. Mitchell's interview with CBC-AM on February 3, 1974. Mitchell's interview with Jody Denberg on KGSR, September 9, 1998. Mitchell's interview with Liane Hansen on NPR's *Weekend Edition*, May 28, 1995. Mitchell's conversation with Jon Pareles at the TimesTalks Luminato Festival in June 2016. Ghomeshi, CBC Music.

51.

ARTICLES: Alex Bruell, "For Mount Rainier's resident wolverine, it's paradise on Paradise," *Courier-Herald* (Enumclaw), October 7, 2021. Alex Bruell, "Joni the Wolverine does it again," *Courier-Herald* (Enumclaw), December 21, 2022. *Chronicle* staff, "Joni the Wolverine: Relentless, Dedicated, Single Mother Births Triplets in Cascades," June 14, 2023. Charles Mudede, "Joni the Wolverine Breeding Like Crazy on Mount Rainier," TheStranger.com, December 29, 2022.

53.

ARTICLES: Jody Denberg, "Taming Joni Mitchell—Joni's Jazz," *Austin Chronicle*, October 12, 1998. OTHER: Mitchell's 2000 interview for the Millennium Project.

ACKNOWLEDGMENTS

Huge, huge thanks to Aimée Bell, as well as to Jonathan Karp, Karyn Marcus, David McCormick, Greg Villepique, Liz Brown, Katherine Barner, Rick Willett, Tony Simon, Matt Diehl, Carolyn Schurr Levin, Jennifer Bergstrom, Sally Marvin, Jill Siegel, Jaime Putorti, Sierra Fang-Horvath, David Yaffe, Susan Morrison, Les Irvin, Chris Bonanos, David Kamp, and Fred Alford.